Feedback in Higher and Professional Education

Learners complain that they do not get enough feedback, and educators resent that although they put considerable time into generating feedback, students take little notice of it. Both parties agree that it is very important.

Feedback in Higher and Professional Education explores what needs to be done to make feedback more effective. It examines the problem of feedback and suggests that there is a lack of clarity and shared meaning about what it is and what constitutes doing it well. It argues that new ways of thinking about feedback are needed.

There has been considerable development in research on feedback in recent years, but surprisingly little awareness of what needs to be done to improve it and good ideas are not translated into action. The book provides a multi-disciplinary and international account of the role of feedback in higher and professional education. It challenges three conventional assumptions about feedback in learning:

- That feedback constitutes one-way flow of information from a knowledgeable person to a less knowledgeable person.
- That the job of feedback is complete with the imparting of performance-related information.
- That a generic model of best-practice feedback can be applied to all learners and all learning situations

In seeking a new approach to feedback, it proposes that it is necessary to recognise that learners need to be much more actively involved in seeking, generating and using feedback. Rather than it being something they are subjected to, it must be an activity that they drive.

David Boud is Professor of Adult Education in the Faculty of Arts and Social Sciences at the University of Technology, Sydney, Australia.

Elizabeth Molloy is an Associate Professor in the Health Professions Education and Educational Research Unit in the Faculty of Medicine, Nursing and Health Sciences at Monash University, Melbourne, Australia.

Feedback in Higher and Professional Education

Understanding it and doing it well

Edited by David Boud and Elizabeth Molloy

Routledge
Taylor & Francis Group

LONDON AND NEW YORK

First published 2013
by Routledge
2 Park Square, Milton Park, Abingdon, Oxon OX14 4RN

Simultaneously published in the USA and Canada
by Routledge
711 Third Avenue, New York, NY 10017

Routledge is an imprint of the Taylor & Francis Group, an informa business

British Library Cataloguing in Publication Data
A catalogue record for this book is available from the British Library

Library of Congress Cataloging in Publication Data
Feedback in higher and professional education : understanding it and doing it well / edited by David Boud and Elizabeth Molloy.

p. cm.

ISBN 978-0-415-69228-1 (hardback) -- ISBN 978-0-415-69229-8 (paperback) -- ISBN 978-0-203-07433-6 (e-book) 1. Communication in education. 2. Motivation in education. 3. Feedback (Psychology) 4. Education, Higher. 5. Professional education. I. Boud, David. II. Molloy, Elizabeth.

LB1033.5.F44 2013

371.102'2--dc23

2012026703

ISBN: 978-0-415-69228-1 (hbk)
ISBN: 978-0-415-69229-8 (pbk)
ISBN: 978-0-203-07433-6 (ebk)

Typeset in Galliard
by Fakenham Prepress Solutions, Fakenham, Norfolk NR21 8NN

MIX
Paper from
responsible sources
FSC® C004839
www.fsc.org

Printed and bound in Great Britain by
TJ International Ltd, Padstow, Cornwall

Contents

Acknowledgements   vii
Contributors   viii

1 What is the problem with feedback?   1
   DAVID BOUD AND ELIZABETH MOLLOY

2 Changing conceptions of feedback   11
   ELIZABETH MOLLOY AND DAVID BOUD

3 Resituating feedback from the reactive to the proactive   34
   DAVID NICOL

4 The impact of emotions in feedback   50
   ELIZABETH MOLLOY, FRANCESC BORRELL-CARRIÓ, RON EPSTEIN

5 Socio-cultural considerations in feedback   72
   ANDREA PAUL, KARA GILBERT, LOUISA REMEDIOS

6 Trust and its role in facilitating dialogic feedback   90
   DAVID CARLESS

7 Written feedback
   What is it good for and how can we do it well?   104
   BRIAN JOLLY AND DAVID BOUD

8 Feedback in the digital environment   125
   BRETT WILLIAMS, TED BROWN, ROBYN BENSON

9 Feedback in clinical procedural skills simulations   140
   DEBRA NESTEL, FERNANDO BELLO, ROGER KNEEBONE

10 Implementing multisource feedback   158
JOCELYN LOCKYER AND JOAN SARGEANT

11 The role of peers in feedback processes   174
RICHARD K. LADYSHEWSKY

12 Utilising the voice of others
The example of consumer-delivered feedback   190
LISA MCKENNA AND FIONA KENT

13 Decision-making for feedback   202
DAVID BOUD AND ELIZABETH MOLLOY

Index   219

Acknowledgements

We would like to thank the teachers and colleagues who throughout our learning experiences have intuitively understood what is important in feedback. We owe them all a debt of gratitude for their persistence and insight. However, we accept sole responsibility for the changes that we made in our own work when their influence was successful!

The impetus for a book on feedback came from a staff and student workshop on how to improve feedback. Thank you to Kara Gilbert, Brett Williams and Robyn Benson who encouraged the idea of writing a book for educators on problems and prospects in feedback.

Thanks also to Joanna Tai for assistance in the final stage of editing, and in helping prepare the manuscript for the publishers.

Contributors

Fernando Bello is a Reader in Surgical Graphics and Computing at the Department of Surgery and Cancer, Imperial College, London.

Robyn Benson is an Adjunct Senior Lecturer in the Faculty of Medicine, Nursing and Health Sciences at Monash University, Australia, with a background in adult education, distance education and e-learning.

Francesc Borrell-Carrió is in the Department of Medicine, University of Barcelona, CAP Cornellà, Catalonian Institute of Health (ICS), Cornellà de Llobregat, Spain.

David Boud is Professor of Adult Education in the Faculty of Arts and Social Sciences at the University of Technology, Sydney, Australia. His webpage is www.davidboud.com.

Ted Brown is an Associate Professor in the Department of Occupational Therapy Faculty of Medicine, Nursing and Health Sciences at Monash University. His webpage is http://www.med.monash.edu.au/ot/staff/brown.html.

David Carless is Professor of Educational Assessment in the Faculty of Education, University of Hong Kong. His webpage is: http://web.edu.hku.hk/academic_staff.php?staffId=dcarless.

Ron Epstein is Professor of Family Medicine, Psychiatry, Oncology and Nursing at the University of Rochester Medical Center, Rochester, New York.

Kara Gilbert is a Course Development Manager at the Berwick and Peninsula campuses, Monash University. She is currently completing her doctoral studies.

Brian Jolly is Professor of Medical Education, The University of Newcastle, NSW, Australia.

Fiona Kent is a physiotherapist and lecturer in the Health Professions Education and Educational Research Unit in the Faculty of Medicine, Nursing and Health Sciences at Monash University, Melbourne, Australia.

Roger Kneebone is Professor of Surgical Education at the Department of Surgery and Cancer, Imperial College, London.

Richard K. Ladyshewsky is Professor and Online MBA Program Leader in the Curtin Graduate School of Business, Curtin University, Perth. Western Australia. His web page is http://www.gsb.curtin.edu.au/gsb/staff-directory?profile=Rick-Ladyshewsky.

Jocelyn Lockyer is Professor, Community Health Sciences and Senior Associate Dean—Education, Faculty of Medicine, University of Calgary, Calgary, Canada.

Lisa McKenna is an Associate Professor and Director of Education in the School of Nursing and Midwifery at Monash University, Melbourne, Australia.

Elizabeth Molloy is an Associate Professor in the Health Professions Education and Educational Research Unit in the Faculty of Medicine, Nursing and Health Sciences at Monash University, Melbourne, Australia. Her webpage is http://www.med.monash.edu.au/education/healthpeer/staff/molloy.html.

Debra Nestel is Professor of Simulation Education in healthcare at Gippsland Medical School, School of Rural Health and the Health Professions Education and Research Unit in the Faculty of Medicine, Nursing and Health Sciences, Monash University, Victoria, Australia.

David Nicol is Emeritus Professor of Higher Education at the University of Strathclyde, Scotland. He has led numerous projects on assessment and feedback. See project website at www.reap.ac.uk.

Andrea Paul is a lecturer in the Faculty of Medicine, Nursing & Health Sciences, Monash University.

Louisa Remedios is Deputy Head of Physiotherapy, Melbourne School of Health Sciences, Melbourne University.

Joan Sargeant is Professor and Director Research and Evaluation, Continuing Medical Education in the Faculty of Medicine, Dalhousie University in Halifax, Canada.

Brett Williams is a senior lecturer in the Department of Community Emergency Health and Paramedic Practice, Faculty of Medicine, Nursing and Health Sciences at Monash University. His webpage is http://www.med.monash.edu.au/cehpp/staff/williams.html.

Chapter 1

What is the problem with feedback?

David Boud
Elizabeth Molloy

We all experience the influence of feedback in our lives and in our work. We are told that we can't park our car in a particular space, and we choose to go elsewhere. Our students tell us that they don't understand a point we have made in class and we find another way of explaining it. We get referees' comments on a paper submitted to a journal, we make revisions and resubmit it. These are familiar examples of everyday feedback. Feedback is a normal part of our lives; it is ubiquitous. If it seems to work so normally and so regularly, why then does it appear to be so troublesome in higher and professional education? Why is it that students complain more about feedback than almost any others parts of their courses? Is what we are doing so wrong, or are there other explanations of what is rapidly becoming a crisis of concern?

One of the key reasons for a focus on feedback is that it is widely accepted to be an important part of learning and it refers to an important part of learners' lives. It is not some minor feature of students' experience. They have probably spent more time on their main assignments than on any other aspects of their study. Feedback is the mechanism through which students discover whether they are successful in their work and if they are on track to meet expectations. It is central in their lives as learners. Through feedback teachers communicate what they value and do not value in what students do. It is a personal channel of communication to students about something in which they have typically invested considerable time and effort. Learners care about their work and they care about how it will be judged.

We suggest in this book that there are explanations for what appears to be troubling and that there are many strategies that can considerably enhance the positive impact of feedback on students and their learning. We will show that part of the present 'crisis' is that we do not have a sufficiently secure idea of what feedback is for us to consistently use it effectively. There are overlooked features of feedback that need to be considered to make it work, and there are many options for what we can usefully do. We expect that by engaging with this book, readers will be able to see feedback afresh and will never again arrange students' tasks in the same way. Many of the approaches discussed here do not involve more ongoing effort by teachers, indeed they may end up spending less time marking, or observing performance *in situ*, but they do require us to take a sober look at what is being achieved through feedback practices and rethink what is of most importance to benefit students.

Why be concerned about feedback now?

More than ever, students are expressing dissatisfaction with feedback in higher education. And more than ever, institutions worldwide are investing resources and time in trying to remedy this 'problem'. There is a substantial risk in finding a simple solution that may raise student ratings of feedback quality in the short term, but fail to address the underlying problem. So, having teachers label many of the things that they do in normal teaching as 'feedback' may increase awareness of the diversity of uses of the term – that it is more than giving comments on written work – but it may also lead to cynicism on the part of both teachers and students that what is important is not improving the quality of feedback, but simply identifying that it may be occurring. The 'let's increase our signposting of feedback' response interprets negative student ratings as a lack of awareness of feedback on their part – that is, a learner deficit, not a problem of teaching and courses. It therefore avoids engagement with substantive educational issues and making decisions about changing teaching, learning and assessment practice. The quick fix misses the underlying problems.

Much of the literature in higher and professional education has focused on the 'delivery' of feedback by teachers to students, as if the most important parts of the process are the actions of teachers. This contrasts with the view taken here that the fundamental justification of feedback must be to change what students can do. The acts of teachers need to be judged in the light of their impact on learning. The process of feedback might be prompted by what teachers say or write, but the process is not concluded until action by students occurs. This means a wider perspective must be adopted that includes what happens prior to teacher inputs – briefing, orientation, nature of the task – and what occurs afterwards – responses of students, subsequent attempts at tasks or submission of work, etc. Feedback, in this view, encompasses a far broader group of activities that includes actions by teachers (and others who contribute to feedback) and by students.

This involves not just focusing on what occurs within the conventional framing of feedback, such as improving the quality of comments and ensuring that they reach students in a timely fashion, but reframing the notion of feedback around the effects on students. Feedback thinking then starts with the design of the program or the unit of study, the selection, location and sequencing of tasks, includes the provision of hopefully useful information and the reception and use of this information by students, and ends with both teachers and students seeing the outcome of feedback in improved performance on subsequent tasks. For feedback to be effective, attention needs to be focused more on what occurs before the generation of comments and what occurs afterwards. This is not to say that the comments themselves are not important, but that in isolation from student engagement, they will not be effective. In particular, evidence of effects is needed, not only to ensure that feedback has been done well, but that it has even occurred at all.

It is timely to think further about feedback now not only for these intrinsic reasons, but because higher and professional education is taking place in a rapidly changing context. There is an increase in the numbers and diversity of students, students are drawn from a greater range of educational experiences than ever before, and fewer assumptions can be made about their prior experience and what that equips them to do now. They are being prepared for increasingly diverse forms of practices and workplaces and this is all occurring in an increasingly cost-constrained environment in which personal attention from teachers and supervisors is severely limited. If it was ever possible to base feedback practices on a common set of assumptions about what student work was, it is not possible now.

Finally, we need to attend to feedback now, not just to improve immediate performance of students on their current tasks and educational outcomes, but to build their capacity to use feedback for their own ends. In the world of work, they will typically not have structured processes of learning. Continuing learning in work will require individuals, together with others (peers, consumers, various resources) to take their own initiatives to seek and utilise feedback in settings in which the imperative is productive work, not learning. To do this they will need to be equipped with high levels of self-regulatory ability so they can plan and manage their performance, monitor themselves and utilise all manner of persons and processes to generate what they need to be effective practitioners. The foundation of this needs to be laid from the very start of their courses and reach a very high level by the end so that they can enter the workforce with all that they will need to manage their own learning. A key part of the attainment of this state (learning to trust their self-evaluative capacity) will need to come from feedback processes. So, a key outcome is not just improvement on the performance of tasks now, but on the capacity to better manage subsequent tasks of different kinds. This is the double duty of feedback.

The problems with feedback

Feedback is under scrutiny from many points of view. The problem of feedback is not a singular one. It arises from many different directions and many different dimensions. For an impact to be made, these issues need to be acknowledged and tackled together. The problems we suggest are ones of perception, of shared meaning, of impact on learning, of burdensomeness and of being judged.

Problem of perception

Students believe feedback, however they define it, is done badly and criticise teachers and institutions for this. This has led to instrumental 'band aid' solutions to address the problem. These quick-fix solutions assume that there is no real problem, students just need to recognise the extensive and worthwhile feedback that is already widespread in their courses. A typical example reported to us was the remarks of a Pro-Vice-Chancellor who encouraged teachers to signal and underline their use of anything that seemed like feedback on every occasion they could think of. She was reported as saying something along the lines of 'remember, when commenting in your lecture on the test just completed say to the students that you are giving them feedback'! Regarding feedback as a problem of perception is a good example of the phenomenon of blaming the student: '*we* are doing the right thing, students just don't seem able to see it'! Teachers are not responding to the feedback delivered by students. Or more correctly, are responding in limited ways that deflect any responsibility for changing their practice.

Problem of shared meaning

Even if both students and teachers acknowledge that there is an issue with feedback, it doesn't mean that they interpret it in the same way as each other. Indeed, they can have quite different perceptions of what the process involves. This means that changes as seen by teachers may not be seen as an improvement from the student perspective. Adcroft (2011), for example, argues that teachers and students each have their own mythologies of feedback which informs their beliefs, attitudes and behaviours in the feedback process. He suggests that these myths create dissonance as the two groups offer different interpretations of the same feedback events. In his study, students perceive that they receive feedback much less frequently than academics perceive that they give it. Students see the feedback they receive as much less multi-dimensional than do academics and they see marks and written comments on assessed work as much more critical to their learning experience than do academics.

Problem of impact on learning

It is impossible to justify the time and effort spent on feedback if it does not have a positive impact on what learners can do. This implies that the main test of the inputs of teachers and others is not in terms of content or style or timing, but in terms of whether they make a difference to what students can produce. What is termed feedback doesn't necessarily lead to a positive effect on learning. Commonly it has no effect because information from teachers is not taken up by students and sometimes it is not even read. In other circumstances, for example when students receive overly critical appraisals of their work, it can have a negative impact on learning (Kluger, A. N. and DeNisi, 1996; Hattie and Timperley, 2007).

Problem of burdensomeness

Marking of students' work can have a tendency to take on a routine character. A well-defined range of comments are made year after year on similar tasks. This can lead to teachers believing that marking is a chore and is done mainly for reasons of generating grades. They can have low expectations that it will improve student performance and become disillusioned and disconnected with it and seek to have it undertaken by lowly paid assistants. Feedback cannot be improved in the long term if it is seen as one of the unpleasant side effects of teaching. Making it satisfying for teachers is just as important as making it worthwhile for students.

Problem of being judged

Receiving what are perceived to be judgemental comments from others does not engender a positive disposition and desire to change. Students naturally resist the views of others that they do not like, and particularly resist those that are not seen as respectful or of being in their own best interests.

The fear of judging students too strongly leads to teachers being mealy-mouthed in their comments and creating comments which are indirect and difficult for students to interpret clearly. It also leads to formulaic responses such as the feedback sandwich – a positive comment followed by a negative one and then another positive. Ironically, part of the solution is the removal of judgemental language from feedback. Learners are open to information they see to be useful to them. However, if that information is couched in terms of judgements or in terms of 'final vocabulary' which leaves no room for response (Boud 1995), then it is more difficult for them to process it and use it to change what they do. They spend time wrestling with the weight of judgement before getting to the useful information.

It can be seen from this initial analysis of the problematic nature of feedback and how it is interpreted and used, that multifaceted solutions are needed. It is not a matter of adding more to our existing conceptions of feedback, or of necessarily looking for new and interesting ways of providing information to students. This is needed, but we also need a richer conception of what feedback is and a broader notion of its scope.

The major issue in feedback from our perspective is that inappropriate ideas about 'the activity' are reinforced by simplistic ideas and misconceptions of what that act is, could be and how it can be effectively utilised. In this book we present the view that feedback constitutes a set of practices, framed by purposeful and dual intentions (to improve immediate work and future work), and nestled within conditions favourable for uptake and use.

What do we mean by feedback?

Feedback, as we are beginning to see, is a slippery term. It is used in an everyday sense within institutions to refer to the making of comments on students' work. It is seen as a helpful adjunct to grading in which specific points are elaborated and guidance for improvement given to students in addition to the allocation of marks. In this colloquial use of the term feedback, the reporting on work to students in a timely fashion is seen as a necessary attribute of feedback. Indeed, many institutions have rules or guidelines which specify that work needs to be returned within two or three weeks of when it was submitted. In this taken-for-granted sense of the term, feedback may also be given verbally, practically or through electronic media. However it still takes the character of teachers, practitioners or indeed other students providing information about particular work.

As we shall discuss in more detail in the next chapter, this is a very teacher-centric view of feedback. It is one that focuses on the activities of the teacher – writing comments, returning work, discussing work verbally – rather than the activities of the learner – seeking information, responding to comments, incorporating what is learned from them in later work. Given the major shifts that have occurred towards taking a more learner-centric or learning-focused view of teaching and learning in higher education, this residue of a teacher focus appears like a relic of the past. Perhaps an emphasis on what students are expected to do in feedback might help transform a tired practice into one that could generate enthusiasm and meaningful action.

Ironically, such a shift of emphasis is not a radical new departure for feedback, but a return to the origins of the term itself. In Chapter 2 where we look to the disciplinary bases from which the metaphor of feedback has been borrowed, such as biology and engineering, we will see that feedback is characterised by its effects – the changes that occur as a result of the application of information – rather than by the inputs into the process: the output of a circuit is altered by feedback or the temperature of an organism is regulated. A view of feedback that more thoroughly respects the traditions from which it emerged might have a lot to offer in education. Many metaphors are extended beyond their scope of applicability. Conversely, the metaphor of feedback has more to offer than it at first sight appears.

While the idea of feedback is elaborated throughout this book, it is useful to start with a working definition on which we can later build. There are many different variations in the literature, but the one we adopt focuses on the learner rather the those who might provide inputs:

Feedback is a process whereby learners obtain information about their work in order to appreciate the similarities and differences between the appropriate standards for any given work, and the qualities of the work itself, in order to generate improved work.

Some of the features of this definition are

- It centres on learners and what they do, rather than what teachers or other parties others do for them;
- It recognises the importance of external standards applicable to work produced and the need for learners to understand what these are;

- It is a process extended over time and is not a single act of reception of information;
- It sees the appreciation of variation between the standards to be applied and the work itself as an important point of focus;
- It positions feedback as leading to action as a necessary part of the process.

The book

This book takes the view that there is currently poor understanding of what feedback is, and even where such an understanding exists, the consequences are inadequately put into practice. There has been considerable development in research on feedback in recent years, and a shift in basic ideas about how it should be thought about, but there is surprisingly little awareness of what needs to be done. The book addresses this gap by providing access to current thinking and research on feedback by those who have been major players in the literature and those who have applied these ideas in real teaching and learning situations. It aims to be a major source and influence on feedback in the higher and professional education area.

It provides a multi-disciplinary and international account of the role of feedback in higher and professional education. Current models for best practice are critiqued and new approaches examined, grounded in secure conceptual foundations. Such a focused untangling of the conceptual roots of feedback is a relatively novel endeavour in the education literature. Many researchers on feedback – both in higher education and the workplace – define effective feedback as constituting clear steps (these steps are rarely contested) and they look for the frequency of these actions within practice.

The book challenges the reader to consider how sensible it is to apply a generic and behavioural set of guidelines to all facets and contexts of feedback and only link it to formally assessed work. It looks to different kinds of feedback processes for different purposes. Oral feedback is examined along with feedback on written work, on experiential learning in the workplace, online and in simulated learning environments. The idea of the teacher acting alone as the source of feedback is challenged. Research on multi-source feedback, the role of peers, and the role of consumers in encouraging learners to reflect on and change practice is presented. Prospects for improving practice will be presented and discussed, reflecting the key conceptual foundations that inform feedback processes.

The book challenges three conventional assumptions about feedback in learning:

1   That feedback constitutes one-way flow of information from a knowledgeable person to a less knowledgeable person.
    We ask the question of 'what would feedback look like if we were working from a model of learning where the learner takes agency to solicit opinion, to self-evaluate and to co-construct strategies for improvement?' We suggest how these features can be realised.

2   That the job of feedback is complete with the imparting of performance-related information.

We argue that a necessary function of feedback is 'closing the loop' where learners and educators create an opportunity to act on the message and detect the quality of subsequent change in action. Without examining the consequences of the feedback message, how can educators calibrate the type and volume of feedback they are providing to learners? We suggest that much of what is currently termed feedback in education today doesn't meet the basic requirement of noticeably influencing learning.

3   That a generic model of best-practice feedback can be applied to all learners and all learning situations

We present reasons for why current advocated feedback models (primarily based on behaviourism) are not appropriate for application in higher and professional education due to variation in context, variation in person and varieties of risk. We emphasise the limited assumptions, inherent in current models, about how people learn. Empirical examples are provided to show how these 'generic best practice feedback frameworks' fall apart with the loading of authentic learning activities in university-based and workplace environments.

The aim of this book is to present a detailed examination and re-conceptualisation of feedback practice within higher and professional education. Although there is a growing body of literature devoted to feedback, distinct gaps remain in our understanding of the process and its impact on professional skills development. This lack of clarity is largely due to the fact that feedback is a complex intervention that is dependent on the characteristics of the learning context, the source of the feedback, the individual recipient, and the message that is generated. It is the multi-dimensional nature of the process that makes the analysis of feedback inter-actions so challenging. Although the book is targeted primarily at educators, it aims to inform all parties in the learner-teacher relationship about how learning can be effectively promoted in both academic and workplace settings.

We move beyond reductionist and behaviourist approaches, such as 'the feedback sandwich' model, to explore novel ways of introducing learners and educators to the theoretical principles underpinning effective feedback. Through the presentation of action research, observational studies, case studies and program implementation and evaluation on feedback, the book provides ideas on how to better prepare teaching staff, learners, peers and consumers to meaningfully engage in written, verbal and electronic forms of feedback in order to maximise learning and teacher/student satisfaction.

The chapters

In contrast to the texts currently available on learning and practice in higher education, this book is not framed as an instructional 'how to do it' guide.

Instead, it aims to challenge and tease out historical and current assumptions of best-practice feedback.

In each chapter the context for feedback is set, and problems and prospects for feedback practice addressed in relation to the literature and authors' own research findings, where applicable. Authors have been asked to focus on application to practice pitched at both providers and seekers of feedback, including, as appropriate, undergraduate and postgraduate learners on campus and in the workplace. This provides practical examples of how educators/supervisors and learners can apply the key chapter messages in their practice.

The first three chapters set the scene for the 'problem' of feedback and provide a rationale for alternative notions of feedback so that it can better fulfil its purpose. A key conceptual argument is the importance of situating the learner at the centre of the process, and shifting our concern to how learners seek and use feedback, rather than how educators give it. Feedback, within this new notion, is seen as a mechanism to help both learners, teachers and others change their practices, and is seen as a process to build learners' self-evaluative judgement over time.

The next three chapters highlight the impact of emotion, culture and relationships, specifically trust, on feedback. Establishing conditions conducive to the uptake of feedback are seen as imperative to its capacity to improve work. There is no attempt to simplify the complexity of the socio-cultural influences on feedback but rather the multiple and intersecting influences are brought out and untangled.

Chapters 7 and 8 focus on different modes of feedback, being written and digital, and the unique advantages of the different methods of engagement are raised. Chapter 9 discusses the potential for feedback in simulated learning environments that enable task attempts in a lower-stakes learning environment than that which has a personal impact on patients or clients. All three chapters emphasise that we need different types of feedback for different purposes.

The last section of the book is devoted to different sources of feedback, beyond the teacher. The potential for peers and consumers to act as useful sources of knowledge is discussed, along with the latest research on multi-source feedback tools, and how these can inform learners' judgements about performance. The value of these 'others' to act as sources of feedback is under-recognised and under-utilised. Finally, in Chapter 13, the editors summarise the key messages in the book, and frame these messages in terms of effective decision-making for feedback. Considered design of feedback in the wider curriculum is needed, along with thoughtful and responsive decisions within episodes. The key message of the final chapter – a thread that connects all chapters of the book – is that feedback implies an expectation that the information generated is going to be used. This is a very different prospect to the sprinkling of hopefully useful information that has come to define itself as feedback in education.

References

Adcroft, A. (2011) 'The mythology of feedback', *Higher Education Research and Development*, 30(4):405-19.

Boud, D. (1995) 'Assessment and learning: contradictory or complementary?', in Knight, P. (ed.), *Assessment for Learning in Higher Education*. London: Kogan.

Kluger, A. N. and DeNisi, A. (1996) 'The effects of feedback interventions on performance: A historical review, a meta-analysis, and a preliminary feedback intervention theory', *Psychological Bulletin*, 119(2):254-84.

Hattie, J. and Timperley, H. (2007) 'The power of feedback', *Review of Educational Research*, 77:81-112.

Chapter 2

Changing conceptions of feedback

Elizabeth Molloy
David Boud

Introduction

Feedback has proved problematic for individual learners, for teachers and for institutions. The lack and availability of it is criticised by students. Teachers bemoan the burden of marking. And leaders of educational institutions wonder why, of all things they have to deal with, feedback creates so much difficulty. There is no shortage of proposals and recipes for action. Is it just a matter of seriously attending to these and ensuring that they are put into practice? If only it were clear what feedback was and how it could be implemented well, then the problems should severely diminish. The fact that so much has been written about the topic and so much energy has been expended without resolving the problem suggests more of the same is not enough. So much has been invested in the idea that it can't be wished away; it has to be confronted. New ways of thinking about feedback are needed. A clear view of current assumptions and practice is needed as a starting point, but it is also important to step back and examine feedback in its wider context to see what it promises and what it might be reasonably be expected to do.

In this chapter we suggest that it is necessary to go back to the origins of feedback in other fields of endeavour: what has it been used for and how it has been used effectively. Feedback is not an idea native to education. It is an enormously powerful and successful concept that has been borrowed from other disciplines and taken up in the field of education. It is from the translation into the educational context that different feedback practices and traditions have sprung, many of which have lost the main feature of the idea and have not proved fit for purpose. New ideas about feedback have been introduced with little evidence of their effects. We start by examining some of these practical schemes, or nostrums, that have embedded themselves in the teaching and learning discourse. And we will highlight how problematising these practices can lead us to thinking about feedback in a different, and hopefully more useful way.

Following this critique of common practices claimed as 'feedback' we wish to consider the idea of feedback in its wider context – first to see what ideas from its successful application elsewhere offer something for education, and then to examine what it is that feedback in education in particular needs to satisfy if it is to be successful.

Two models for practising feedback will be introduced and discussed, drawing extensively on a framework we have proposed in a recent paper (Boud and Molloy, in press). The first of these is built directly on the origins of feedback in other disciplines and identifies the key characteristic of feedback as a noticeable change in learners. The second model builds on the first, but it adds the unique feature of educational feedback: that the learner has volition and agency. It treats the learner not as if they were a passive object responding to a stimulus, but as a thinking, acting person. In this model, feedback is positioned not as an episodic act linked to marking of assessed work, but rather as situated *as part of* the overall design of the curriculum with a clear function to perform. The implications for practice in these two frameworks will be considered, including generating dispositions for teachers and learners to effectively take up these forms of feedback, along with features of curriculum design.

Challenging the Nostrums

Reports of learner dissatisfaction with feedback, whether in the educational or workplace setting, lead us to re-examine the ways that what is commonly termed 'feedback' is being enacted. In professional development there are a number of assumptions or recipes that are sometimes promoted as 'best practice'. Dissecting these nostrums can provide revealing insights into how feedback is viewed, carried out and evaluated. While some may argue that 'a little bit of knowledge is better than nothing', we suggest that professional development that provides quick tricks or formulaic approaches to practices such as feedback can be detrimental through encouraging educators to take up practices that deviate from the main purpose of feedback. In other words, quick tricks or nostrums that are not contextualised in a sound theory or evaluated practice may do more harm than good.

Nostrum 1: All feedback is good feedback

Many accounts of feedback in education begin with the claim that feedback drives learning and that learning or performance is optimised through the provision of feedback to students. If we look at the evidence, particularly the very helpful comprehensive systematic reviews by Hattie and Timperley (2007) and Kluger and DeNisi (1996), it is clear that some feedback has no effect on learning or performance, and in fact, there can be negative effects. Empirical work in psychology and healthcare suggests that feedback is a complex process and can have both positive and detrimental effects on performance depending on the task, the learning setting or the learner's motivation in approaching the task. For example, research by Kluger and Van Dijk (2010) and Ilgen and Davis (2000) indicated that critical feedback provided without sufficient strategies for improvement could undermine task performance and motivation for subsequent mastery of tasks, projecting students into a state of 'learned helplessness'.

This lack of productive impact of feedback on learning is not limited to episodes of critical or harsh commentary to learners. Ende's (1983, 1995) studies indicated that feedback characterised by praise had little impact on learners' performance, and if anything, had the potential to provide learners with over-inflated perceptions of how they executed tasks. These findings from both experimental and observational studies suggest that not all feedback is good feedback, and rather, that the potency of feedback as a process in learning is contingent on context, timing, and learner and educator attributes and skills.

Nostrum 2: The more the merrier

An overwhelming institutional response to student satisfaction surveys in higher education relating to the 'feedback problem' has been 'we must give more feedback' or 'we must ensure that students understand all comments as feedback'. This is either because student questionnaire responses are taken literally, or because one of the hypotheses to explain students' poor feedback ratings is that students don't recognise many examples of performance infor-mation, such as that given in lectures, as feedback.

The need for commentary on students' work, with clear, collaboratively devised strategies to improve performance on subsequent tasks is real. Whether increasing the frequency of commentary or the amount of commentary (how much is said, or critiqued) might be contested. Or at least, it should be tested. The landscape of assessment in higher education changed considerably from the 1960s with a focus on multiple assessment episodes to drive and to gauge achievement of standards (Rowntree, 1977). This change in approach was stimulated by arguments about the lack of validity of once-off assessments in a standard format and also the reported stress on students in completing single high-stakes examinations. There should now be more opportunities structured within programs to give and receive feedback, yet students appear to be more disillusioned with feedback than ever. Why is this so?

One explanation might be that the frequency or volume of feedback does not necessarily equate to meaningfulness or usefulness of feedback to learning. Rather it may be that the conditions in which feedback episodes sit have a larger bearing on the student experience of whether or not engaging in feedback is worthwhile. For example, continuity of the learner-educator relationship so that educators develop a close understanding of the learners' work over time (including how the work changes in response to feedback) may be more important than the volume of feedback provided in the program.

Moving from the program level to the episodic level of feedback provision, the concept of 'the more the merrier' can also be challenged. A study by Molloy (2009) of feedback in the clinical workplace found that physiotherapy students, when confronted with a large volume of feedback on their performance, found it difficult to prioritise the messages, and therefore were challenged to implement changes based on the information exchange. Large amounts of feedback may simply increase their cognitive load (van Merriënboer and Sweller, 2005) so much that they can't process what is available. Research is needed into what constitutes a suitable amount and type of feedback in order to both motivate learners to change their behaviours or approaches while at the same time not swamping them with information they cannot process.

Nostrum 3: Feedback is telling

There appears to be an assumption in feedback practice that what the educator does is the most important part of the feedback process. That is, educators' skills in observing learner performance, detecting points for improvement and then delivering this information in an artful way (exercising sensitive linguistic choices) are *the* determinants of feedback efficacy. While not diminishing the importance of educators, we observe that this view fundamentally misses the point. Feedback needs to be framed in terms of what learners do – what educators do is only a means to this end. Unfortunately, many professional development initiatives for improving feedback are anchored in this nostrum (Molloy and Boud, 2012). However, as Carless et al (2011) pointed out, 'tinkering with feedback elements such as timing and detail is unlikely to be sufficient [in generating good feedback]. What is required is a more fundamental reconceptualisation of the feedback process' (p. 2).

There has also been recent literature, written from a constructivist perspective, about how to engage learners as active players in feedback (Butler and Winne, 1995; Boud, 2000; Hounsell, 2007). These proposals are grounded in the notion that students are central to the process of learning, and that the feedback and strategies for improving practice should be collaboratively devised between learners and educators. Despite these recommendations, many of the feedback models remain teacher-centric, and many verbal feedback interactions are didactic exchanges of educator opinion on what went wrong and what needs to happen to enable improvement.

Molloy's (2009) observational study of verbal feedback in clinical education revealed that on average the feedback exchanges lasted for 21 minutes, and that the average input from physiotherapy students was 2 minutes within this encounter. In post-session interviews, educators acknowledged the monologic nature of the feedback sessions and attributed this to lack of time to engage in a legitimate conversation. Some indicated that they did in fact extend invitations for students to self-evaluate in line with best practice principles, but privately hoped that these invitations would not be taken up:

> We've all got time restraints so you know, saying 'what did you do well?' and then giving feedback, it all takes extra time and that's an issue as well. And you know, I find myself saying to the learner 'OK, what did you think [about your performance]?' and then hoping inside me that they'll be really quick about what they want to tell me.

(Molloy 2009 p. 134).

Other educators in the study justified their 'telling' style because of a lack of trust in students' judgements. They were concerned that inaccurate student self-evaluations would require energy to contest with counter-data and counter-arguments and conceded to acquiescing to known transmissive rituals whereby the expert tells the novice. They seemed to be saying that if only the students would listen to them more attentively, then all would be well. The findings suggest that educators may be more focused on securing short-term outcomes including efficiency and harmony of the exchange (with a lack of contested viewpoints) rather than committing to longer-term outcomes such as developing learners' capacity for self-evaluation in practice.

Undoubtedly it is important for educators to establish conditions favourable for the exchange and uptake of performance information. Student-centred practices are only achieved through focusing initially on what teachers do. However with modelling, with increasing exposure to standards of practice and familiarity with teaching and learning expectations, learners should be able to progressively seek the feedback they need. They need also to be able to commit to self-evaluation alongside externally generated feedback. By allowing students agency in feedback practices, educators can better cue into learners' needs for feedback and help generate meaningful and achievable strategies for improvement. 'It is helpful to remember that what the student does is more important in determining what is learned than what the teacher does.' (Sheull, in Biggs 1993, p. 73).

Nostrum 4: Feedback ends in telling

That feedback *ends* in telling is unfortunately one of the most followed and pernicious nostrums in the feedback business – that is, a seemingly common acknowledgement by educators that the work of feedback is done once performance information is imparted. Definitions of feedback are promoted that emphasise the act of reflecting back to the learner the 'reality' of the performance, so that feedback serves as a mirror to performance (Molloy, 2009). The 'seeing' or 'replaying' or 'diagnostics' of feedback is only one function of the process however. Sadler (1989), in his seminal paper, described three essential components of feedback which include: information on the goal of performance, information on the executed performance, and finally and most importantly, strategies to address the gap between task goal and task performance. A study in medical education by Fernando et al. (2008) found that of all the feedback encounters recorded, only 50 per cent of these included strategies for how the learner could improve. The seemingly high focus on the diagnostic element of feedback, and the lack of emphasis on how the learner can move forward in their practice – the bridging-the-gap component in Sadler's account of feedback – is alarming. Without helping learners devise ways to move forward in their learning, Sadler has said that this information is not feedback at all, merely 'dangling data' (Sadler, 1989, p. 121). Worryingly, much of the feedback literature in higher and professional education is on how to improve the telling techniques of the educator so that they can more skilfully dangle the data (Boud and Molloy, in press).

In principle, devising strategies for learner improvement would not appear to be too onerous or too taxing a demand for the educator. Indeed, they should be a normal part of what teachers do. The lack of engagement in this key component in feedback could potentially be explained by a lack of expectation that this is part of the deal. That feedback does end in telling. The second component in challenging this nostrum is that educators have a responsibility to set subsequent (and related) tasks for the learner so that learners have an opportunity to demonstrate change in their behaviour. This subsequent demonstration of performance is part of completing the feedback loop – it is the output component of the process. The pivotal nature of this output component of the feedback loop will be explored in detail later in this chapter. The 'closing of the loop' provides opportunities to the learner, and also opportunities for educators, to evaluate the quality of their educational messages and advice. For example, if the student does not improve their performance in the subsequent task, the educator may need to rethink the way in which they have constructed the performance information and practice advice.

This observation and analysis of future task performance provides essential feedback to the educator on their own skills as a teacher. Without this, how can the educator know that they have acted appropriately? Yorke (2003) argued for the importance of conceptualising formative and summative assessment as a mechanism to help the teacher. 'The act of assessing has an effect on the assessor as well as the student. Assessors learn about the extent to which they [the students] have developed expertise and can tailor their teaching accordingly' (p. 482). In order to be realised, this notion relies on two things: reasonable continuity of the educator-learner relationship, and a record of knowledge of student work, so that educators can observe subsequent performances. This in turn requires the setting of subsequent tasks that enable learners to exercise similar competencies or address similar standards and noticing the changes that have or have not occurred. With the increasing fragmentation of programs where experts deliver discrete topics/modules, and the shortening placements in professional workplace learning, these two conditions are becoming harder to meet.

Picking the nostrums apart

In summary, what we wanted to reveal is that these nostrums, or rules of thumb, live in practice and are perpetuated through word of mouth, literature and professional development initiatives. They are decisive and relatively simplistic. And what they all assume is that feedback is a fairly simple idea; easy to execute. The nostrums serve to mask the complexity of feedback and direct attention to considerations that are probably not the most important ones.

Our intention is not to seek to generate a list of 'better nostrums' in an attempt to improve feedback practices. Rather we emphasise the elemental features of feedback and seek to elicit the implications of these for practice. We focus on what feedback exists to do, and how can it do that effectively.

Rethinking feedback: Revisiting origins

Feedback, as a process, was not founded in the field of education. Corrective feedback became important through the rise of mechanisation in the industrial revolution. An engine, for example, could be regulated through gauging its output (i.e. how much steam was produced) and feeding this 'performance information' back into the system to control it. Similar features can be seen in the way that a thermostat works today to control a building's temperature. The controller stores the reference value (e.g. 24 degrees), compares it with the current, measured value (i.e. 21 degrees) and on the basis of this comparison, provides an output that enables correction (raises the room to 24 degrees through a surge in heat).

Feedback has been prominent in considerations of biological processes – for example, how organisms could adapt to changing conditions and yet still maintain controlled internal conditions needed for survival. Homeostasis is perhaps the most sophisticated feedback loop we can draw upon, enabling the body to regulate variables such as pH levels and temperature regardless of inputs that threaten to undermine the delicate balance. Feedback in both engineering and biological examples involves the control of a system by reinserting into the system the results of its performance.

Feedback became part of an area of study concerned with regulation, order and stability of complex systems. In the 1950s, these principles began to be talked about in the newly created field of cybernetics (Wiener, 1954), and eventually education (Ende, 1983). The system in focus was no longer the steam engine or a biological process, but the learner. External performance information was provided to improve a learner's subsequent performance – that is, to help make it correspond more closely to the reference value, which were the standards for good work. The difference in the application to education is that humans have the capacity to think and make judgements as to whether performance targets have been reached. Information does not act automatically, it has to be processed by learners and they have to decide whether to act upon it to lead to a changed output. The neglect of this vital stage led to a distortion of research and neglect by teachers of a necessary feature of feedback.

Because of this focus on the input of information, feedback theory in education tended to ignore the role of the learner in the process, and positioned them akin to a mechanical system whereby a certain stimulus (information from a teacher) was likely to result in a predicable response in learner behaviour. It is not surprising that feedback became a practice where a more experienced person tells a less experienced one about how they can do things better.

What was lost from the theoretical framework of feedback when applied to education (apart from the volition of the learner) was consideration of the change in the learner's subsequence performance as a result of the information input. As argued by Wager and Wager (1985), feedback became to be seen as any type of information provided to learners after they have engaged in a learning task. The mutation in definition meant that that notion of a learner comparing actual performance with intended performance and then changing subsequent performance was lost. This left an attenuated concept of feedback in education that has inhibited development ever since.

Rethinking feedback: Mark 1

Feedback, as applied to education, had become synonymous with 'telling', where educators were seen as responsible for providing accurate information to learners on the observed task. Underpinning this notion is the assumption that if students can only adhere to the advice provided, they can improve their performance. This, in turn, assumes that the information that educators provide is accurate, meaningful, unambiguous and realistic, and that it enables this change to occur. Apart from disregarding the agency of the learner in this process (ignoring what they think is important, what they want to achieve, what they are able to achieve), it places enormous pressure on the educator to see all, know all and say all. No wonder the literature tells us that feedback is hard to give, as well as hard to take (Molloy and Boud, 2012). In our earlier conceptual paper (Boud and Molloy, in press) we proposed two ways to think about feedback in education. These notions, or models, we described as Feedback Mark 1 and Feedback Mark 2.

Feedback Mark 1 leans on a key premise of feedback from the engineering or biological conceptualisation. That is, information about their current level of work is available to learners in order to affect the quality of subsequent work. The process occurs in order to produce higher-quality subsequent work, not solely as an act of communication from educator to student. There needs, of course, to be a way of determining whether this change has occurred in the direction desired, because the feedback effect cannot be judged by looking at what the educator does:

> *If the information which proceeds backwards from the performance is able to change the general methods and pattern of the performance, we have a process which may very well be called learning.*

> (Wiener 1954, p. 71)

Without this visible detection of change, we have a process we might call the imparting of 'hopefully useful information', which it would be inappropriate to label 'feedback'.

In challenging nostrums in feedback practice earlier in the chapter, we saw how most of the espoused principles of good practice are centred on improving the information-imparting ability of the educator. Feedback Mark 1 goes beyond this to focus on what this information is used for. See Figure 2.1.

Figure 2.1 Feedback Mark 1: Input and output components of the system

The information provided to students is used to influence their subsequent task performance. This output manifest in performance on the later task is a central part of the feedback process. Conventionally, the tendency is to label the first box titled 'information to student' as feedback, and therefore to feel that the job of feedback is complete at this junction. Until a response to it has been made and identified by the educator, this remains 'hopefully useful information'. As represented in the Figure, feedback is part of a system that necessarily involves both input from others and output from the learner.

Figure 2.1 represents the feedback loop for learners, but Feedback Mark 1 also provides an important feedback process for those who offer feedback information. See Figure 2.2.

The provider of information receives useful data about whether the input offered to the learner has had a desirable effect in improving their performance. Using this data, the educator can adjust the information they provide to maximise the possibility that it will have a positive influence on learners. They do this in two ways. First, through observing the effects in subsequent tasks by the same student. Second, through providing hopefully improved information to students in the next cohort on the original task. This is an essential feedback loop for the purpose of educator skill development:

> *The act of assessing has an effect on the assessor as well as the student. Assessors learn about the extent to which they [the students] have developed expertise and can tailor their teaching accordingly.*
>
> (Yorke 2003, p. 482).

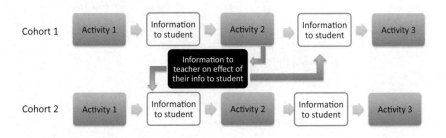

Figure 2.2 Educators adjust information provided to students over time.

For example, if a learner approaches Activity 2 in the same way as Activity 1, with no modification of their work in the direction desired, the educator has good cause to question their own advice, and to think of alternative strategies to help the learner change their approach to their work. The learner's response, as depicted by Activity 2, acts as data to help the educator refine their own 'feedback skills'. Educators calibrate their ability to provide useful information to students through comparison of the comments they provide with the student's work in the subsequent task. This enables more effective information to be provided for students in (a) later tasks for the same students, and (b) the same task for the next cohort of students.

The other key premise of Feedback Mark 1 is that students, following performance information from the first activity, must engage in a second activity that is constructed to allow their changed performance in the desired area to be demonstrated and noticed. This means that the design of the subsequent activity ('Activity 2' as pictured in Figure 2.1) needs to contain some overlapping features to enable the learner to demonstrate the change in performance. This concept is represented in Figure 2.3.

The design of tasks or activities needs to be such as to ensure overlap of some key learning outcomes. The 'nesting of tasks' enables the feedback loop to be completed through detecting the effects of earlier information provision in subsequent tasks. Figure 2.3 shows not only the overlap of learning outcomes (nesting) but also that task complexity may increase as the learner develops over time.

The question arises, what should the overlapping material include? Clearly, it is inappropriate and unnecessary for basic material that can be demonstrated as learned through a single iteration to be repeated. This leaves such things as core

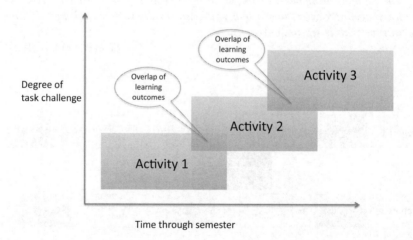

Figure 2.3 Feedback as iterative and nested task design

or threshold concepts (i.e. key ideas that are challenging to appreciate but funda-mental for further study: Meyer and Land, 2005); academic skills, such as writing and other forms of communication; and discipline-specific material that requires continuing practice to fully learn. The old notion that different assessment tasks should test quite discrete learning outcomes is not compatible with such an output-oriented notion of feedback.

So here lies Feedback Mark 1 – a conception of feedback for education that draws from the biological and engineering origins of feedback. Feedback Mark 1 reminds us that feedback is a system whereby learners use external information on performance in order to narrow the gap between intended and executed performance. Learners need to be provided with subsequent opportunities to demonstrate change in performance after they receive this information, and the subsequent activity should share some overlapping learning outcomes with the original task. The benefit of 'doing feedback' in this way is for both the learner and the educator (through seeing the results of the information transfer).

We should note that an implication of Feedback Mark 1 is that educators require knowledge of what were the earlier comments and what use of them the student made before they provide a second iteration of information to the student. Discrete, fully anonymised marking can be disruptive of effective feedback. It might be undertaken, but it is far more resource-intensive and may limit the quality of feedback information.

Could we promote Feedback Mark 1 and feel justified in saying that the conceptual work of this book is done? We could certainly argue that feedback practices, if they resembled Mark 1, would be more effective than what is currently implemented in conventional educational practice. However, we can't rest here because Feedback Mark 1 still represents the learner as resembling a machine. We need to go further and examine the implications of a rather obvious feature of students: they are human beings who make their own choices about what they do. Feedback Mark 2 builds on Feedback Mark 1 and seeks to take account of the learner as an agent in the process, capable of self-evaluation, and capable of taking on, or ignoring, aspects of the externally provided information, depending on their perceived use for it.

There is a further pragmatic need to move beyond Feedback Mark 1. It may simply not be possible to fit in sufficient numbers of tasks in which feedback is utilised within the typical higher education course and level of staffing to achieve the desired effects. If students can be more actively mobilised, then better use might be made of necessarily limited information.

Rethinking feedback: Mark 2

Feedback Mark 2 introduces a new discourse of feedback in learning. It departs from Feedback Mark 1, because it is based on the notion that learners are neces-sarily active and volitional. They do not have passive and predictable responses to given inputs. Mark 1 sees teachers or educators having full control of the feedback process. Learners need to play their part, but this role is constrained to what is provided to them by others. Feedback Mark 2 sees students as having significant agency and choice. They are regarded as being capable of soliciting and using feedback rather than being recipients of the 'inputs' of others. Most importantly, Mark 2 acknowledges that the impact of feedback extends beyond immediate subsequent task performance. The premise of Mark 2 is that feedback, as a process, has a role in developing students' continuing evaluative judgement that has a more sustainable impact on learners. Feedback is seen not only as having an influence on immediate tasks but of building students' capability for making judgements about their subsequent work.

This is an important feature of what Boud (2000) has termed sustainable assessment. He called for students to necessarily be active players in their assessment within programs and noted that 'acts of assessment need both to meet the specific and immediate goals of a course as well as establishing a basis for students to undertake their own assessment activities in the future. To draw attention to the importance of this, the idea that assessment always has to do double duty is introduced' (p. 151). This 'double duty' of assessment and feedback is acknowledged in Feedback Mark 2, where the act of feedback not only has the potential to positively impact subsequent attempts at an activity or task, but also plays a key role in helping learners to develop informed judgement (Molloy, 2009).

Butler and Winne (1995) also identified the importance of positioning the learner at the centre of the feedback process and recognised that the learner actively makes links between their goals in learning, the strategies or approaches they use to achieve this target and their actual performance outcomes. This comparative process may propel the student to alter their conception of the learning goal and standards or may cause them to alter the strategies they employ to try to reach the goal. The external feedback provider, whether that is a peer, practitioner or educator then provides additional external information that helps to further inform the 'adjustment process'.

There is ample literature in the health sciences describing the poor capacity that humans have in isolation for accurate self-assessment (Eva and Regehr, 2005). Indeed, this is one of the reasons why it is so important to help develop it. This very tendency to lack objectivity when it comes to 'self' is why external feedback is so important for learning. Our ability to judge our own actions in a way that reflects others' judgement of our actions is highly variable and can be influenced by a number or factors related to disposition, environment and practice opportunities. For this reason, particularly when entering any aspect of a field as a novice, humans need external performance information to help calibrate their own judgement about how things are going. Even though effective self-assessment may be difficult to achieve, there is evidence that supported practice at self-judgement can improve reliability of ratings (Eva and Regehr, 2005).

The student's comparison of the internal appraisal and external appraisal of performance is a key process in development as a learner. It enables them to interpret what is required for any task, and to design strategies to reach the task goal. The external information may be significantly different to students' own internal judgement of the 'work' and this may help to calibrate the learner's judgement (Boud et al., submitted for publication). The ability to 'accurately' judge one's own work and the work of others is arguably one of the fundamental competencies required in the workplace (Boud and Falchikov, 2007).

If students are to take a greater role in making judgements about their learning, then our models of feedback need to be adapted to take this into account. A necessary feature of such a model is that students are expected to take more of an initiatory role. The obvious place where this can begin is in identifying the kinds of input from others that would be most helpful to them. Depending on the kinds of prior educational experience students have had, this may be a challenging process for some. Any lack of confidence on their part in doing so and in identifying the kinds of information they need speaks more to the inadequacies of their earlier experiences than the importance of being able to take a proactive approach to feedback. It is common for students to be resistant at first to seeking specific comments, so this process typically needs to be introduced carefully to them.

The second important expectation of Feedback Mark 2 is that students follow through and actively utilise the information they have solicited in subsequent work. The importance of having later activities in which students can demonstrate their utilisation of hopefully useful information is no less in Mark 2 as in Mark 1. The role students take in actively soliciting and using feedback is represented in Figure 2.4.

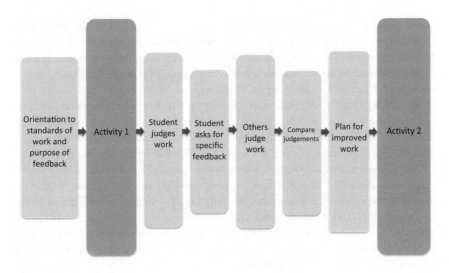

Figure 2.4 Mark 2 Feedback: Active role of students in soliciting and using feedback

The seven distinguishing features of this representation of Feedback Mark 2 are:

1   Students are orientated not only to standards of work (learning outcomes) but also to the purpose of feedback. With this explicit orientation, students are more likely to see feedback as a process they can use, rather than a tool imposed on them.

2   Students judge their own work and are encouraged to articulate this judgement (self-evaluation).

3   Students seek or solicit feedback on those aspects of their work that matter to them most (for example, asking the external source to comment on particular aspects of their performance that require improvement). This serves to cue educators and external providers of information into what to focus on to best help learners achieve their goals. This honesty in acknowledging limitations in their own practice does leave them vulnerable, and this honesty can be compromised if students are overly attuned to the summative assessment process – that is, they are always attempting to 'show their best selves' to the educator.

4   Educators or 'others' provide performance information to the learner.

5   The learner then engages in a comparative process where they combine the internally and externally generated judgements and decide how to meaningfully interpret these messages.

6   The comparison of judgements, and how these relate to the standards or goals of work, are used to generate a plan for improved work.

7   The strategies are implemented in the subsequent participation in later tasks.

While this model is presented as a single sequence described in procedural detail, it would be possible to envisage other representations of Feedback Mark 2. Other arrangements are possible so long as the central active role of the learner as initiator and decision-making is present, and so long as the feedback loop is completed through the production of subsequent work.

Feedback Mark 2 as illustrated in Figure 2.4 has two purposes; first, to improve the quality of the immediate subsequent work (as represented by Activity 2) and, second, to develop capacity for long-term evaluative judgement which can be applied to future circumstances. This is where feedback has a role in developing sustainable learning practices, akin to the 'double duty' role of assessment discussed above. Changing the way that we think about feedback, as a process to help harvest evaluative judgement (needed for self-monitoring, self-regulation, and working with and evaluating others), has implications for the way that both learners and educators approach the feedback process. This next section unpacks this further, to address the question: what is the agenda for feedback in this Mark 2 conception?

Changing conceptions in feedback: Practice implications

If we are moving away from educators 'giving feedback' to students, what is it that educators should now be doing? Do they now become marginalised as students move to the centre of the process where their volition, agency and motivation are acknowledged? We suggest that the challenge for educators is just as great to create conditions favourable for productive feedback, but their emphasis or focus needs to change. Overall, the educator's role in feedback in this new view is twofold: first, influencing the nature of the course and type of curriculum features, and second, focusing on behaviours and conditions within a single episode or encounter. These curricular, or 'macro', features are presented in Table 2.1, and include examples of how Feedback Mark 2 principles may play out in practice.

This renewed conception of feedback challenges us to go beyond the commonplace idea of providing hopefully useful information to students about their work. It views feedback as a complex *system* that needs to permeate the curriculum, rather than an activity that appears within it from time to time. In this conception learners need to be orientated to their own roles as co-producers of learning, the purpose of feedback as being beyond immediate performance control or improvement and their role in soliciting feedback. It also requires them to be oriented to cueing educators or others to aspects of performance that require critique and improvement. Enactment of Mark 2 also needs educators to be thoughtful in curricular design, including scheduling of nested and incremental tasks that allow for learning to be demonstrated after the exchange of internally and externally generated performance critique. Encouraging students to take on the role as feedback generator as well as seeker, positions them away from the 'passive recipient' role, reliant on comments and instruction from expert teachers. The dual role also gives students a first-hand taste of the complexity of feedback, reminding them that skilful feedback involves information that is hard 'to give', not just hard to take, which is akin to taking them backstage so they see the inner workings of the curriculum that they are in fact part of, rather than be witnesses (or consumers) of it. Finally, creating opportunities for students to give and receive feedback encourages students to fully engage in understanding learning outcomes, as without appreciating the performance benchmark, there is no capacity to give feedback.

Along with the macro, there are of course the micro considerations of feedback practice, all of which are written about extensively in the higher and professional education literature. These include principles of giving and receiving feedback (see, for example, how students may do this for each other: Boud, 1995, pp. 200-6). Principles such as these, which can guide episodic feedback interactions, may be helpful, particularly if framed within a curriculum design that honours the sustainable notion of feedback. Other examples of guidelines for episodic feedback practices are presented in Table 2.2. Key underpinning principles include that feedback should be co-produced and should be based on clear intentions

Table 2.1 Curriculum features characteristic of Feedback Mark 2 (reproduced with permission from Boud and Molloy, in press).

Feature	Examples
Learners orientated to the purposes of feedback	Explicit learning outcomes relating to developing judgements and collaboration with peers, clear expectations that students actively participate in classes and that information received will lead to action
Learners participate in activities promoting self-regulation	Activities to build student engagement and foster self-regulation through self-testing of understanding, students reflecting on how the standard required compares to their execution of the task, or planning what information they need to meet learning outcomes
Learner disposition for seeking feedback is developed	Development of feedback seeking skills through early practice activities including identification of appropriate criteria, formulating comments on others' work, practice in identifying what kind of comments are needed on assignments
Opportunities provided for production of work	Opportunities for students to produce work of the kind that is central to learning outcomes through multiple tasks well-designed for this purpose, not all of which might be formally graded
Calibration mechanisms	Channels to enable learners to check knowledge sources, develop understanding, calibrate their judgement against expert work and peer work, regular opportunities to judge their own work before it is marked
Incremental challenge of tasks	Development of sequences of tasks that progressively and realistically challenge learners, assessment tasks progressively build capacity to tackle more complex problems
Nested tasks to allow for 'feed forward'	Timing and design of tasks to permit input from others (teachers, peers, practitioners, learning management systems, as appropriate) and self on each task, to be utilised to benefit performance on subsequent tasks
Learner as 'seeker and provider'	Opportunities to practice giving as well as receiving of feedback. Orientation of learners to dimensions of the target performance (they need to engage with the desired learning outcomes, so they can make and articulate a comparative judgement)

(to help learners improve their work). Many of the guidelines are based on the importance of others providing specific and timely comments and using first-hand data and behaviours (which are remediable or have the capacity to change). Even though on one level, these guidelines appear to be driving the model of 'feedback as telling', they also encourage student agency in that behaviours, not 'persons' are critiqued (implying capacity for change in subsequent tasks), and that the student is encouraged to reflect on their behaviours or actions and the potential underpinning reasons behind the work. This approach seeks to be intrinsically empowering for learners, compared to educators making and articulating assumptions around students' motivations about their approach to work.

Table 2.2 Examples of episodic feedback guidelines, drawn from Ende (1983)

1. Educator and student work as allies
2. Well-timed and expected
3. Based on first-hand data
4. Limited to behaviours that are changeable
5. Phrased in descriptive language
6. Specific performances not generalisations
7. Subjective data should be labelled as such
8. Actions are emphasised, not assumed intentions behind the actions

The following case studies illustrate how Feedback Mark 2 might be enacted in order to maximise learning opportunities for students. This is in no way prescriptive, or empirically tested for effectiveness, but rather illustrative of how Tables 2.1 and 2.2 may come to life in practice.

Case Study 1: A first year arts/social science student

Students are introduced to the idea of what constitutes good work through working in groups on the task of discriminating between the qualities of three short typical assignments. They are asked to identify how they differ from each other and what is good and not so good about each. They create a list of what should be found in a good assignment of this type.

Subsequently they produce their own assignment and attach their own statement of what is good and not so good about it.

After tutor marking, this is returned to the student with commentary from the tutor that focuses on the accuracy of the student's own analysis of their work. Examples are provided in areas in which the student appears unable to make good judgements, e.g. 'you indicated that you were concerned with the sequencing of the arguments. I thought the way that you sequenced the essay was sensible and effective. What I did notice, is that your key point in each paragraph was buried within the third to fourth sentence. Next time, try to position your key argument in the first sentence of each paragraph and see whether this format is easier to navigate as a reader.'

The second assignment covers different subject matter, but requires students to do some of the kinds of analysis they engaged in for the first. Before submission, students exchange their final draft with another student and use the earlier agreed features of a good assignment to provide comments to each other. After revision, when handing it in, students are asked to indicate specifically the areas in which they want comments from their tutor. They receive detailed comments only on the areas specified and commentary about the areas on which they may have found it profitable to ask for guidance.

The third assignment covers different subject matter again, but there is some overlap in the learning outcomes from the second. For this, students are asked to judge their work against explicit criteria. Tutors use the same criteria and provide comments about reasons for discrepancies between student judgements and their own. In this way, the tutor is providing commentary on both the calibre of the work produced, and the calibre of the learner's judgements about their own work.

Case Study 2: A third year social work student on hospital placement

A student studying social work starts a placement at an acute hospital, in a ward that specialises in acute spinal injuries. On the first morning of the placement, the social work supervisor provides the student and her peer with a tour of the hospital ward, including introductions to other team members, orientation to systems on the ward including patient records and a timetable for the four-week placement. The supervisor suggests that after morning tea, she would like to sit down with the two students and spend an hour discussing mutual expectations of the placement, and what the students see as their strengths and deficits in practice to date. Both students had experienced two placements prior to this spinal injury rotation so were able to draw on their past exposure and performance. The student found it helpful to hear about her peer's experience, and it was comforting to know that they shared similar concerns about what they found difficult and what they needed to improve on. The supervisor stated upfront that she wanted the students to actively seek feedback, and that she expected that they would self-evaluate prior to her providing her own commentary on their performance on the ward.

Although it is tempting to launch the students straight into practice (the 'roll up your sleeves and do' approach), the supervisor had experienced first hand the value of sanctioning a half-day for discussions around mutual expectations and learning needs. Asking the students to identify what they viewed as their strengths and weaknesses in clinical practice provides the supervisor with cues about how to allocate tasks (selection of patient profile with associated degree of complexity) and what aspects of practice to provide feedback on. This approach means that the feedback is more likely to be tailored to the needs of the individual learner, and therefore more meaningful than if driven solely by the supervisor's agenda.

In the afternoon, the student is observed taking a patient's history. The patient is a 24-year-old male, whose spinal injury in a car accident had left him without any movement in his lower limbs. Although most of the points concerning the patient's medical status are covered, the student neglects to ask any questions relating to the patient's social history, including occupation, living situation, and activity levels prior to the car accident. After the episode, the supervisor and student sit down in the office and discuss the performance. The student is asked to provide her own account of the episode first, and her strengths in the history taking are accurately described. The supervisor validates this judgement, and adds that she noticed that no questions were asked relating to the patient's social situation. The student replies that these questions were purposefully left out, because she didn't want to upset the patient who had just lost function, and was unlikely to want to talk about his involvement in basketball that he would never return to. The supervisor acknowledged the rationale behind the purposeful omission ('I know where you are coming from') but highlighted the importance of gathering this information to help in goal-setting and in establishing rehabilitation plans with the patient.

The next day, the student is asked to take a history with a new patient on the ward (in line with the output principles in Feedback Mark 2). In the feedback session afterwards, the student acknowledges that she again failed to adequately gather the information she needed, as she felt the required line of questioning was too invasive and too distressing for the patient. Rather than observe a repeat attempt at the task, the supervisor suggested that the student observe her peer in taking a history, with the instructions to 'think about why he is asking the questions, how he is phrasing the questions, and what you would do similarly or differently in the same situation.' This provides the student with cues to observe performance (what to watch for, rather than passively observing), and positions her as a voyeur (lower stakes) rather than a doer. This break from practice provides the student with an opportunity to observe 'good practice' and to reflect on how her own practice approach deviates from these standards.

The key illustrative points in Case Study 2 are that the supervisor protected time in a busy setting to orientate learners to expectations of the work, and also the supervisory relationship (including feedback process). Post-performance discussion, the supervisor provided an opportunity for the student to approach a similar, overlapping task. When the learning outcomes were again not achieved, the supervisor was creative in adapting the learning strategy, and instead suggested that the student shadow her peer in order to see modelling of the expected clinical behaviours.

Finally, we acknowledge that a move to Feedback Mark 2 might in some courses represent a substantial challenge to existing practice and ways of thinking. Careful thought needs to be given to the transition from the common practice of provision of hopefully useful information to a student-engaged feedback process. In making this transition, we have been greatly encouraged by the many initiatives of the First Year Experience movement – that is, the groups of educators worldwide that have focused on how students can be assisted in making the transition into an academic environment to become fully engaged as active learners within it. Kift, Nelson and Clarke (2010) write of 'transition pedagogy', and it is a kind of transition pedagogy that may be required in some courses to enact Feedback Mark 2. The introduction of the full process represented in Figure 2.4 may create such initial resistance in some classes that the whole rationale for it may be doubted. In such situations, there is no substitute to working up to it slowly, by providing multiple opportunities for students to take the initiative, to become engaged and to show tangible respect for their involvement. Feedback Mark 2 cannot exist independently of an environment that supports what it represents. In some situations, the starting point might be not the feedback practices per se, but the ways in which students are engaged in the course.

Conclusion

Looking at feedback in a different way, with features that incorporate helping learners to look beyond the present assignment as well as improving immediate tasks, has the potential to significantly change practices on the ground. The reported dissatisfaction of learners with feedback, and the amplifying tone of this dissatisfaction, needs to be taken on as feedback to us as educators. Rather than repeating the same practices but with greater frequency or intensity, we argue for new notions of feedback, based on placing the student at the centre of the process, rather than positioning them as passive recipients of educators' comments. This demands a shift away from formulaic modes of learning where both parties (commonly the educator and student) are complicit in participating in the transmissive-style rituals that have been reported in observational studies of feedback (Molloy, 2009; Fernando et al., 2008; Ende et al., 1995). Cultivating a student disposition for seeking and using feedback, and seeing the benefits of feedback as a tool for them to build sustainable learning practices, requires educator skill at the macro (curriculum design) and micro (task episode) level. This chapter has outlined the importance of:

1   Creating conditions for students to develop as learners with agency, including establishing engagement, i.e. developing self-monitoring, self-regulation, capacity to make good judgements.
2   Designing programs/courses and generative learning tasks that position students to identify and engage with standards and criteria, and seek sources of feedback and utilise these in changing their work.
3   Establishing dialogical processes to enable students to clarify and explore standards and criteria and to help orientate educators to their learning needs.

4   Sequencing activities and tasks so that students have the opportunity to reapply their learning to new situations to show how they have benefitted.
5   Providing opportunities for students to track the development of their skills and expertise over time.

The re-conception of feedback, as presented by the notions of Feedback Mark 1 and Mark 2, has been driven by the 'feedback problem' which doesn't seem to be improving, despite featuring as a 'must improve performance outcome' by universities internationally. In exploring the roots of feedback, in its native contexts of engineering and biology, we exposed the extent to which feedback practices in education have deviated from this original purpose and function. Feedback Mark 1 revealed the importance of students responding to performance information with change in their subsequent attempt at overlapping tasks. This relies on educators creating opportunities for learners to use the information to produce improved work (Boud, 2000; Nicol and Macfarlane-Dick, 2006). The limitation of Feedback Mark 1 is that it ignores the volition of the learner, and assumes that the learner will respond in a consistent way to the input (information). Feedback Mark 2 builds on Mark 1 (takes the good parts) but expands the notion to incorporate the learner in the process. The model assumes that the learner can seek and give feedback (rather than acting as the receptor), that the learner's own self-judgement contributes to how feedback is used, and that this practice opportunity (to see how your own judgement compares to external appraisal) is integrated with other such episodes of comparison, to generate the learner's capacity for informed judgement. In other words, that what has been traditionally seen as once-off pieces of feedback are collected as a string of data points to help to build an internal 'radar' for sensing when work hits the mark, exceeds it, or falls short. Mark 2 promotes feedback as a strategy for improving work, and for improving future work through the harvesting of evaluative judgement.

The practice implications for feedback using this notion have been highlighted in Tables 2.1 and 2.2 and discussed through case studies. There is of course potential or predicted resistance to incorporating these changes in educational programs. Firstly, the incorporation of explicit learning outcomes based on 'student as agent, and student as giver and receiver of feedback' means that the curriculum content needs to be reprioritised and shifted. All educational designers can relate to the fear of 'crowding the curriculum' (Dalley et al., 2008) or worse, pushing out disciplinary content, to fit in 'lofty ideals of creating the reflective, lifelong learner'. Educators may look at Table 2.1 and fear that the promoted activities will be pushing out the substantive content of the program. Our own concern is that we are already including outcomes in the curriculum that are not attainable and pretending otherwise. There is also the very real concern that students themselves 'won't buy it'. Literature, particularly in professional education (Molloy and Keating, 2011), reports that students very early in their programs decipher what they see as essential and peripheral content. Activities and assessments that students deem to be aligned to becoming a teacher/nurse/psychologist, which are typically those with a focus on technical skill acquisition, are taken more seriously. This barrier should be anticipated, and we need further research and further dialogue about how to demonstrate (not convince) to students the importance of becoming 'not a student, but a learner'. The proof needs to be in the eating of the pudding, and we suspect that students need to operate in this model, 'to do feedback and monitor the results' in order to see the value in it.

While we argue for less concern with what educators 'do' in giving feedback, such as dimensions of when to give feedback and how to structure the information, this is not to be ignored. Instead we argue for the priority of having a better understanding of how students seek, interpret and use information about their performance.

References

Biggs, J. (1993) 'From theory to practice: A cognitive systems approach', *Higher Education and Research Development*, 12:73-85.

Boud, D. (1995) *Enhancing Learning through Self Assessment*, London: Kogan Page.

Boud, D. (2000) 'Sustainable assessment: rethinking assessment for the learning society', *Studies in Continuing Education*, 22(2):151-67.

Boud, D., Lawson, R. and Thompson, D. (submitted for publication). Does student engagement in self-assessment calibrate their judgement over time?

Boud, D. and Falchikov, N. (2007) 'Developing assessment for informing judgement', in Boud, D. and Falchikov, N. (eds) *Rethinking Assessment for Higher Education: Learning for the Longer Term*, London: Routledge.

Boud, D. and Molloy, E. (2012) 'Rethinking models of feedback: the challenge of design', *Assessment and Evaluation in Higher Education*, DOI:10.1080/026029 38.2012.691462.

Butler, D. L. and Winne, P. H. (1995) 'Feedback and self-regulated learning: a theoretical synthesis', *Review of Educational Research*, 65(3):245-81.

Carless, D., Salter, D., Yang, M. and Lam, J. (2011) 'Developing sustainable feedback practices', *Studies in Higher Education*, 36(5):395-407.

Dalley, K., Candela, L. and Benzel-Lindley, J. (2008) 'Learning to let go: the challenge of de-crowding the curriculum', *Nurse Education Today*, 28(1):62-9.

Eva, K.W. and Regehr, G. (2005) 'Self-assessment in the Health Professions: A Reformulation and Research Agenda', *Academic Medicine*, 80(10 Suppl.):S46-S54.

Ende, J. (1983) 'Feedback in clinical medical education', *Journal of American Medical Association*, 250:777-81.

Ende, J., Pomerantz, A. and Erickson, F. (1995) 'Preceptors' strategies for correcting residents in an ambulatory care medicine setting: A qualitative analysis', *Academic Medicine*, 70:224-9.

Fernando, N., Cleland, J., McKenzie, H. and Cassar, K. (2008) 'Identifying the factors that determine feedback given to undergraduate medical students following formative mini-CEX assessments', *Medical Education*, 42(1):89-95.

Hattie, J. and Timperley, H. (2007) 'The power of feedback', *Review of Educational Research*, 77:81-112.

Higher Education Funding Council for England. (2011). *The National Student Survey: Findings and Trends. 2006-2010.* Bristol: Higher Education Funding Council for England.

Hounsell, D. (2007) 'Towards more sustainable feedback to students', in Boud, D. and Falchikov, N. (eds) *Rethinking Assessment for Higher Education: Learning for the Longer Term*, London: Routledge.

Ilgen, D. and Davis, A. (2000) 'Bearing bad news: Reactions to negative performance feedback', *Applied Psychology: An International Review*, 49:550-65.

Kift, S., Nelson, K. and Clarke, J. (2010) 'Transition pedagogy: A third generation approach to FYE – A case study of policy and practice for the higher education sector', *The International Journal of the First Year in Higher Education*, 1(1):1-20.

Kluger, A. N. and DeNisi, A. (1996) 'The effects of feedback interventions on performance: A historical review, a meta-analysis, and a preliminary feedback intervention theory', *Psychological Bulletin*, 119(2):254-84.

Kluger, A. N. and Van Dijk, D. (2010) 'Feedback, the various tasks of the doctor, and the feedforward alternative', *Medical Education*, 44:1166-74.

Molloy, E. (2009) 'Time to Pause: Feedback in Clinical Education', in Delany, C. and Molloy, E. (eds) in *Clinical Education in the Health Professions*, Sydney: Elsevier.

Molloy, E. (2010) 'The feedforward mechanism: a way forward in clinical learning?', *Medical Education*, 44:1157-9.

Molloy, E. and Boud, D. (accepted for publication) 'Feedback models for learning, teaching and performance', in Spector, J. M., Merrill, D. M. and Elen, J. (eds) *Handbook of Research on Educational Communications and Technology*, New York: Springer.

Molloy, E. and Keating, J. (2011) 'Targeted Preparation for Clinical Practice' in Billet, S. and Henderson, A. (eds), *Promoting Professional Learning: Integrating experiences in university and practice settings*, Springer: Dordrecht, The Netherlands.

Meyer, J. H. F. and Land, R. (2005) 'Threshold concepts and troublesome knowledge (2): Epistemological considerations and a conceptual framework for teaching and learning', *Higher Education*, 49(3):373-88.

Nicol, D. and Macfarlane-Dick, D. (2006) 'Formative assessment and self-regulated learning: A model and seven principles of good feedback practice', *Studies in Higher Education*, 31(2):199-218.

Rowntree, D. (1977) *Assessing Students: How Shall We Know Them?* London: Harper & Row.

Sadler, D. R. (1989) 'Formative assessment and the design of instructional systems', *Instructional Science*, 18(2):119-44.

van Merriënboer, J. J. G. and Sweller, J. (2005) 'Cognitive load theory and complex learning: recent developments and future directions', *Educational Psychology Review*, 17:147-77.

Wager, W. and Wager, S. (1985) 'Presenting questions, processing responses, and providing feedback in CAI', *Journal of Instructional Development*, 8(4):2-8.

Wiener, N. (1954) *The Human Use of Human Beings: Cybernetics and Society*, Oxford, England: Houghton Mifflin.

Yorke, M. (2003) 'Formative assessment in higher education: Moves towards theory and the enhancement of pedagogic practice', *Higher Education*, 45(4): 477-501.

Chapter 3

Resituating feedback from the reactive to the proactive

David Nicol

Introduction

In higher education, the word feedback inevitably conjures up a situation of 'production' and the delivery of a 'response': the student produces an assignment and the teacher delivers comments. The premise underpinning this chapter is not in itself original, but it needs to be stated at the outset: In any feedback situation, the responding agent is never just the teacher. A view that restricts feedback agency to the teacher ignores the active role of the learner and the ubiquity of inner feedback processes. Learners are always generating internal feedback when they produce a piece of work, even in the absence of a teacher. This inner feedback is a by-product of task engagement; it derives from the learner's inner monitoring and evaluation of discrepancies between current and intended performance, the latter determined by some mix of students' own goals and what they think the teacher is looking for. And when external feedback is provided it does not operate alone, it will trigger and also add to learner-generated feedback, at times confirming, supplementing or conflicting with it. For the most part, research on feedback has ignored the complexity of these inner mental processes, although there are some notable exceptions (Butler and Winne, 1995). This chapter draws together some ideas to address this gap. It reviews feedback from a cognitive perspective and suggests ways of harnessing and strengthening inner feedback processes. It also identifies some limitations with current feedback research.

In this chapter, it is assumed that the purpose of feedback in higher education is to develop the students' capacity to make evaluative judgements both about their own work and that of others. This is a position shared by some assessment researchers (Boud, 2007; Cowan, 2010; Sadler, 2010) and it is also consistent with my earlier papers where I stated that feedback should serve the function of progressively enabling students to better monitor, evaluate and regulate their own learning independently of their teachers (Nicol and Macfarlane-Dick, 2006; Nicol, 2009). Both making evaluative judgements and evaluating and monitoring one's own learning rely on internal feedback processes, and are activities that students must learn to do for themselves. The question addressed here is how we can enhance students' skills in this area.

Feedback as reflective knowledge building

The argument in this chapter is that for feedback to foster evaluative judgement two cognitive processes must be consciously and systematically exercised and developed, namely, evaluation and knowledge building. First, students must be given explicit opportunities to reflect on and evaluate their own work in relation to a feedback input, either an input provided by an external agent (e.g. teacher) or an input that is generated by the student herself, for example, by engaging in self-review. Strong evaluation skills are necessary if students are to be able to identify gaps in their understanding, misconceptions, discrepancies, errors, structural deficiencies, other perspectives or weaknesses in the work they produce. Second, students must also have explicit opportunities to use the results of these evaluative processes to repair misunderstandings and to build a better understanding. This entails knowledge building – filling knowledge gaps, restructuring current representations of content and/or creating new or modifying pre-existing mental models. Knowledge building is important as it provides an identifiable reference point that can be used to gauge whether feedback processes have had any effect. If feedback processes do not result in any knowledge building then arguably they have had no impact. Key issues for learning here are the nature, extent and validity of this knowledge building as well as its visibility.

I use the term 'reflective knowledge building' to represent both processes of evaluation and knowledge building. Obviously these two mental processes overlap and inter-relate in complex ways. However, it is argued here that both are necessary if feedback is to result in enhanced learning. The term 'reflective knowledge building' is borrowed from Roscoe and Chi (2008), who used it to describe the tutor's own learning when they engage in some forms of peer tutoring. In their studies the 'reflective' component within reflective knowledge building refers to the tutor's monitoring and evaluation of their own understanding as they tutor; as such, it is quite consistent with the usage here.

If it is agreed that feedback processes are only effective if they result in reflective knowledge building then two questions arise: (i) what is the best way to design feedback processes so that they explicitly support the elicitation of reflective knowledge building, and (ii) what kinds of reflective knowledge building activities are most productive for the development of evaluative judgement? Below, three different feedback scenarios, and the different ways in which they might promote productive reflective knowledge building, are examined.

In this chapter, any assignment produced by a student is referred to as student work. The types of assignment of interest are those which require a complex written response such as an essay, a report, a case study, a design specification, a position paper, etc. While this context gives some focus to discussions about feedback, many of the arguments would also be relevant to feedback in other contexts.

Teacher feedback and reflective knowledge building

By far the most common feedback intervention in higher education is for teachers to provide written comments on students' assignments. The assumption is that students will use these comments to update their knowledge and to improve their performance in subsequent assignments. However, there is a great deal of concern about the effectiveness of such feedback in higher education. In the UK National Student Survey (NSS), for example, students invariably report that they are less satisfied with feedback than with any other aspect of their course; they report that they don't get enough feedback from teachers, that it is often not timely and that it does not clarify things they do not understand. This has led many institutions in the UK to put in place interventions to address these issues and to enhance the quality of teacher comments: these include more detailed feedback, faster turnaround times for feedback on assignments and more attention to providing corrective advice. I believe that while these interventions might have a beneficial impact on scores in the NSS, they will not necessarily have a big impact on student learning, as they are based on a very narrow conceptualisation of the relationship between feedback and students' knowledge construction.

Cognitive perspective

For teacher feedback to result in knowledge building a complex array of cognitive processes needs to take place in the mind of the student. Students must decode the feedback messages contained in the comments, internalise and reflect on them, evaluate and compare them against their own work, identify discrepancies and inconsistencies in specific areas of that work and revise or reconstruct their knowledge networks based on the inner feedback that these processes generate. As well as identifying the need for local repairs in the assignment at hand, ideally students would also need to create some permanent revisions to their knowledge networks that can be brought to bear when they are asked to tackle a new but similar assignment in the future. The latter is necessary if learning is to be transferred to new contexts.

From this perspective, even if the quality of the comments is as high as can be from the teacher's perspective – for example, they are timely, detailed and clearly written and thus meet the NSS requirements – this feedback can be ineffective for a variety of reasons. First, students might ignore the comments, reject them or judge them irrelevant. This would negate the possibility that the feedback results in knowledge building. Second, students might read the comments but not decode them as intended because they are written in a discourse they are unfamiliar with or they are filtered and distorted by pre-existing beliefs and subject matter misconceptions. Third, students might successfully interpret the feedback message as intended but still have difficulty in connecting it and evaluating it in relation to what they have produced; in other words, they may not be able to make comparative judgements or may not perceive its relevance or how it connects. Finally, even if they achieve all of the above, students might still not revise their knowledge networks or, importantly, be able to transfer their learning to new contexts. Hence, while the quality of the teacher comments is important, it constitutes only one component of the overall feedback process. Feedback effectiveness relies as much on what goes on in the students' mind and on what they do with the comments, and on what these lead them to do, as on what the teacher provides.

Enhancing reflective knowledge building with teacher feedback

How might we make it more likely that teacher comments will lead to reflective knowledge building in ways that support the development of evaluative judgement?

At a simple level, this could be achieved by asking students to rephrase teacher comments in their own words and articulate what they understand them to mean and how they might use them to inform future work. Rephrasing the comments requires that students decode and evaluate them in relation to their work; while saying how they might use them would require that they make inferences about them beyond the assignment that they have produced. A short proforma with questions could be used as a prompt for this activity: e.g. What did my comments mean to you? If you had to re-edit this essay then how would you apply my feedback? What actions will you take as a result of this feedback? Another approach might be to return assignments in a tutorial and ask students in small groups to discuss the comments they received and to formulate action plans for improvements in subsequent work. This would achieve similar benefits; however, the peer dialogue would enrich the students' cognitive processing and their evaluation of the teacher's comments, and their resulting action plans. Other approaches involving peer dialogue are outlined in Nicol (2010a).

Perhaps the most productive way of promoting reflective knowledge building would be to sequence students' assignments so that the feedback information that is provided by teachers on earlier work can be directly applied in subsequent work. In this case, students might be required at submission to comment on how they had used the earlier feedback in the new assignment. The application of feedback advice in new assignments would directly call into play a range of cognitive processes – decoding and evaluation of the feedback, constructing new knowledge and transfer; examples here are multi-stage projects that lead to the build-up of more complex outputs and overlapping tasks where the second task builds on the knowledge and skills in the first task. A related approach is the so-called patchwork text. This involves a sequence whereby students produce a range of linked writing outputs (e.g. an essay, a report, a case example) which they then 'stitch' together to create a final integrated written assignment; the key idea here is that earlier feedback on each writing task would inform the next and the final output (Winter, 2003). Such assignment sequencing could be made much more effective, however, if the feedback provided by teachers was recorded so that both the teacher and the student could easily revisit earlier feedback when they tackle future assignments.

Still another sequencing approach that promotes reflective knowledge building is to have students rewrite their assignment after receiving teacher comments on a first draft. Rewriting is not only important from a learning perspective but it is also important from a research perspective, as the revisions students make to their drafts provide an identifiable record of changes in their knowledge and under-standing. This would allow teachers, and in turn researchers, to investigate what kinds of comments actually have an effect on learning rather than which comments students perceive as helpful, which is the focus of much current feedback practice and research. Redrafting after feedback would also align academic practice with the realities of writing activities as they occur in professional practice. However, redrafting is often criticised by those who believe that students who receive a lot of feedback from teachers will end up submitting work that they could not produce on their own, and that this gives them an unfair advantage in summative assessments. Whether this is true depends in part on what kind of feedback the teacher provides; redrafting the students' work would be quite different from asking students questions about it or pointing them to sources where they might update their understanding. It also depends on whether the assignment is intended as a high-stakes or a low-stakes developmental activity.

Teacher feedback: a principle for good practice

The above examples all share the assumption that for teacher feedback to result in reflective knowledge building any planned instance of such feedback should always be followed by an evaluative response from the student. The challenge is to make this normal practice. For this to happen an intervention at the policy level might be required, not just encouragement at the practice level. For example, this could be explicitly stated as a guiding principle in educational policy documents; e.g. *teacher feedback should be planned in ways that ensure that students are provided with explicit opportunities to evaluate and/or to act on it.* This principle might also inform the data gathered through course evaluation and review procedures.

Self-review and reflective knowledge building

In this section I move away from the teacher as the initial source of feedback input and focus on planned scenarios where students evaluate their own work and produce their own feedback commentary: that is, the starting point for evaluative judgement is an activity initiated by the student, not the teacher. I call these scenarios *self-review*.

There are a number of reasons for this switch of focus. First, in this chapter it is assumed that the purpose of feedback is to develop the students' capacity to make evaluative judgements on their own without the help of an external agent. I believe that self-review directly calls on and exercises this capacity whereas the mere receipt of teacher feedback does not. Secondly, it could be speculated that developing the students' own ability to make judgements about their work will ultimately make them better at utilising teacher feedback. Thirdly, some research suggests that the more feedback teachers give, the more reliant students become on their teachers, usually the weaker students; they continually strive to create responses that meet what they think is the teacher-recipe rather than thinking for themselves (Orsmond and Merry, 2009). Developing students' confidence in their own ability to evaluate is necessary if we are to wean these students off this dependency relationship.

Cognitive perspective

There is a long history of research in cognitive science on the benefits of, and on the mental processes elicited by, self-review activities. For example, Chi et al. (1994) and Chi (2000) have shown that when students are asked to comment verbally on their own understanding of a written text as they read it (e.g. about the human circulatory system) or on the problem solving approach they are using (e.g. while solving physics problems) their learning is significantly better than when they are not required to provide commentaries. Chi et al (1994) call this process 'self-explaining': they maintain that self-explaining forces learners to monitor and evaluate their own understanding and that this results in their identifying gaps in their knowledge (e.g. missing links, misconceptions, incorrect assumptions, procedural errors) and in their constructing inferential knowledge to fill those gaps. In other words, self-explaining results in students evaluating their own knowledge and generating inner feedback in a way that helps them see for themselves where they need to make improvements in their understanding.

Even though self-explaining has often focused on verbal explanations and on students explaining the meaning of a text produced by others rather than on students providing written reviews of an assignment they have produced, I would argue that similar kinds of evaluative and knowledge building processes are at play. Indeed, I might be inclined to go further and argue that the process of producing written rather than verbal explanations might actually lead to deeper evaluation and knowledge building. This is an area, however, that really warrants further research.

In the published literature, accounts of self-review are usually discussed within the context of self-assessment research where students mark (or grade) as well as comment on their own work. Also, the investigative focus of that research has not so much been on commenting, but rather on the degree to which these marks/grades are consistent with those that might be awarded by teachers (e.g. Stefani, 1994). Such marking considerations are of less interest here, as from a reflective knowledge building perspective it is the production of the feedback commentary that is critical as, arguably, this requires deeper levels of cognitive engagement and knowledge elaboration than the production of a mark, which can often be an impressionistic and intuitive process. In this chapter, therefore, the interest is in scenarios where students review some work, their own or that of others, and produce a written commentary, often comprising a justification for their evaluative decisions.

Enhancing knowledge building through self-review

If the purpose of self-review is to trigger self-explanations, that is, to get students to evaluate the work they have produced and to comment on it, then an important consideration is the criteria that are used to frame these commentaries.

In higher education, self-review usually involves asking students to evaluate their work with reference to the assessment criteria. Invariably, students provide both a mark and a commentary detailing the strengths and weaknesses in relation to these criteria. Taras (2010), however, notes problems with this approach in that some students are reluctant to comment on weaknesses in their work, believing that this will have a negative impact on teacher-awarded marks. Another approach that addresses this issue, as it does not require pointing out weaknesses, is to ask students to decide on a mark for their work and to produce a justification for that mark in relation to the criteria through the commentary.

While giving experience of evaluating their own work in relation to assessment criteria will help students learn about academic standards and about how marks are awarded, I believe that this approach on its own is rather limiting, especially if the aim of self-review is to develop a broad range of evaluative capabilities. In the professions, practitioners make evaluative judgements all the time; however not all judgements start with, or are tied to, explicit criteria and certainly they have nothing to do with marks. Some judgements are about relative quality, others about the value of different perspectives, still others about the trade-offs involved in taking different decisions or in acting in different ways, and so on.

From this wider vantage point, I believe that three principles are important in relation to criteria for self-review by students. First, if self-review tasks are to develop evaluative judgement and elicit productive knowledge building, students must have many opportunities to evaluate their work from reference points different from those which they used to produce the work. For example, the review criteria might call on students to summarise their own work before handing it in, to identify hidden assumptions, to explore alternative perspectives on an issue, to identify the centre of gravity in a piece of writing, or the most compelling argument or most convincing evidence, etc. Importantly, many of these judgements will require holistic rather than analytic appraisals, a capability that, according to Sadler (2010), is not being sufficiently developed in higher education.

Second, evaluation criteria should also tap into the subject domain in ways that help develop disciplinary thinking (even though they might also go beyond a single discipline, for example, if the course aim is to foster inter-disciplinary thinking). From a disciplinary perspective, students might, for example, make judgements about the relative merits of different design decisions in engineering, about the soundness of a diagnosis in medicine, about the most elegant solution to a mathematical problem or about the validity of decision-making in business or social work.

Third, students should have some opportunities to formulate their own criteria for reviews so that they both have experience in deciding what kinds of evaluative criteria are important and in appraising their own performance against those criteria (Boud, 1995). This is vital if students are to become autonomous and lifelong learners, able to set their own goals and evaluate their progress in achieving them.

As well as broadening the scope of evaluation criteria, I also believe that opportunities for self-review should become a regular, rather than an infrequent, activity in courses and programmes. A first step in achieving this might be for self-review to be stated explicitly as a learning outcome in course documentation, e.g. *'at the end of this module students will have developed the capacity to evaluate the quality or impact of their own work'*. It is rather surprising that learning outcomes of this kind are not already common practice in the disciplines, given the robustness of the research on self-explaining and the fact that the ability to review the strengths and weaknesses in one's own work might be seen as one of the cornerstones of critical thinking.

Teacher feedback and self-review

Although I believe self-review should be more widely integrated into the curriculum, I am aware that there are some issues in the application of this method. In particular, students sometimes find it difficult to create the distance or detachment required in relation to their own work; as such they might not be able to view their own work objectively, believing that it conveys a meaning different from that experienced by the reader, or they might have ideas about their work that they are not able to express in writing.

The above issues can be addressed, however, through the provision of teacher feedback. Instead of just commenting on the students' assignments, teachers might productively comment on the outputs of students' self-reviews. Such an approach would give students useful reference points from which they could calibrate their own evaluative judgements, i.e. compare their evaluations against the appraisals of others with more expertise. This approach is also consistent with the advice in Hattie and Timperley's (2007) recent review of feedback, where they argue that the transfer of learning is more likely when teachers focus their feedback comments on students' regulatory abilities rather than on their performance in the task itself. Interestingly, in this perspective, self-review does not replace the need for teacher feedback; rather it changes its focus.

Peer review and reflective knowledge building

So far, in this chapter I have identified some potential limitations with teacher feedback from a cognitive perspective and suggested some improvements. I have also proposed self-review as a fundamental approach to harnessing inner feedback processes in ways that would strengthen students' evaluative capabilities. However, I believe that these enhancements will only take us so far.

In professional and workplace settings and in life beyond university, feedback rarely comes from a single source. Rather, faced with multiple sources of feedback, the task is usually to evaluate, weigh up, reconcile and respond to different and sometimes quite contradictory feedback perspectives. Also, in professional life, graduates are not just consumers of feedback but they are also producers; they will be invariably required to evaluate and comment on the work of others from a range of perspectives. I believe that these considerations need to be taken on board in the design of feedback in higher education. I therefore here propose a third feedback scenario, peer review, that might help to address these aspects, and that I think offers the greatest promise for the development of evaluative judgement (see also Nicol, 2010b).

Peer review is defined here as a process whereby students evaluate and make judgements about the work of their peers and provide a feedback commentary. In the educational literature this is usually discussed in the context of peer assessment, a scenario where students usually mark (or rate) as well as comment on the work of other students. In that research, as with self-assessment, the dominant focus has been on whether the marks provided by peers correlate with those that teachers might award. I believe that the benefits to be derived from peer commenting might sometimes be undermined by this focus on marking (see Kaufman and Schunn, 2011) and that more research is required to separate out these potentially conflicting variables.

In peer review, students normally act both reviewee and reviewer. As reviewee, they receive feedback from peers. As reviewer, they evaluate the work of peers and generate a feedback commentary. I first examine these aspects separately and then consider their combined effects.

Cognitive perspective: Receiving reviews

From a cognitive perspective the receipt of feedback from peers is similar to the receipt of teacher feedback – that is, whether it results in reflective knowledge building depends on what students do with it. Fortunately, in most peer review scenarios students produce a draft assignment and have opportunities to evaluate and use the feedback they receive to make revisions to their drafts. Hence, peer review complies with the good practice principle identified in the section on teacher feedback. Also, because peer review usually involves the reworking of the assignment, researchers have been able to identify some benefits from the receipt of peer feedback when compared with teacher feedback; these include greater quantity and variety of feedback, the receipt by students of multiple 'readings' of their work, and feedback in a language and discourse that is easier for students to understand (van den Berg, Admiraal and Pilot, 2006).

Some studies have even shown that students perceive feedback from peers as more helpful than teacher feedback (Falchikov, 2005), and one controlled study has demonstrated that when students received feedback from multiple peers they made more complex revisions to their draft assignments than students who received feedback from a single peer or a single teacher (Cho and MacArthur, 2010). In this study the researchers provide direct evidence of knowledge updating through a detailed analysis of the revisions that students made.

Cognitive perspective: Producing reviews

While there has been some research on the receipt of feedback from peers, surprisingly few studies have specifically investigated the reviewing process within peer review. In an earlier paper, I proposed that having students review and give feedback to peers was likely to be a more powerful and effective learning process than receiving feedback from peers (Nicol, 2011). My arguments were that reviewing, unlike receiving reviews, (i) requires that students make evaluative judgements about others' work and justify those judgements, thus directly calling on high levels of cognitive processing; (ii) requires that students exercise assessment criteria many times thereby helping them to internalise them, known to enhance learning (Rust, Price and O'Donovan, 2003); (iii) exposes students to different approaches to the same assignment, which helps them appreciate that in complex tasks quality can be produced in different ways; (iv) involves writing feedback commentaries which helps students acquire disciplinary and tacit knowledge. I also argued that experience in carrying out peer review would significantly enhance the students' capacity for self-review.

In their research on peer tutoring, Roscoe and Chi (2008) have shown that when students are required to produce explanations of conceptual ideas for others, in this case peers, they actively monitor, evaluate and rehearse their own understanding. The result is that the students' own knowledge and understanding is enhanced as a by-product of the production of these explanations. I believe that reviewing the work of peers invokes similar mental processes. It requires that students evaluate texts produced by peers to identify errors, gaps in understanding, misconceptions and alternative viewpoints in those texts and that they also construct written feedback commentaries. In doing this, the students' own ideas about the subject domain become available for self-evaluation and updating. Essentially, reviewing elicits both external and internal evaluation processes. However, I believe that reviewing the work of peers goes beyond just the 'explaining' processes outlined by Roscoe and Chi (2008). Students are not just explaining a text they have read, rather they are 'evaluating' it against criteria to produce a feedback justification. In addition, these processes take place in a context in which students themselves have already produced a text in the same subject domain. Hence the cognitive processes are even richer and much more complex than those proposed by Roscoe and Chi (2008).

My own recent research on peer review provides some specific insights into the complexity of students' reflective knowledge building processes. This research, which will be reported in detail elsewhere (Nicol, Thompson and Breslin, in preparation), drew on focus group interviews and survey data from a number of peer review implementations. Here I only provide brief details of some critical findings relevant to the reviewing component within peer review.

I found that when students are asked to make judgements about the work of peers, they start the reviewing process by comparing the peer work against an internal representation of their own work. This is inevitable given that students have just produced work in the same domain themselves; hence their own work is the standard or benchmark for any comparison. The result is that reviewing always results in students reflecting back on their own work and using the feedback they generate from the comparison to inform that work. Evidence for this is that when students have opportunities to update their work after reviewing and before receiving reviews, most will do so. Also, when reviewing, students not only compare their own work with that of peers but also, if they complete more than one review, they will compare and evaluate the work of one peer against that of another. This generates another source of internal feedback that is also used to inform their own work and the review commentaries that they produce. There are, therefore, multiple and overlapping acts of evaluation involved in reviewing. However, although it is the students' internal representation that serves as the catalyst for making evaluative judgements, it is the criteria provided by teachers that usually frames the students' feedback commentaries. This is important, as the criteria provide some external guidance about what to look for when making comparative judgements.

Overall, the most important finding from my research is that, unlike feedback receipt, reviewing the work of peers results in students actively engaging in multiple evaluative acts and in their generating their own internal feedback: feedback that is directly used to build new knowledge and understanding and that is directly acted on, if there are opportunities to do so. This is the essential argument in this chapter and the benefits are captured succinctly in the following student quote:

> I think when you are reviewing...[the work of peers]...it's more a self-learning process, you're teaching yourself; well, I can see somebody's done that and that's a strength, and I should maybe try and incorporate that somehow into my work. Whereas getting...[teacher]... feedback you're kind of getting told what to do; you're getting told this is the way you should be doing it, and this is the right way to do it. You're not really thinking for yourself.... I think...[reviewing]... would help you not need so much of teacher feedback, if there was more of this. Whereas, I think if you're not being able to do...[reviewing]... then you will always be needing more...[teacher feedback]...

The findings I have described above, based on my own research, need further corroboration; however, even at this stage I believe they cast feedback processes in an interesting new light. At the very least, they suggest that students can generate quite powerful feedback on their own through reviewing and, importantly, that they perceive this feedback as useful, even to the extent that it might reduce the need for teacher feedback. In my view, this empowering potential of reviewing has been under-researched in higher education.

Enhancing reflective knowledge building through peer review

There are many ways of designing peer review and of integrating it into other teaching practices. However, in the context of this chapter, the main challenge is to design it in ways that enhance its capacity to elicit reflective knowledge building and to develop evaluative skills. Here are some considerations from that perspective.

First, within practical limits, the number of reviews that students undertake should be maximised. This is because the more reviews students produce, the wider the range of examples of work they are exposed to and the more opportunity they have to gain practice in making evaluative judgements of work of different quality. Put another way, the wider the range of examples, the greater the potential for knowledge construction.

Another approach to enhancing reflective knowledge building is to enrich peer feedback processes with opportunities for dialogue. For example, a teacher I recently worked with implemented peer review in a computing course. In this course, students in groups of four produced a draft report on a web-based application they had developed and then received anonymous written feedback from individual students from other groups. This was supported by an online peer feedback system. The result was that each group received eight to ten individual reviews on their draft, increasing the likelihood that some would be of high quality but without individual students incurring a high workload in reviewing. As well as revising their drafts, each group also produced a written reflective report on the value of the feedback they received. Hence this design resulted in rich peer feedback dialogue, with the students in groups both discussing the feedback they received as well as the revisions they would make to their report. These peer discussions would also have contributed to the evaluative and knowledge building processes.

Peer review designs can also be strengthened by integrating peer reviews and self-reviews. This is important as a key goal of peer review is to enhance the students' ability to evaluate their own work. For example, students might be asked first to review the work of peers and then to review and comment on their own work. This directly calls on students to use their evaluation of others' work to inform their own. In one version of this design, students are asked to provide a commentary stating how they might improve their work based on their reviewing experiences but are not asked to make any actual revisions to their assignment. This approach allows the teacher to evaluate directly what students are learning from their reviewing experience. It also helps address the concerns of some teachers that students will plagiarise from the work of peers. Another approach is 'requested feedback' where students first carry out a self-review to identify the aspects of their work on which they would like feedback from peers; for example, they might attach a cover sheet with feedback questions when they submit their assignment. This self-review would both sensitise the student to weaknesses in their own work and would help the reviewer target some feedback to students' perceived needs. This approach could be usefully extended by asking students, once they have received the peer reviews, to comment on their value, thereby initiating further knowledge building; over time this would help develop students' skills in peer reviewing.

The criteria that frame the students' feedback production in reviewing are also critical as they provide the catalyst for both evaluation and knowledge building. In the section on self-review I outlined some considerations that might guide the formulation of criteria for different kinds of evaluative judgement. I believe these same considerations should apply in the implementation of peer reviewing, where they would probably have even greater impact. It is also important to note here that the mere act of making evaluative judgements will invoke a range of tacit criteria that extend beyond those that are formally defined.

Finally, it is possible to influence the kinds of reflective knowledge building that occur through manipulations of the topic of the work produced and reviewed. It is common for the topic of, or brief for, the work that students produce to be exactly the same as that of the work to be reviewed. In this case, students are exposed to alternative approaches and ideas which can be useful if students have little knowledge in the topic domain or if they are new to peer review. If, however, the intention is to enhance the scope of students' reflective knowledge building well beyond that of the original work, then it is helpful if topics for production and review are different. An intermediate position might be for them to be different but in the same topic domain.

The role of the teacher

Taken together, the findings on peer review suggest a dual role for the teacher. One role is to design peer review scenarios that give students regular opportunities to generate their own feedback and to make use of it to revise their own work. This would extend students' knowledge building while at the same time develop their critical faculties. Another role is to provide feedback comments that support, validate and strengthen students' ability to generate valid feedback. This will mean teachers spending less time providing routine feedback on assignments and more time providing comments on the quality of students' own feedback production. The provision of an expert perspective would help students learn how to calibrate their own evaluative capabilities; however, care would be required so that this expert input does not undermine the calibration that would naturally derive from peer feedback processes. I believe that such shift of focus would not necessarily lead to an overall workload increase for teachers. Indeed, in my own studies I found that a great deal of routine feedback advice was actually provided by peers, thus freeing up teacher time to comment on higher-order issues.

Conclusion

In this chapter, I have examined feedback processes from a cognitive perspective. I have suggested that knowledge restructuring by students can be initiated by external feedback provided by a teacher or by fellow students (e.g. peer comments) or it can be initiated by activities carried out by the student themselves – for example, when they engage in self-review or produce comments on the work of others. Furthermore, I have argued that, no matter which of these two inputs is the catalyst for knowledge restructuring, it is the inner feedback that students generate that is critical, as this is what mediates and shapes the knowledge construction process and the outputs that students produce.

The main issue I discussed in this chapter was how to enhance the power of these inner feedback processes in ways that would develop the students' own capacity to make evaluative judgements. One suggestion I made was that when teachers provide feedback they should also prompt students to evaluate it and to make a structured response to it. This would ensure that received feedback actually leads to knowledge restructuring. A second recommendation I made was to increase opportunities for students to engage in reviewing activites, and in particular peer review. My own research has shown that reviewing the work of peers is perceived by students as a 'self-teaching' process where the feedback they generate on others' work is reflected back to inform their own work in ways that build new knowledge and understanding. Students also believed that reviewing might even reduce their need for teacher feedback.

To conclude, in the light of the above, I would argue more generally that as well as focusing on enhancing the students' use of teacher feedback, much greater attention should be paid in higher education to the production of feedback by students as this is a more direct means of eliciting knowledge restructuring than feedback receipt, and not least because the ability to construct feedback is a fundamental professional skill that has been somewhat neglected in higher education.

References

Boud, D. (1995) *Enhancing learning through self-assessment*, London: Kogan Page.

Boud, D. (2007) 'Reframing assessment as if learning was important', in Boud, D. and Fachikov, N. (eds) *Rethinking Assessment for Higher Education: Learning for the Longer Term*, London: Routledge, 14-25.

Butler, D. L. and Winne, P. H. (1995) 'Feedback and self-regulated learning: a theoretical synthesis', *Review of Educational Research*, 65(3): 245-81.

Chi, M. T. H., de Leeuw, N., Chiu, M. H. and La Vancher, C. (1994) 'Eliciting self-explanations improves understanding', *Cognitive Science*, 18:439-77.

Chi, M. T. H. (2000) 'Self-explaining: The dual processes of generating inferences and repairing mental models', in Glaser, R. (ed.) *Advances in instructional psychology*, Mahwah, NJ: Lawrence Erlbaum.

Cho, K. and MacArthur, C. (2010) 'Student Revision with Peer and Expert Reviewing', *Learning and Instruction*, 20(4): 328-38.

Cowan, J. (2010) 'Developing the ability for making evaluative judgements', *Teaching in Higher Education*, 15(3): 323-34.

Falchikov, N. (2005). *Improving assessment through student involvement*, London: Routledge-Falmer.

Hattie, J. and Timperley, H. (2007) 'The power of feedback', *Review of Educational Research*, 77(1): 81-112.

Kaufman, J. H. and Schunn, C. D. (2011) 'Students' perceptions about peer assessment for writing: their origin and impact on revision work', *Instructional Science*, 39: 387-406.

Nicol, D. and Macfarlane-Dick, D. (2006) 'Formative assessment and self-regulated learning: A model and seven principles of good feedback practice', *Studies in Higher Education*, 31(2): 199-218.

Nicol, D. (2009) 'Assessment for learner self-regulation: enhancing achievement in the first year using learning technologies', *Assessment and Evaluation in Higher Education*, 34(3): 335-52.

Nicol, D. (2010a) 'From monologue to dialogue: improving written feedback in mass higher education', *Assessment and Evaluation in Higher Education*, 35(5): 501-17.

Nicol, D. (2010b) 'The foundation for graduate attributes: developing self-regulation through self and peer assessment', QAA Scotland, Enhancement Themes. Online. Available at: <http://www.enhancementthemes.ac.uk/resources/publications/graduates-for-the-21st-century>

Nicol, D. (2011) 'Developing students' ability to construct feedback', QAA Scotland, Enhancement Themes. Online. Available at: <http://www.enhancementthemes.ac.uk/resources/publications/graduates-for-the-21st-century>

Nicol, D., Thomson, A. and Breslin, C. (in preparation), 'Feedback for learning: Is giving better than receiving?', to be submitted to *Assessment and Evaluation in Higher Education*.

Orsmond, P. and Merry, S. (2009) 'Processing tutor feedback: a consideration of qualitative differences in learning outcomes for high and non-high achieving students', paper presented at *Fostering Communities of Learners*, 13th EARLI Conference, Amsterdam, 25-29 August.

Roscoe, R. and Chi, M. (2008) 'Tutor learning: the role of explaining and responding to questions', *Instructional Science*, 36: 321-50.

Rust, C., Price, M. and O'Donovan, B. (2003) 'Improving students' learning by developing their understanding of assessment criteria and processes', *Assessment and Evaluation in Higher Education*, 28(2): 147-64.

Taras, M. (2010) 'Student self-assessment: processes and consequences', *Teaching in Higher Education*, 15(2): 199-209.

Sadler, D. R. (2010) 'Beyond feedback: Developing student capability in complex appraisal', *Assessment and Evaluation in Higher Education*, 35(5): 535-50.

Stefani, L. A. J. (1994) 'Peer, self and tutor assessment: Relative reliabilities', *Studies in Higher Education*, 19(1): 69-75.

van den Berg, I., Admiraal, W. and Pilot, A. (2006) 'Peer assessment in university teaching: evaluating seven course designs', Assessment and Evaluation in Higher Education, 31(1): 19-36.

Winter, R. (2003) 'Contextualising the patchwork text: addressing the problems of coursework assessment in higher education', *Innovations in Education and Teaching International*, 40(2): 112-22.

Chapter 4

The impact of emotions in feedback

Elizabeth Molloy
Francesc Borrell-Carrió
Ron Epstein

> *Knowing about the relevance of feelings in the processes of reason does not suggest that reason is less important than feelings, that it should take a backseat to them or that it should be less cultivated. On the contrary, taking stock of the pervasive role of feelings may give us a chance of enhancing their positive effects and reducing their potential harm.*
>
> (Damasio, 1994, p. 246)

This chapter focuses on the effect of affect in feedback. Emotion is an important dimension in the seeking, giving, receiving and use of feedback. Many current models of feedback are predicated on a framework of equal provision of positive and negative feedback in order to create an encouraging learning environment, and to reduce the potential for defensive reactions from the learner. These content and linguistic considerations are often anticipatory, rather than responses to learners' own reactions to feedback conversations. Observational studies of verbal feedback have suggested that despite these good intentions to support the learner, rituals of feedback can result in vaporous or 'vanishing' outcomes where the constructive messages for improvement of practice can not be deciphered.

The chapter discusses the extent to which emotions can act not only as a barrier but also a stimulus in the learning process. The impact of corrective feedback on learners' esteem will be highlighted, along with how different learner tendencies or profiles may predict responses to external judgement, ranging from open to defensive. Strategies to help promote desirable affective engagement in feedback processes will be discussed. The provision of future-referenced strategies for change can potentially negate feelings of failure. Self-evaluation is described as a key strategy to reduce the emotive impact of feedback and to reduce pressure on the educator to act as the 'bearer of bad news'. The authors also argue that self-evaluation should be viewed as a skill that can be cultivated as a habit, not only to maximise the learning potential in feedback through limiting unproductive emotions, but also to help individuals operate and co-operate in a reflective mode within their day-to-day professional practices.

Lack of time, adherence to a well-rehearsed 'feedback script', lack of trust in learner ability, lack of trust in educator intentions, and expressions of power through language can influence both stakeholders' ability to engage in a collaborative model of feedback. Goffman's 'face work' (1955) and Harré's 'positioning theory' (1999), both arising from discursive psychology, are drawn upon to help explain the unproductive feedback interactions described in the literature in higher and professional education. Practical strategies to facilitate learner agency in learning will be identified so that feedback is seen as a tool for the learner, rather than a tool used on the learner. The key properties to consider in designing effective feedback, and avoiding emotionally charged feedback in order to impinge on dialogue, receptivity and positive action, are distilled at both program (macro) and episodic/interactional (micro) levels.

Emotion as part of learning

There is a large body of literature devoted to the role of emotion in learning (Gigerenzer, 2007; Boud and Walker, 1998; Damasio, 1994), and an increasingly strong discourse exploring the relationship between assessment and emotion (Falchikov and Boud, 2007). Feedback, as a set of practices geared for learning and closely linked with assessment, is an inherently emotional business. Not only can feedback invoke an emotional response during an encounter – for example during a verbal feedback exchange or while reading written feedback on an assignment – it can have long-lasting impact, beyond its intent (Ende et al., 1995). As Falchikov and Boud (2007) reported in their exploration of the relationship between assessment and emotion,

> In some cases the interaction between the learner and the assessment event is so negative that it has an emotional impact that lasts many years and affects career choices, inhibits new learning. (p. 144)

Within the classroom or the practice setting, individuals at any point on their path from novice to expert are able to recount a 'painful feedback anecdote' that caused them some sort of emotional discomfort. This capacity of feedback to stir up emotion – a challenge to baseline ease or certainty – is why it can motivate behaviour both in positive and negative directions. If learners are provided with information that they have to wrestle with, reflect on, experiment with, this can act as a potent stimulus for learning and for reconsidering new ways of knowing and doing. It may not feel comfortable, certainly in the beginning, but there are ample studies to indicate that feedback as a stimulus has a more powerful impact on learning than any other variable in education, including class size and teacher experience (Hattie and Timperley, 2007).

When it comes to emotions and feedback, what we read about most is the capacity of feedback to do harm to the learner. Ilgen and Davis (2000) report that the impact of feedback can be linked to confusion, anxiety, embarrassment and crisis of confidence. There is in fact a complete sub-set of literature devoted to the sensitivities of feedback, and the human tendency to respond defensively to criticism (Latting, 1992; Ilgen and Davis, 2000; Ende et al., 1995). This range of unpleasant emotions experienced by the learner is not surprising given that learners are typically positioned as novices within the learning relationship. In their self-positioning as 'novice' they are concurrently elevating the teacher to a place of authority (Molloy, 2006). This concept of the dynamic relational positioning of one person to another is described as part of Harré's (1999) positioning theory. Analysing learner-educator interactions in feedback through the lens of positioning theory may provide useful insights into what works and what does not work in feedback (Molloy and Clarke, 2005; Molloy, 2009). In a typical feedback episode, a more experienced or knowledgeable 'other' typically focuses on the learner's performance and picks out deficits in performance that need to be remedied. Learners are likely to register this impact of 'judgement' through some sort of experience of emotion, particularly if the message is delivered in a tone of finality that leaves no room for learners to contest the viewpoint. Although the judgement is made about students' work, students themselves can see work as a presentation, or a manifestation of their own amateur knowledge, ideas or behaviours (Hyland, 1998). Even if they tell themselves that feedback is about the task or performance, they can interpret the constructive criticism as an affront to their self or person.

Learners have been described as agents that have filters through which they process information and make sense of it (Dewey, 1933). As outlined in Chapter 2, this book sees feedback in the context of students being active participants in their own learning, consistent with descriptions of constructivist models of learning (Wertsch, 1997). Despite acknowledgement of the benefits of promoting learner as agent, the bulk of feedback literature and feedback practices enacted on the ground still tend to pull heavily on behaviourist views of feedback. In other words, best-practice principles are often founded on the idea that feedback occurs in a contextual vacuum, in which learners will respond reliably and consistently to a given stimulus provided by the teacher (Boud and Molloy, 2012). Given this stance, protocols for effective feedback are pitched at the educator, are one size fits all, and are focused on how they can better 'deliver' the message to enable improvement in performance. By virtue of this positioning of the educator as teller, the learner becomes the passive receiver (Molloy and Clarke, 2005). Without a sense of ownership in the process or content of feedback, it is not surprising that students often don't act on feedback, or in fact, don't go to the effort to even read written feedback (Hattie and Timperley, 2007).

Emotion can have both a positive and negative impact on learning (Falchikov and Boud, 2007). Enjoyment of a topic or practice may encourage learners to spend more time on the task, and therefore result in optimal learning. On the other hand, if learners anticipate that they have not mastered a skill, this may motivate them to study harder, and therefore the perceived inadequacy (emotional discomfort) can have a positive impact on subsequent learning and performance. Some learners, however, who identify a lack of mastery and don't think they have the capacity to develop this over time, may give up and declare that they are not fit for the task or work. These variable responses, depending

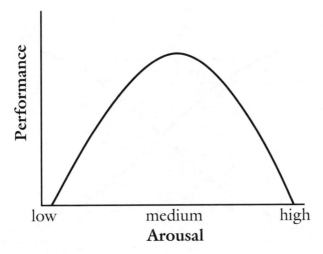

Figure 4.1 The stress-performance curve

on the learner's disposition, prior experience and motivation, make it difficult to provide generic models on 'how to give effective feedback'.

Research indicates that learners characteristically perform best – that is, receive information, make links, retain knowledge, and apply knowledge to different situations – when they are operating in a context of a somewhat tempered ground of emotion or arousal (Apter, 1989; Chanock, 2000). Individuals need a certain amount of stress or arousal to function well. Low arousal results in sub-optimal performance, as does high arousal (Figure 4.1).

Apter (1989) adapted this stress-performance curve to further deconstruct 'the optimal work zone' (Figure 4.2), where good work is achieved in this tempered ground of emotion/arousal. On the horizontal axis, Apter's model represents the degree of arousal of the learner, typically measured in levels of adrenaline and alertness, and on the vertical axis, 'hedonic tone' or the degree to which the learner is enjoying themselves (or not), is represented. Four emotional states that we often register and work within are represented on the four corners of Figure 4.2, with optimal work capacity pictured in the middle. In this area, optimal cognitive processing is seen to occur. Ideally, both learners and educators would seek to create these 'tempered' or moderate conditions when engaging in feedback to maximise the learning potential of the practice. As Chanock stated, 'feedback can become obscured by emotional static' (2000, p. 95).

Many feedback guidelines do, in a way, acknowledge principles from Apter's (1989) notion of an optimal cognition zone. For example, guidelines impress upon the educator the importance of providing feedback to the learner in a 'safe environment' away from consumers in the workplace (e.g. pupils in a school setting, patients in a health setting or consumers in a retail setting). Feedback constructed away from the 'coal face' means that learners may be better able to engage in the

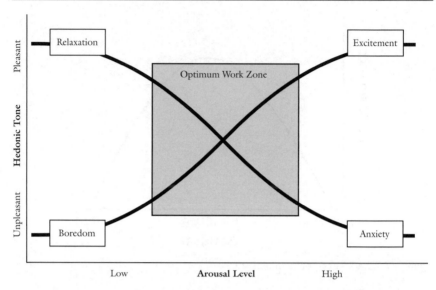

Figure 4.2 Apter's (1989) model of emotional reversal theory. Reproduced with permission from Borrell-Carrió, F. and Epstein, R. (2004) 'Preventing clinical errors: a call for self-awareness', *Annals of Family Medicine*, 2:310–316.

discussion and take away important information that can improve their future work. Likewise, studies report on the benefit of delayed feedback (post-task performance) if the learning encounter has proven highly emotive or distressing (Hattie and Timperley, 2007; Ende et al., 1995), e.g. immediately after a medical treatment that has been ineffective in keeping a patient alive or immediately after a failed attempt at a performance where the learner's emotions are already heightened. These temporal and geographical dimensions of feedback are important. However, the acknowledgement of the impact of emotion on feedback efficacy needs to extend beyond these practical implications of when and where to provide feedback as ways to protect the learner's self-esteem. The equation needs to account for more complexity, and therefore multiple 'feedback practice strategies' depending on the factors at play.

Research on feedback has indicated that recipients of feedback typically find the process difficult and confronting (Ende, 1983; Henderson et al., 2005; Molloy, 2009), occupying the space depicted as the 'anxiety quadrant' on Apter's Model. Less talked about is the emotional experience of educators in providing, and in anticipation of providing, this performance information. These characteristic educator responses will be described later in the chapter, and may provide clues as to why feedback is seen as so problematic by learners, teachers and institutions. So, given that research indicates that feedback often takes place in Apter's anxiety quadrant (or in fact, the act causes both parties to relocate into the anxiety quadrant), two questions need to be asked. Why is the act of feedback so inherently challenging for the learner? And, given its potential to generate negative reactions, do we in fact need it all?

External and internal feedback: Making sense of judgements

An increasing number of studies point to the inadequacy of self-assessment alone as a vehicle for performance improvement, particularly for novices (Eva and Regehr, 2005 and 2008). As humans, we tend to hold a number of biases in the way that we judge our own performance, and often we don't have a clear or shared understanding about what it is we are trying to achieve (performance standards, or task target). Studies show that poorly performing learners have over-inflated self-perceptions of performance, and that conversely, high performers are overly critical, and tend to underrate their performance when compared to external, experienced judges (Dunning et al., 2004). For this reason, external information relating to performance ('external feedback') is extremely important in narrowing the gap between actual demonstrated performance and the goal of performance. For the purposes of this chapter, information on performance provided by an external source will be termed 'external feedback', and internally generated judgements will be labelled 'internal feedback'. We ascribe to the definition and conceptual representation of feedback presented in Chapter 2 (see Figure 2.4) that feedback is in fact a process of seeking, receiving, interpreting (making sense of internal and externally generated information) in order to change the output (subsequent performance). The whole process is feedback, not just the 'provision of information' by an external other.

This broader 'process model' of feedback, represented as Feedback Mark 2 (Boud and Molloy, 2012, and Chapter 2) considers the integral role of the learner in feedback. The model calls for a greater level of commitment in considering how the learner seeks information, interprets information and uses this data to fuel their subsequent performance. One of the major challenges of feedback, as a process, is that there can often be a dissonance or conflict between the external feedback provided and feedback internally generated by the learner (Sargeant et al., 2010). A key job of the learner, in interacting with their environment and in seeking or being a recipient of external feedback, is that they need to interpret this data for themselves. In other words, the external feedback is sifted for 'quality' or 'utility' based on the learner's prior experience, values, motivation, perception of the status of the 'teacher' or 'other', and own judgement about how they viewed their performance on task. Over time, it is postulated that this process of sense-making and interpretation allows the student to operate within a self-regulated model of learning (Butler and Winne, 1995). Ultimately, as professionals and workers become more experienced, the amount of direct external feedback and instruction (certainly from a teacher or supervisor) is reduced. One hypothesis for this progressive withdrawal of direct observation and instruction is that external feedback acts as a mechanism to build self-regulation (Boud, 2000; Nicol and Macfarlane-Dick, 2006; Butler and Winne, 1995). A self-regulated learner relies more heavily upon, or trusts, their internally generated feedback:

> Self-regulated students are thus aware of qualities of their own knowledge,
> beliefs, motivation, and cognitive processing—elements that jointly create
> situated updates of the tasks on which the students work. This awareness
> provides grounds on which the students judge how well unfolding cognitive
> engagement matches the standards they set for successful learning. (Butler
> and Winne, 1995, p. 245)

So, intuitively, based on the above assumption, we could conclude that learners
would flock to feedback opportunities in order to improve their performance and
to hasten their path towards self-regulation. Why, then, is feedback seen as so
problematic and so capable of generating high emotions, despite best intentions?

One answer is that people have a particular view of themselves and the way
that they operate in the world, and the constancy of this view creates a feeling
of calm. Incoming data that contradicts or challenges this internal perception is
naturally confronting (Gilbert and Wilson, 2000), like a stone in the shoe that
demands action, or at least, consideration. For example, if a learner believed that
their performance on Task A was excellent, and received external feedback to the
contrary, they have on their hands a judgement dissonance or judgement gap. In
the feedback literature, there is ample written on the 'performance gap' where
there is a difference detected between actual performance and goal of performance (Sadler 1989). The less-discussed 'gap' is that of the judgement gap, or
the difference between internal and external perceptions of behaviour/perfor-
mance. Butler and Winne (1995), in their theoretical discussion of feedback, do
in fact deal with this complex issue very well. They draw on the work of Chinn
and Brewer (1993), who described six typical reactions of the learner when
external feedback varies from their own internal judgement (summarised in Table
4.1). The common maladaptive responses are presented, along with potential
coinciding dialogue that learners may be telling themselves or others, in order to
reconcile the internal and external judgement variability.

Table 4.1 The judgement gap: Maladaptive responses to external information
on performance (based on the work of Chinn and Brewer, 1993)

Maladaptive response	Examples of the learner's 'inner dialogue' when faced with internal and external feedback dissonance
1. Ignore the external feedback	Feedback? What feedback?
2. Reject the external feedback	I think the feedback is wrong. It's not accurate, and I don't trust the teacher's opinion.

3. Review the feedback as irrelevant	That is all good and well, that comment. But it doesn't relate to my job as a dietician. It doesn't help me in any way.
4. Refuse to see connection between the internal and external feedback	I thought my overall performance as a 'teacher' in that class was good. The supervisor has picked out some negatives about how I came across to the students, but that's not the point. The point is that I taught the right stuff in the lesson, and that's the main thing.
5. Re-interpret the external feedback to align with internal judgement	The supervisor said that I'm on the right path to becoming a doctor – that my level of practice is where it should be. But then he did pick out some deficits about the way I did the physical examination, so clearly, I'm not where I should be. This confirms my view that I'm not good enough to be a doctor.
6. Act on the feedback in a superficial/placatory manner	For the purposes of this assignment, I'm happy to take on board the suggested changes to the essay, i.e. I will use those headings to give it structure, but that's not how I'm going to write long-term, it's not my style.

In each of these responses the influence of the externally provided feedback on subsequent behaviour change is minimal. The common responses suggest that the impact of external feedback on learning is contingent on how the information is filtered through a student's existing beliefs and motivations for learning. If educators are mindful of these characteristic student responses, it may alert them to reasons why learners might not be changing their behaviour in response to performance information. Addressing the dissonance in internal and external judgements through dialogue may be much more productive than the educator providing the same message but louder, or offering the same message from a slightly different angle.

One way to counter these maladaptive tendencies may be to give the learner opportunities to initially express their own judgement or self-evaluation, and the reason why they thought their performance should be viewed in that particular light. This may cue both learner and educator to consider alternative interpretations of judgement, and also help highlight the learner's beliefs or epistemological values that they hold (Butler and Winne, 1995). For example, through this dialogue, the trainee doctor (see point 5 in Table 4.1) may articulate that she sees expertise as a fixed construct, as either 'you have it or you don't', rather than as a spectrum of capability that is time- and context-dependent.

There could be long-lasting benefits in airing this assumption, and offering counter-arguments as to why it might not be a productive attitude to hold onto. By shifting expectations, or values, this can help the learner recalibrate their internal judgements, i.e. the trainee doctor may then see that his performance is appropriate for his level of experience and that there is room for improvement, no matter how experienced a practitioner. Moulton and Epstein (2011) argue for learners to replace a static and fixed identity, such as 'I am a good doctor', with an evolving and complex identity that acknowledges that competence is fragile, fluid and context-dependent. This argument reflects the work of Dweck (2000), who suggested that the ability of feedback to do good work depends on the world-view of the individual learner. Students who responded poorly to feedback were more likely to be inhabiting a 'fixed' or entity view where they saw their ability as a capped and finite construct. In contrast, those learners who responded to feedback with subsequent positive behaviour/performance change adopted an 'incremental perspective' where they viewed their ability as malleable and contingent on effort, motivation and environmental conditions. Those learners with a fixed view of their own capacity had a tendency to interpret feedback relating to failure *at task* as failure *of self* and this response served to demotivate action.

This makes us consider that creating optimal emotional conditions for feedback may not be a simple matter of tinkering with the mechanics of the individual feedback episode itself. The success or lack of success of feedback may hinge on the learners' interpretation of 'competency' and their view about their own capacity to change. Orientating learners to this 'fluid' construction of identity and competency may minimise the threat of feedback to self-esteem.

The difficulty in dealing with conflicting data about self or performance is that a differing external data point challenges the learner to reconsider their own prior notions of self. There is a tendency for humans to want to present as a consistent and unchanging entity. Goffman (1955) and Harré (1999), in their theses about the construction and maintenance of self, argue that 'face' is a mask that changes depending on the audience and the nature of the social interaction. Typically, people strive to maintain the face they have created in social situations and they are emotionally committed to their faces. This means that they tend to feel good when their faces are maintained and conversely they feel emotional pain when they have a loss of face, or a challenge to their identity that they have worked hard to establish. Goffman (1959) suggests that in social encounters others use 'politeness strategies' to maintain each others' faces. Some of the effort that educators have reported in trying to provide feedback that is sensitive to the learner (Molloy, 2009; Ende et al., 1995) can be interpreted under the umbrella of politeness strategies, according to Goffman's notion of how ideas about self are preserved over time.

The extent to which people are defensive or protective of their view of self in feedback depends on personality, experience and levels of confidence (Eva et al., 2012). For example, some learners with high levels of confidence have reported feeling more receptive to advice about how they can improve, whereas novices are more likely to exhibit fragile confidence and defensive mechanisms towards critical external feedback. Individuals who are attuned to the purpose of feedback – to help improve learning/performance – can acknowledge the initial discomfort experienced as a recipient of criticism but can rationalise the emotion on the basis of the message doing 'good things'. As a learner in Eva et al.'s (2012) study stated:

> *If it's negative it always feels a bit painful. But it's true, when you look upon yourself and you know she's [the educator's] right, you can place it in a way.*
> (Midwifery student, Eva et al., 2012)

This student's reflection also highlights the impact of the perceived status, or credibility of the provider. If learners trust the expertise or knowledge of the source, and also trust the source's intention (that they have the learner's best interests at heart) they are more likely to be able to process and utilise the feedback, even if the message challenges their own internal judgement. Hearing this insight from learners reinforces the notion that feedback efficacy is not necessarily about what is said by the source, but instead, how external feedback is interpreted by the learner. As highlighted in Chapter 2, feedback is more than 'telling'.

The six maladaptive strategies presented in Table 4.1 reflect learners' attempts to ameliorate the pain of critical external feedback. This defensive tendency has been described by psychologists as the 'psychological immune system' or a set of cognitive strategies that serve to protect the learner from experiencing negative emotions (Gilbert and Wilson, 2000; Isen, 1993). There may be occasions where these defensive mechanisms are productive in enabling the learner to preserve a sense of positive self-efficacy and to cope with their complex learning environment. However, when the learner's psychological immune system is working in overdrive there are two common responses. First, the learner avoids feedback opportunities. And second, the learner deflects external information when it is made available, holding tightly to their own interpretation of events (Eva et al., 2012). In both these responses, the psychological immune system is successful in preserving face, but is doing little to help with learning. Students who are aware of these self-protecting mechanisms and who have experienced, first hand, the benefit of taking on external feedback and observing the subsequent positive change, are more likely to use feedback for its intended purpose. Unfortunately, the feedback approaches of some educators, in terms of intention, content and delivery method, are so poor that the psychological immune system does in fact perform a service to the learner.

Feedback as an emotional business: how do educators respond?

Learners as recipients of 'bad news' get plenty of space in the feedback literature, but what about the educators' role in feedback? Is there enough knowledge about how 'the bearers of bad news' experience emotion, or react to emotion? Examination of the literature seeking educator perspectives on feedback highlights that acting as the source of external feedback can be as equally stressful as assuming the recipient position. First, educators are conscious of the importance of collecting observational data and making 'correct' diagnostic decisions about the student's performance (Molloy, 2009). Second, they may doubt their own knowledge about the goal of performance (e.g. do I really know what a good systematic review should look like? Am I a credible enough source to judge whether the learner has met these practice standards?) And third, they may be concerned about offending or upsetting the learner (Ende, 1983; Molloy, 2009). As Higgs et al. (2004) reported,

> giving feedback that preserves dignity and facilitates ongoing communication between the communication partners, but that also leads to behavioural change, is a challenge. (p. 248)

Much of this anxiety is around the anticipation of upsetting the learner through presenting an overly critical account of their work. Ironically, this anticipation of leading the learner out of the 'neutral emotion zone' can result in the educator propelling themselves into a hot zone of anxiety where their own decision-making or work may be compromised. This anticipatory fear of eliciting emotion is explored next.

Fear of feeding emotion: introducing the feedback sandwich

A number of models and guidelines in the literature are designed to preserve the dignity and feelings of learners in feedback. The 'feedback sandwich' – where negative feedback (the meat) is sandwiched between layers of positive feedback (the bread) – is probably the most well-known model of feedback in professional development circles, and potentially one of the most undermining of attempts to encourage good practice (Molloy, 2010). Its very design is revealing about how educators consider feedback, and it is worth unpicking, layer by layer, the messages that it gives learners about feedback. In the feedback sandwich model, the educator is assigned the task of making the sandwich, handing it over, and the students must digest it. Implicitly this analogy diminishes student agency. The hard-hitting 'negative feedback' is seen as the meat in the middle. This is encased (or softened) by slices of 'bread' that constitute the 'positive feedback' on performance. The rationale, of course, is that if you warm up the student with flattery and warm down the student with another dose of flattery, the criticism in the middle will be easier to digest. It's a model of disguise.

  The very labelling of 'positive' and 'negative' feedback provides students with not-so-subtle messages that praise is good and useful and that highlighting an aspect of performance that needs improvement is negative. In contrast to this, research on feedback suggests that praise can be unhelpful and that accurate information about performance is what is desired and effective (Shute, V. J., 2008). Kohn's (1999) synthesis of studies on praise concludes that people actually do inferior work when they are enticed with praise, grades, or other incentives. He postulates that we need to move beyond the use of carrots (particularly indiscriminate praise) or sticks if we want to improve learning and improve workplaces. There has been such a sweeping reform in school-based education to avoid criticism and comparison of students' performances, and the replacement has been praise. It is not surprising that learners, after transition into higher education or workplace-based learning, feel ill-equipped to process information formulated for the purpose of improvement. For these learners, the psychological immune system is forced into overdrive as these individuals may have no orientation to, nor practice in, how to use these judgements for positive change.

Ironically, if we revisit the definition of feedback in Chapter 1, and return to the three principles espoused by Sadler (1989), the meat in the sandwich is the only part of the concoction that we could truly define as a part of feedback. It is the meat in the middle that challenges the student to improve their practice. So if we have to stick to the reductionist positive and negative terminology, shouldn't the meat be the 'positive' layer?

The other problem with the feedback sandwich, apart from its attempt to disguise helpful information to aid students in their learning, is that students learn very quickly to anticipate the linguistic ritual (Molloy, 2010). Students have reported that these predictable routines tamper with authenticity (telling it how it is) and therefore strict adherence to models such as the sandwich are likely to invite an equally tokenistic response from students in feedback encounters (Molloy, 2009).

Ende (1983) acknowledged the inherent danger in educators anticipating an emotional response in learners through feedback. He coined the concept of 'vanishing feedback' where the educator neglects to raise an important performance issue for fear of eliciting a negative reaction from the student. The student, in fearing a negative appraisal, may support and reinforce this educator avoidance of 'telling it how it is'. The message and the potential for learning that it carries can be lost due to the perceived threat of judgemental feedback on learner self-efficacy. As Hounsell (1987) pointed out, students can become

> locked into a cycle of deprivation as far as constructive feedback is concerned. Since feedback fails to connect, it comes to be viewed as insignificant or invalid, and so is not given considered attention. At the same time the activity within which it is offered is seen increasingly as unrewarding, and so it is approached perfunctorily, thus rather lessening the likelihood that a more appropriate conception might be apprehended. (p. 117)

Feedback designers seem to like the metaphor of ingesting and digesting. The sugar-coated pill is another analogy to describe a way to make a bitter-tasting agent (however useful to the user) more palatable for the recipient. A coating of flattery ('positive feedback') may ease the pain of the learner, whilst the active ingredient – information on how performance can improve – does its work. This is a one-step improvement on the sandwich because at least the analogy acknowledges that constructive performance information is of benefit to the learner. The sugar coating may make it go down better at the start, but again, research indicates that learners are very savvy as to what constitutes honest appraisal (Eva et al., 2012) and what constitutes ritualistic coating to encourage digestion. The sugar, or the reinforcing feedback, still has a disguising function.

Maybe the work of the enteric-coated pill is the best descriptor yet. The enteric pill has a coating to prevent the medication from dissolving in the stomach, where it is vulnerable to being broken down by acids in the stomach. The coating is designed to dissolve in the small intestine, enabling absorption of the drug so it can do the job it is designed for. In this model, both the reinforcing (coating) and the corrective components of the feedback (drug) have roles to play. They are both active ingredients in making the drug effective, not fillers, nor disguisers that are designed to protect the emotions of the receiver. If anything, these compensatory or protective sugar-coating measures position learners as lacking capacity to seek or hear messages that may challenge them. It puts limits on what we think they are capable of doing.

Giving effective feedback is not just about how to structure information to make it palatable, it is about generating conditions and developing skills conductive to the uptake and application of feedback. We may need to give more consideration to factors such as orientation to feedback purpose, practice in giving and receiving it, practice with self-evaluation as a way to build confidence in internal judgements, trusting the educator (in their intention to help) and better building of the learners' knowledge of standards of practice. Using these strategies we are more likely to build robust learners, capable of seeking and using feedback, rather than learners with fragile confidence and over-active psychological immune systems that don't let anything through.

Educator Linguistic Choices

The language of feedback impacts on the way learners hear and interpret messages. The effect of linguistic choices in feedback, both in the oral and the written mode, are explored in this book in Chapter 5 and Chapter 7. One of the dangers in a more knowledgeable person providing performance information to a less knowledgeable or experienced person is the creation of a one-way transmission of information. This linguistic dynamic can be particularly unproductive if educators use an authoritative or judgemental voice in feedback. This 'telling' mode of performance information exchange implies that the educator viewpoint cannot be contested. A number of studies of feedback in professional education have highlighted the negative influence of teacher power on students' confidence and learning (Ende, 1983; Molloy and Clarke, 2005; Carless, 2009). Even a single poor evaluation can have a devastating impact on the student's future in terms of the specialty or activities they choose to pursue.

The language positions feedback information as fact, rather than as a subjective construct that can be negotiated with the learner. The trap in using this tone is that it can inhibit the learner's agency in comparing and making sense of internal and external judgements. Carless (2009) highlights the 'finality' of one-way written or verbal comments that do not invite any learner supplementation or modification. Boud (1995, following Rorty, 1989) labels this phenomenon as 'final vocabulary' and criticises its use in leaving the learner with no room for manoeuvre or self-regulation.

To further complicate this very real issue of educator/expert power in feedback, studies have shown that learners are often complicit in generating this one-way transmission of information (Molloy, 2009). Often, they deflect opportunities for self-analysis – 'sticking your neck out' – because of the risk that their own perception may be inaccurate. Also, many students, particularly those involved in workplace learning, have been conditioned to appear deferential, even when they might be more perceptive than the attending teacher/supervisor. The professional practice culture has a significant bearing on the learning practices of students and this implicit expectation of 'deferring to expertise' forms part of the hidden curriculum within the workplace.

To counter this deferential culture, teachers may need to encourage the student to take a one-up position in an authentic way so that they can speak more honestly from their own experience. For example, saying 'Only you can know what was going on in your mind, so to help you figure out where your reasoning went askew, could we talk about your process of thinking when you were examining the client?' can be a way of fostering reflection and valuing the learner's judgement. These educator prompts can encourage students to take up these habits of self-questioning during their own practice (Borrell-Carrió and Epstein, 2004). For example, learners may ask themselves 'how might my previous experience affect my actions with this patient?' or 'what would a trusted peer say about the way I managed this situation?'. The questions posed within a feedback exchange may act as a form of modelling for learners to adopt this moment-to-moment reflective stance in their practice. This capacity is known as 'self-monitoring' or 'mindfulness' (Epstein et al., 2008; Moulton and Epstein, 2011).

Generating conditions conducive to feedback

This chapter has highlighted that feedback is an intrinsically emotional business because of its focus on the learner, and how they need to improve to reach a given standard. When any discrepancy between internal and external judgement occurs, there is likely to be some feeling of discomfort generated for the learner. In particular, learners that view expertise or competence as a fixed entity are more likely to interpret constructive feedback as a threat to self. With orientation to feedback purpose, and also practise opportunities to seek and use feedback, it is hoped that learners start to build increasingly able internal judgement systems that are open to seeking and interpreting alternative external data points that may extend their learning.

Unfortunately, acknowledgement of the emotional nature of feedback has resulted in the generation of models and educator-driven practices that undermine the very purpose of feedback. In essence, these 'gently gently' practices are predicated on fear of eliciting an emotional learner response, and therefore burying important constructive messages for learners to take up into their subsequent practice. Table 4.2 summarises the dimensions that educators may consider when formulating feedback in a program. They are divided into macro, or program-level characteristics to consider, as well as the micro, or *in situ* elements that may have a bearing on the effectiveness of feedback. These elements have been distilled to create a reflective framework for educators to consider their feedback practices from the anticipatory or preparatory perspective (before they encounter the student), to the perspective of when they are working with the student within a feedback episode. The framework encourages educators to take up reflective habits – to consider the impact of what they do on students' learning. In other words, we are encouraging educators to take up mindful feedback practices.

Table 4.2 Framework for considering emotional dimensions in feedback

Dimensions to consider when providing feedback	Educator self-prompts
MACRO DIMENSIONS	
Orientation of students to the **purpose of feedback** – as a tool for the learner, to help the learner improve subsequent performance	Have I briefed the learner/s on the role of feedback, and my own role in helping the learner to see how they can improve? Have I highlighted the traps of 'vanishing feedback' and my commitment to generating strategies together that can be taken forward?
Providing **opportunities for learners to solicit** feedback, including cueing educators to focus on certain aspects of their performance. This empowers the learner to be an agent in learning, rather than a recipient, responsive to the educator's agenda.	Have I extended this invitation at the start of the unit/placement? Do I continue to prompt the learner to ask what they would like help on (i.e. what they want me to focus on when I watch them perform a task, or when I read their submitted work)?

Making clear expectations of *learner self-evaluation* as part of the feedback exchange (and if necessary, refraining from providing external feedback until after the self-analysis is offered). Again, this positions the learner as active within the process, and can ameliorate the emotion raised by 'being told' the performance is sub-optimal (self-analysis of deficiencies is much more empowering than being told your deficiencies).

Have I verbalised this expectation and the rationale for the value of self-evaluation?
    Have I expressed to learners that it is OK to make mistakes in self-judgement or to have a mismatch in internal and external feedback? That this weighing-up of discrepancies in judgement is essential to calibration?

Continuity of learner-educator *relationship*

Is there a sustained learner-educator relationship so that I can observe subsequent task performances and close the loop? Is there more likely to be trust built when the learning relationship can develop over time and we both learn the tendencies and characteristics of each other?

Opportunities for *repeat task* performance

Was the student able to use the feedback, and have I commented on the extent to which they have achieved the goals set in this subsequent performance?

MICRO DIMENSIONS

Source of external feedback

Who is in the best position to provide feedback to the learner – peers, multiple supervisors/teachers, consumer? What is the advantage of triangulating data from these multiple sources? Will it strengthen the 'performance picture' for the learner? Will it take the pressure off me as the all-seeing, all-knowing teacher?

Mode of information exchange – written, verbal, video-tape

What will be the most effective mode for the learner? What can written feedback achieve that verbal can not, etc?

Location of feedback exchange

Where is the best place for engagement in feedback? Where will the learner feel 'safest', where will the message be best taken up?

Timing of feedback	Shall I give feedback at the time of performance? i..e. in situ or immediately post-performance, delayed, at half-way point in the unit or placement. Is there any value in feedback at the end of semester or at the end of the placement?
Information flow (one- v. two-way conversation)	Who did most of the talking? Did we respond to each other's input or did we stick to our own agendas in what we wanted to raise in the discussion?
Power/positioning dynamics (verbal content)	How did I position myself in relation to the student? Did I use inclusive/ encouraging language? Did I use any 'final vocabulary' that the student felt unable to contest? Did I allow enough time for student responses or questions? Did the student lose face in front of a wider audience through the feedback process?
Power/positioning dynamics (non-verbal)	What was my body language conveying to the learner? Was I open, did I show any signs of irritation, were we seated at the same level?
Educator **responsiveness** to student input	How did I respond to students' questions/comments? Did I validate the student's self-evaluation where appropriate?
Content (balance of comments relating to confirmation of good aspects of performance and need for improved performance)	What areas did my comments focus on? Was there an emphasis on how to improve performance in relation to standards of good work?
Specific supporting data (provision of examples of *behaviour or work that needs improving*)	What specific behaviour did I refer to? Did I ensure that I was commenting on aspects of work or behaviour, and NOT the person? Did I at any point provide any broad brush generalizations that are unlikely to affect capacity to do better future work?
Strategies for improvement (future-referenced)	Once deficits were identified, did I make suggestions for how to improve the work? What strategies for improvement did we devise? Did the student think that these were achievable?

Summarising/clarification for shared meaning	Did I check that the student shared or understood my analysis? Were we on the same page? If it was a verbal feedback episode, did I suggest that the student make a written record of the key take-home messages, for reasons of cognitive load and to provide a reference point for the next performance discussion?

A number of considerations including program design for student agency, power symmetry, message content, and future-referenced, clear strategies for improvement are emphasised in the reflective framework. If students are engaged in this model of feedback where they act as agents, we anticipate that feedback could be based on honest dialogue, rather than tricks of dialogue as a mechanism to minimise damage. This open exchange should mean that learners have a clear concept of what they are aiming to achieve (the target performance) and how their own task attempt measured up to the target. However, we know from the literature that speaking openly for the good of the learner – 'sometimes you need to be cruel to be kind' or 'students learn best from teachers that challenge them' – is rarely well achieved. The discussion of performance information, including the performance gap analysis, requires sensitivity, and certainly skill and experience from both students and teachers to make it work. It requires not only comments on students' work, but a commitment to showing what the target performance can look like and what might be the likely consequences if learners do not take up the desired behaviours. For example, 'if you call patients by their first name on first meeting, without an invitation to do so, this could be interpreted as rude or lacking respect. I find that it's often best to use Ms or Mr X in the first instance, and then change tack and apply the less formal approach if you're invited to do so'.

As outlined earlier in the chapter, the tendency for a defensive stance from learners is likely to be heightened if their own self-judgement differs from the external judgement. Also, defensiveness may be amplified when the learner is significantly invested in achievement of the standards. For example, the learner may not be so concerned by average scores on a theory-based exam where they invested little in preparation/study, but may be devastated if they receive poor feedback on their classroom teaching placement when they are working hard, committed to improving, and starting to form a professional identity. In these circumstances, factors including the perceived credibility of the educator by the student (Eva et al., 2012), the trust in the learning relationship (Carless, 2009), the timing of the feedback (Hattie and Timperley, 2007), the phrasing of the feedback (Molloy, 2009), and the amount of support provided before and after the feedback encounter (Nicol and Macfarlane-Dick, 2006) are likely to influence how the message is heard and taken up into practice.

The importance of learner orientation to the purpose of feedback is possibly the most neglected factor in this discourse about learner fragility in the reception of feedback, as is the importance of providing learners with opportunities to practise giving and receiving feedback in low-stakes or non-threatening environments, for example, with peers (Ladyshewsky, 2006). If learners believe that feedback is a process that is for them, to help them, rather than a practice imposed upon them by 'gatekeeping educators', the defensive tendency may be negated. Henderson et al. (2005) wrote a strong commentary on the need for orientation of learners to the purpose and practice of feedback in the academic environment so that feedback encounters in the workplace were not seen as suitable for the brave-hearted only. Carless in Chapter 6 of this book also highlights the importance of building trust in the educational relationship. Perhaps both parties can afford to be more direct in feedback encounters the more that mutual trust is established, and the more that learners experience the benefit of feedback in building their capacities. Generating feedback that is both sensitive and challenging is not an easy feat, and requires 'mindful educators', responsive to learner reactions and learner performance outcomes.

Conclusion

Emotions are part of learning, and therefore part of feedback. Psychological studies show us that certain emotions, with accompanying levels of arousal or stress, can hinder learning and performance. It is therefore important that both learners and educators work together to generate conditions that are optimal for seeking and using feedback for learning. As it is currently enacted, feedback practices are often not fit for purpose. The anticipation of emotive reactions from learners seems to have paralysed educators' honesty, and has reduced face-to-face verbal feedback encounters to predictable linguistic rituals where not much is said at all. The disguised messages, as promoted in models like the feedback sandwich, position learners as incapable of digesting and making sense of performance information. And with this volume of indiscriminately sprinkled praise in our classrooms and workplaces, it is no wonder that learners feel stung when they hear constructive feedback about how they can improve their work. In such cases, defensive mechanisms, labelled by Gilbert and Wilson (2000) as the 'psychological immune system', are activated to protect the learner's internal judgement. This discomfort related to internal and external judgement dissonance can lead to learners avoiding feedback opportunities or discounting feedback.

Learners need practice at making sense of their own internal judgements and how these measure up to external judgements. This, over time, enables calibration, and an increased reliance on self-monitoring and feedback seeking from other sources, other than the teacher. Educators need to design feedback at both a program and an episode-based level to empower learners to be active in the process. They also need to engage in a cycle of continual reflection themselves to measure the impact of their feedback on learning outcomes. The aim of feedback is to help build robust learners, not just for the end purpose of seeing them cope, or cope extremely well, in the formal educational setting. We want to help create mindful learners who have capacity for self-monitoring, and the motivation to use feedback from multiple sources in their workplace.

References

Apter, M. (1989) *Reversal Theory: Motivation, Emotion and Personality*, London: Routledge.

Borrell-Carrió, F., Epstein, R. (2004) 'Preventing clinical errors: a call for self-awareness', *Annals of Family Medicine*, 2:310-16.

Boud, D. (1995). 'Assessment and learning: contradictory or complementary?', in Knight, P. (ed.) *Assessment for Learning in Higher Education*. London: Kogan Page, 35-48.

Boud, D. (2000) 'Sustainable assessment: rethinking assessment for the learning society', *Studies in Continuing Education*, 22(2):151-67.

Boud, D. and Molloy, E. (2012) 'Rethinking models of feedback for learning: the challenge of design', *Assessment and Evaluation in Higher Education*, DOI:10.10 80/02602938.2012.691462.

Boud, D. and Walker, D. (1998) 'Promoting Reflection in Professional Courses: the challenge of context', *Studies in Higher Education*, 23(2):191-206.

Butler, D. L. and Winne, P. H. (1995) 'Feedback and self-regulated learning: a theoretical synthesis', *Review of Educational Research*, 65(3):245-81.

Carless, D. (2009) 'Trust, distrust and their impact on assessment reform', *Assessment & Evaluation in Higher Education*, 34(1):79-89.

Chanock, K. (2000) 'Comments on Essays: do students understand what tutors write?', *Teaching in Higher Education*, 5(1): 95-105.

Chinn, C. A. and Brewer, W. F. (1993) 'The role of anomalous data in knowledge acquisition: A theoretical framework and implications for science instruction', *Review of Educational Research*, 63:1-49.

Damasio, A. (1994) *Descartes' Error: Emotion, Reason and the Human Brain*, New York: Harcourt Brace.

Dewey, J. (1933) *How we think. A restatement of the relation of reflective thinking to the educative process*, Massachusetts: DC Health.

Dunning, D., Heath, C. and Suls, J. M. (2004) 'Flawed self-assessment: Implications for health, education, and the workplace', *Psychological Science in the Public Interest*, 5:69-106.

Dweck, S. (2000) *Self-Theories: Their Role in Motivation, Personality, and Development*, Lillington, NC: Psychology Press.

Ende, J. (1983) 'Feedback in clinical medical education', *Journal of American Medical Association*, 250:777-81.

Ende, J., Pomerantz, A. and Erickson, F. (1995) 'Preceptors' strategies for correcting residents in an ambulatory care medicine setting: A qualitative analysis', *Academic Medicine*, 70:224-9.

Epstein, R., Siegel, D. and Silberman, J. (2008) 'Self-monitoring in clinical practice: a challenge for medical educators', *Journal of Continuing Education in the Health Professions*, 28(1):5-13.

Eva, K., Armson, H., Holmboe, E., Lockyer, J., Loney, E., Mann, K. and Sargeant, J. (2012) 'Factors influencing responsiveness to feedback: on the interplay between fear, confidence, and reasoning processes', *Advances in health sciences education*, 17:15-26.

Eva, K. W. and Regehr, G. (2005) 'Self-assessment in the Health Professions: A Reformulation and Research Agenda', *Academic Medicine*, 80 (10 Suppl.), S46–S54.

Eva, K. W. and Regehr, G. (2008) '"I'll never play professional football" and other fallacies of self assessment', *Journal for Continuing Education in the Health Professions*, 28:14-19.

Falchikov, N. and Boud, D. (2007) 'Assessment and emotion: the impact of being assessed', in Boud, D. and Falchikov, N. (eds) *Rethinking Assessment in Higher Education. Learning for the Longer Term*, London: Routledge.

Gilbert, D. T. and Wilson, T. D. (2000) 'Miswanting', in Forgas, J. (ed.), *Thinking and feeling: The role of affect in social cognition*, Cambridge: Cambridge University Press.

Gigerenzer, G. (2007). *Gut Feelings: the intelligence of the unconscious*. New York: Viking.

Goffman, E. (1955) 'On Face-work: An Analysis of Ritual Elements of Social Interaction', *Psychiatry: Journal for the Study of Interpersonal Processes*, 18(3):213-31.

Goffman, E. (1959) *The presentation of self in everyday life*, Garden City, NY: Doubleday.

Harré, R. and Van Langenhove, L. (1999) *Positioning Theory*, Oxford: Blackwell Publishers.

Hattie, J. and Timperley, H. (2007) 'The power of feedback', *Review of Educational Research*, 77:81-112.

Henderson, P., Ferguson-Smith, A. and Johnson, M. (2005) 'Developing essential professional skills: a framework for teaching and learning about feedback', *BMC Medical Education*, 5:1-6.

Higgs, J., Richardson, B. and Abrandt Dahlgren, M. (eds) (2004) *Developing practice knowledge for health professionals*, Oxford: Butterworth Heinemann.

Hyland, F. (1998) 'The Impact of Teacher Written Feedback on Individual Writers', *Journal of Second Language Writing*, 7(3):255-86.

Hounsell, D. (1987) 'Essay writing and the quality of feedback', in Richardson, J., Eysenck, M. W. and Piper, D. W. (eds), *Student Learning: research in education and cognitive psychology*, Milton Keynes: Open University Press.

Ilgen, D. and Davis, A. (2000) 'Bearing bad news: Reactions to negative performance feedback', *Applied Psychology: An International Review*, 49:550-65.

Isen, A. M. (1993) 'Positive affect and decision making', in Lewis, M. and Haviland, J. M. (eds), *Handbook of emotions*, New York, NY: Guilford Press.

Kohn, A. (1999) *Punished by rewards: The trouble with gold stars, incentive plans, A's, praise, and other bribes*, Boston: Houghton Mifflin Co.

Ladyshewsky, R. (2006) 'Building cooperation in peer coaching relationships: understanding the relationships between reward structure, learner preparedness, coaching skill and learner engagement', *Physiotherapy*, 92(1):4-10.

Latting, J. (1992) 'Giving corrective feedback: A decisional analysis', *Social Work*, 37:424-30.

Molloy, E. and Clarke, D. (2005) 'The positioning of physiotherapy students and clinical educators in feedback sessions', *Focus on Health Professional Education: A Multi-disciplinary Journal*, 7:79-90.

Molloy, E. (2009) 'Time to Pause: Feedback in Clinical Education', in Delany, C. and Molloy, E. (eds), *Clinical Education in the Health Professions*, Sydney: Elsevier, 128-46.

Molloy, E. (2010) 'The feedforward mechanism: a way forward in clinical learning?', *Medical Education*, 44:1157-9.

Moulton, C. and Epstein, R. (2011) 'Self monitoring in surgical practice: Slowing down when you should', in Fry, H. and Kneebone, R. (eds) *Surgical Education: Theorising an Emerging Domain, Advances in Medical Education 2*, DOI 10.1007/978-94-007-1682-7-10. Springer Science, 169-82.

Nicol, D. and Macfarlane-Dick, D. (2006) 'Formative assessment and self-regulated learning: A model and seven principles of good feedback practice', *Studies in Higher Education*, 31(2):199-218.

Rorty, R. (1989) *Contingency, Irony and Solidarity*, Cambridge: Cambridge University Press.

Sadler, D. R. (1989) 'Formative assessment and the design of instructional systems', *Instructional Science*, 18(2):119-44.

Sargeant, J., Armson, H., Chesluk, B., Dornan, T., Eva, K., Holmboe, E., Lockyer, J., Loney, E., Mann, K. and van der Vleuten, C. (2010) 'The processes and dimensions of informed self-assessment', *Academic Medicine*, Epub Apr 2, 2010.

Shute, V. J. (2008) 'Focus on formative feedback', *Review of Educational Research*, 78(1):153-89.

Wertsch, J. (1997) *Vygotsky and the formation of the mind*, Cambridge: Harvard University Press.

Chapter 5

Socio-cultural considerations in feedback

Andrea Paul
Kara Gilbert
Louisa Remedios

Introduction

Internationalisation of education and workplaces is driving increased emphasis on the role of communication in professional curricula. Educators must incorporate functional, professional and technical skills with explicit communication skills. The cultural diversity of students and educators highlights the need for feedback approaches that deconstruct and take into account cultural factors that impact on the provision of effective, efficient and accessible feedback across personal, pedagogical and professional dimensions of learning and teaching. To add further complexity, feedback on learning is consistently poorly evaluated by students in national and university-based surveys of higher education (as noted by Boud and Molloy in Chapter 1). To address this, new perspectives on feedback are being defined and integrated into effective learning and teaching strategies, as illustrated throughout this volume. Building on this work, the authors of this chapter introduce a previously unconsidered dimension to feedback, that of socio-cultural literacy. Helping students to achieve professional competence via the development of socio-cultural literacy is crucial to building effective feedback processes in the learning and teaching cycle and for generating appropriate professional applications of propositional knowledge.

We examine social, cultural and workplace factors that impact on the content, delivery and reception of feedback from both educator and student perspectives, in relation to the needs of culturally diverse students who interact with multicultural peer and consumer groups in professional settings. Essential to our approach is that *all* students, irrespective of ethno-linguistic and cultural background, come as novices to the work-based learning environments of professional practice. We emphasise the links between socialisation experiences of students and the specific cultural and linguistic functions in work-based practices. While our own experiences and the examples we draw on for this chapter are located in clinical learning environments, the socio-cultural framework for feedback we present has broad applications across professional work-based practices. We outline an approach to workplace feedback that integrates skills and approaches from two disciplinary areas: work integrated learning and applied linguistics. Both 'macro' (overall structure) and 'micro' (detailed deconstruction) approaches to feedback are discussed and we use case scenarios to illustrate the applications of the framework to learning and teaching practice.

Feedback in professional learning contexts

Although there are many resources on feedback, there appears to be no clarity or consensus on the definition of feedback in professional education, with a diversity of theoretical and explanatory models for providing and responding to feedback (e.g. Ende, 1983; Nicol and Macfarlane-Dick, 2006). Variability in the type, quantity, quality and timeliness of feedback provision to students is also evident (Molloy and Clarke, 2005). In spite of the apparent discrepancies of practice, numerous studies attest to the significant contribution of feedback to the professional learning experience and outcomes of students (e.g. Norcini and Burch, 2007). Yet, the complexities of work-based learning environments regularly challenge feedback strategy. Inconsistencies in learning and teaching experiences persist due to a number of factors, including limited time and resources and often only minimal communication between faculty advisors and workplace supervisors.

How feedback is structured and perceived is impacted not only by the unusual demands of specific workplace environments but also by the inter-action and relationship between teacher and learner as fostered in what is often regarded to be an apprenticeship system of learning. In clinical practice, for example, the professional trainee must acquire not only the content knowledge and skills of a specific discipline but also the range of interactional skills specific to the clinical culture, building effective relationships with both colleagues and patients. Moss and McManus (1992) determined that students deemed interactions with senior medical staff to be especially anxiety-provoking, possibly confounded by the intimidating feedback methods of some consultants and the public experience of displaying one's knowledge. Conversely, a tendency for clinical educators to soften their corrections as a strategy for preserving student self-esteem and autonomy in learning has led to trainee difficulty with recognising and misinterpreting feedback (Ende et al., 1995). Frequently, experts experience difficulty in communicating explicitly their tacit knowledge and attitudes, making feedback 'cryptic and acontextual' (Haber and Lingard, 2001).

The interactions of linguistic, cognitive and social traditions challenge student, educator and practitioner understandings of feedback and feedback processes, further confounded by the demands of work-based environments. In Australia, the United Kingdom, Canada and the United States, there is a growing inter-nationalised healthcare workforce mirroring a multicultural community served by hospitals and clinics. Although enculturation into a homogenous professional identity is a goal, both educators and learners must accommodate significant cultural diversity during clinical training, which represents a particular challenge.

In this chapter, we provide a framework for educators to make explicit in their feedback the rules, practices and cultures of professions, including the discourse strategies for enabling learners to participate effectively in the feedback conversation and acquire professional skills.

Fostering positive interaction in the learning and teaching experience to support a dialogue between the learner and the educator is essential in the feedback process, particularly in workplace cultures with strong oral traditions in learning, such as clinical practice. Recent work supports the 'feedback conversation' as the main tool for the clinical supervisor (Webb et al., 2009). However, there are few resources available to equip educators with explicit strategies for deconstructing and realising the socio-cultural dimensions of their practice in feedback conversations.

Socio-cultural and interactional competence in feedback

In drawing links between language and professional culture, Peräkylä and Vehviläinen (2003) refer to professional stocks of interactional knowledge (SIK) as the 'organised knowledge (i.e. theories or conceptual models) concerning interaction, shared by particular professions or practitioners'. In other words, professionals operate with the distinct qualities (i.e. knowledge, skills and behaviour) and preferred linguistic and discourse patterns of their profession, which may be regarded as a distinctive professional culture.

Lave and Wenger's (1991) emphasis on the socio-cultural practice of learning reinforces the role of language and culture in skills acquisition of the profession. Over time, through a process of socialisation, vocational learners acquire the so-called professional stock of interactional knowledge (SIK) to participate and practice effectively. Key stressors in this process are exposure to new learning environments, teaching styles, workload, and performance expectations. Additional impacts on professional learning and performance for students include cultural factors in workplace communication and behaviours, access to clinical learning opportunities, and the role of communication in assessment.

While educators typically recognise errors in technical and professional skill sets, they often fail to identify and respond effectively to student behaviour that is in cultural conflict with the learning context. Students experiencing socio-cultural conflict with their learning context, particularly when situated in work-based settings, are often deemed to have problems with communication, behaviour or attitude and so feedback is usually focused on addressing their deficits rather than assets in learning. We argue in the vein of Haber and Lingard (2001) by urging educators to (a) communicate how context influences the selection and appropriation of knowledge in professional practice, and (b) make explicit the tacit rules of practice and ensure that students understand the relevance of feedback.

Considering some of the prevalent socio-culturally embedded challenges for educators, tools are needed to:

1   Understand non-participation or passivity and support effective assertiveness in the workplace;
2   Enable successful negotiation of unspoken hierarchies in the workplace;
3   Increase 'organisation' with respect to specific professional tasks, e.g. case taking and presenting information to a colleague, in clinical learning;
4   Exemplify empathy, 'good' client rapport and reassurance; and
5   Deconstruct any mismatch between professional and workplace expectations and norms, and the culturally mediated experience, assumptions or expectations of the learner, whether they are second language speakers from outside Australia or local students acculturating to the requirements of a new workplace.

A socio-cultural framework for guiding feedback practice in work-based learning

Organisational frameworks for professional tasks and specific communicative skills have been deconstructed and outlined across a number of settings. Most formal and informal professional assessments using observational methods require feedback to be structured according to curriculum competencies (Saedon et al., 2009). Such feedback addresses poor performance or deficits in skills and/or professional behaviour, albeit embedding positive aspects of performance. While such approaches are generally structured and positive, students' recognition and management of the social and cultural dimensions of clinical workplace practice are rarely embedded into the assessment criteria for performance and behaviour. The existing frameworks do not 'unpack' and integrate into feedback conversations the learner's underlying socio-cultural value systems or culturally mediated patterns of communication that may impede learning or performance in the workplace. They do not illustrate *how* to tap into the learner's socio-cultural value system to navigate challenging or sensitive feedback in a manner that supports the learner's interpretation of feedback and facilitates and encourages subsequent appropriate action.

Our feedback framework equips the educator and learner with a strategy for integrating the socio-cultural dimensions of learning into the focus and method of feedback, and enables an effective conversation for enhancing learning and supporting professional participation and development. We refer to the framework as the Socio-Cultural Feedback Framework and SCFF (Figure 5.1).

The SCFF outlines three important dimensions of the learning context that impact the feedback conversation: (a) Metadiscourse (viz. 'talk'); (b) Sources (viz. 'participants'); and (c) Socio-cultural systems. These dimensions are identified along the left side of Figure 5.1 and explained in the following section. We show how socio-cultural competence underpins all feedback practices, consistent with previous work on professional identity formation (Webb et al., 2009).

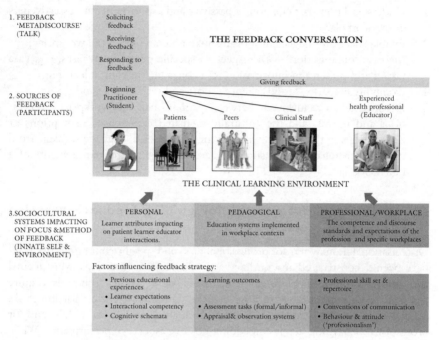

Figure 5.1 The Sociocultural Feedback Framework (SCFF)

'Metadiscourse' of feedback

Metadiscourse is the 'talk about talk', 'the means by which propositional content is made coherent, intelligible and persuasive to a particular audience' (Hyland, 2005, p. 39). Speakers use several devices to convey meaning, to organise and to emphasise, for example: to state intentions ('I'd like to introduce another problem', 'to sum up'); to hedge or qualify information ('might', 'appears to', 'in my opinion'); to show connection between ideas ('therefore', 'in addition'); to intensify or emphasise information ('importantly', 'it is clear that', 'I think this is essential'). Particularly relevant to a socio-cultural framework, metadiscourse subtly reveals a community's preferred practices, values and ideals (Hyland, 2005). Students benefit from learning explicitly about strategies for structuring content and conveying intentions in their talk, as this equips them with socially and professionally acceptable methods for soliciting, receiving and responding to feedback.

'Sources' of feedback

There are a number of potential participants in the educational setting of the workplace. Using the example of clinical settings, educators' feedback is more formally structured and predictable than that given by patients or health care professionals without a formal teaching role in the clinic. Feedback is often public and immediate, to preserve patient safety while granting students limited responsibility to implement clinical skills and be directly involved in patient care. Informal feedback can also be indirect and non-verbal (e.g. a patient grimace may indicate that an IV cannula has been poorly inserted). Educators must ensure that students recognise and value these 'other' interactions as feedback supporting their learning, and support the student to actively elicit, accept and respond appropriately – for example, acknowledging patient discomfort.

'Socio-cultural Systems' impacting feedback

We define three socio-cultural systems operating within the professional learning environment that effect the focus and method of feedback. First, 'Personal Systems' refers to the attributes of the learner that impact the triad of patient-learner-educator interactions in the clinic. Second, 'Pedagogical Systems' refers to the educational models that strive to ensure consistency and 'best practice' across work-based learning structures. Third, 'Professional Systems' orientate feedback strategies to the standards of the profession, encompassing competency, skills sets and behaviour. We will briefly outline each of these now.

'Personal Systems', which usually evolve out of previous culturally grounded experiences, impact on the learner's approaches to participating in feedback. *Previous educational experiences* affect a student's approaches to work-based learning tasks, so feedback must support the student's understanding of the learning opportunities in this professional environment. *Learner expectations* affect attitudes and responsiveness towards feedback and educators must understand students' ambitions to shape their feedback accordingly. *Interactional competency* (combining linguistic and cultural skills) affects the ability to develop cooperative relationships between participants in the work-based learning environment so feedback must nurture strategies for interacting and communicating effectively with colleagues and clients to create desirable learning opportunities. Finally, *cognitive schemata* are conceptualisations of knowledge, the cognitive units or mental models of one's experience, beliefs or practices that permit one to encode and make sense of cultural and social experiences (Sharifian, 2003). Students' acquisition of professional knowledge and expertise requires accessing relevant work-based experiences and unpacking the cultural and social nuances of work-based practice, and this should be built into feedback provisions.

'Pedagogical Systems' significantly influence expectations about feedback practice. With *learning outcomes, assessment tasks* and *appraisal criteria* typically generated out of university institutional practices which are distinct from professional practice, there may be tension between the idealised educational system and the reality of work-based learning contexts (Billett, 2009). The pedagogical culture of the clinical workplace, for example, is a hybrid of idealised university and real workplace worlds, comprising best feedback practice, shaped by clinical and time constraints and historical views of efficiency. Educators need to realign students' expectations about learning with the reality of work practice by clarifying the learning outcomes, assessment tasks and the standards for feedback practice.

'Professional Systems' add an overarching complexity to feedback practice. Practice knowledge encompasses not only the application of professional skill sets (e.g. history taking, physical examination, team management) but also participating effectively in the 'language of practice' (Webb et al., 2009, p. 58). Australian workplace hierarchies are not always clearly marked, indicators of deferral can be subtle, and the relationship between supervisors and subordinates is managed differently (Hofstede and Minkov, 2010). Psychological positioning, institutional practices and social rhetoric of the professional discourse community inform the development of the professional. Educators must unpack and make explicit the implicit rules or norms of thinking and acting based on a value system that is unique to the profession (Webb et al., 2009). Familiarisation with the standards, values and ways of belonging to the community of practice is the basis of a cultural literacy that allows safe and effective professional socialisation.

The feedback conversation: Structuring communication and deconstructing clinical performance

The SCFF offers a standard method for accommodating the socio-cultural dimensions of learning and practice into feedback. Educators can use the framework to systematically consider the range of socio-cultural factors across the levels of metadiscourse, sources of feedback and socio-cultural systems potentially impacting the student's learning and then integrate their analysis of socio-cultural factors into relevant feedback for the students.

Additionally, educators may need to make explicit for the learner the ways we create interaction, meaning and appropriacy in communication (Thomas, 2000). Figure 5.2 illustrates a framework for guiding a critical analysis of the culturally determined components of *communication in interaction*.

In this framework (Figure 5.2), *communication style* is constructed by a speaker's language use and inherent *values and attitudes*, which manifest differently across cultures. Orientation to *Collectivism* (focus on inter-dependence and group goals) or *Individualism* (independent role and responsibility) affects goal priorities, assertiveness, conflict management and maintenance of harmony. *Power Distance* (attitude to unequal distribution of power) affects how speakers enact relations, politeness and formality. Degree of *Ambiguity Tolerance* describes the degree of threat felt from uncertainty and a lack of structure. Low tolerance invokes anxiety, avoidance of uncertainty and a need for detailed structure, high tolerance indicates a greater comfort with unknown and unstructured situations. *Task versus relationship focus* describes the perception of relationship building as a basis for or irrelevant to task completion. Attitudes to gender roles (viz. *gender positioning*) and how we enact these roles also affect our professional interaction

INTERACTION   COMMUNICATION STYLE   INTERACTIONAL CATEGORIES   INTERACTIONAL FEATURES

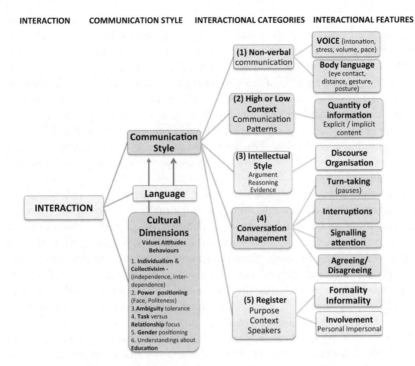

Figure 5.2 The Communication in Interaction Framework (CIF)

style and priorities. Researchers into workplace and intercultural communication have identified that it is productive to apply these culturally mediated attitudes and values to understanding the ways in which *all* individuals, regardless of nationality or cultural background, operate in their work environment (Trompenaars and Hampden-Turner, 2010).

In Figure 5.2, we define five broad *interactional categories* (non-verbal communication; high/low context communication patterns; intellectual style; conversation management; and register) with relevant *interactional features* in an outline designed to support educators with unpacking the specific communication practices for (a) building feedback as dialogue; and (b) enabling students to interact effectively with a range of participants in their work-based learning contexts. These categories and features of interaction are explained below.

Non-verbal cues in communication include *voice* in speech production (e.g. intonation and stress) and *body language* (e.g. eye contact). These are important for establishing and maintaining interpersonal relationships, managing identity and conveying attitudes and feelings, but are often interpreted differently across cultures. While learners may be aware of some communicative meanings, they may not understand diametrically opposed messages associated with any given verbal cue. For example, limited eye contact may signal a number of different attitudes, including internal reflection, disinterest or respect.

High or low context communication patterns have been characterised across societies or groups. In a high context culture, long-term relationships and inter-actions in a specific environment generate shared meanings and understandings of practice and knowledge and so communication tends to be less verbally explicit, i.e. unspoken information is 'implicitly transferred during communi-cation'. In a low context culture, more emphasis is placed on making behaviour and beliefs explicit and so communication is more literal and precise, i.e. a lot of information is exchanged explicitly through the message itself and rarely is anything implicit or hidden. Workplace environments are generally regarded to be low context cultures, which has implications for learning and teaching approaches.

Intellectual styles are regarded by many as culture-specific and while this view might lend itself towards unnecessary cultural stereotyping of cognitive practices, it allows us to acknowledge the impact of cultural traditions on the uses of argument, selection of evidence and methods of reasoning in intellectual activity. Many professions are grounded in an oral culture. Novices must learn and apply the discourse standards of their given professions for effectively articu-lating their knowledge and reasoning in the oral culture of their workplace. This means becoming familiar with the professionally preferred ways to structure and organise information in spoken discourse.

Resources for *managing conversations* become crucial to the beginning practi-tioner keen to operate effectively in the work-based learning environment. How to monitor turn-taking conventions, negotiate speaking with others, implement socially acceptable interruptions, build solidarity and positive relationships, and support or challenge other participants in the numerous array of work-based interactions are elements of conversation enacted with specific conventions of delivery within professional contexts.

Register describes how language and communication varies based on social context, our relationship to other speakers and the purpose of our interaction. Communication differs in the degree of formality or informality and personal or impersonal engagement, which are partly determined by the power differential between speakers.

Typically, when learners first observe an expert modelling work-based tasks, they understand that professional goals were achieved or that the task was done well but often are unable to 'see' the specific task and communication strategies that will allow them to improve their own performance. The deconstruction of interaction allows supervisors and learners to examine task implementation and the concurrent communication required to achieve the skill set required for a given task. Supervisors will often need to explicitly teach communication strategies for initiating and navigating a feedback conversation, reassuring those learners who find it difficult to understand or accept feedback. Feedback must illustrate how to appropriate underlying beliefs, values and assumptions and select language that conforms to professional norms. The ways in which these underlying values and attitudes may have a direct bearing on the feedback conversation and the clinical communication of individuals are explored in the cases below.

Case scenarios

These case scenarios demonstrate how to apply the frameworks (SCFF, including the CIF) in encounters between trainees and supervisors. This application develops a consistent strategy for supervisors to:

1   Deconstruct the observable aspects of learner performance, accommodating the socio-cultural dimensions of learning in the workplace;
2   Guide the focus of feedback conversations with students, addressing the sociocultural systems and interactional communication features potentially impacting on performance; and
3   Scaffold learning opportunities to help students overcome barriers to improving performance.

Scenario 1: The 'quiet' non-participating student

Learning context: History-taking in a medical bedside tutorial

Ken, a third year international medical student, has recently commenced his first year of clinical learning placement. He and five other students attend Dr Karen Clarke's weekly bedside tutorial. Karen has noticed that Ken never volunteers to take a patient history or do an examination. He does not answer many questions, although his level of knowledge appears fair. Today, as Ken takes a history from a 28-year-old female patient called Mary, Karen can see that Ken has not practiced. She notes that he (a) continues to call Mary 'Mrs McConnor' despite her request to be addressed simply as 'Mary'; (b) poses questions ad hoc barely giving Mary time to answer; and (c) fails to elicit sufficient information on Mary's medical problems. When Ken asks Mary about her occupation, Mary makes a joke about being a 'professional' mother, emphasising the fact that she is not 'paid' for her profession. Ken fails to respond to Mary's joke and continues his questions. Mary starts providing less information and becomes observably less engaged with Ken. Later, after the ward session, when presenting Mary's case to the tutorial group, Ken's information is disorganised and he fails to provide sufficient evidence to support his conclusions on Mary's health problems. As Karen gives feedback to Ken, he reclines back deeply in his seat, assuming a very relaxed and casual posture which makes him appear disinterested.

Karen refers to the SCFF to help her identify socio-cultural systems underpinning Ken's behaviour. She decides to explore the following issues:

1   Participation in tutorials;
2   Time management in an unstructured clinical environment; and
3   Ability to access ward learning.

These personal, pedagogical and workplace factors that Karen extracts from the SCFF are elaborated below to show how they provide Karen with useful starting points for generating a dialogue with Ken about his learning and help her to unpack the learning barriers impacting Ken's engagement in the workplace.

1   Low participation in tutorials: Karen learns that Ken's previous learning occurred in teacher-centered environments with written rather than practicum-based assessment. In this he excelled. When Karen says that his minimal tutorial participation is affecting his assessment, Ken shows concern. He reluctantly admits he doesn't want to 'look stupid' in front of the group and so avoids clarifying knowledge he feels he should be getting from text books. He tells you he is not used to doing poorly – *'everyone is so smart in my group'* – and he feels this loss of face keenly – *'I don't want to waste every-one's time'*. His expectations of tutor and learner roles are not being met – *'I don't like spending so much time discussing when the tutor should tell us ... I'm in university to learn from experts, not students like me who don't know much'*. Ken also finds it difficult to get a turn in tutorial discussions – *'everyone speaks so fast and the discussion changes before I can say anything'*.
2   Time management in an unstructured clinical environment: Ken is also challenged by the pedagogical systems operating in the clinical setting. There are few set lectures or tutorials and students self-schedule their weekly bedside, clinical skills and problem-based tutorials. Ken lacks the time management skills to initiate, organise and structure his own practical learning experi-ences. The public performance of clinical skills practice is challenging and he is uncomfortable with the feedback process. *'It's stressful being watched by so many people, and corrected in front of the patient and the group'*. He perceives feedback from his peers as not useful and potentially incorrect.
3   Inability to access ward learning: Ken is surprised that his peers have easy, friendly relationships with patients, registrars and nurses, and even senior consultants. In his home country, this informality would be considered inappropriate. Ken lacks the communication conventions needed to gain access to ward-based learning opportunities: *'The residents and nurses are so busy, it's rude to interrupt their work to introduce myself to ask for information about patients or for teaching'*.

Having developed an understanding of the socio-cultural systems impacting Ken's approaches to learning, Karen is able to offer Ken strategic feedback.

Karen starts with ward-based learning. She suggests that Ken revise his learning strategies, since 'knowing' rarely transfers into practical ability without considerable practice. She emphasises participating in discussions and clinical activities and active participation in clinical skills acquisition. Karen reassures Ken that while his peers may appear confident, they will also be anxious about their own performance in public demonstrations. She notes it is important to acknowledge one's limits and seek supervision for partially mastered skills. She draws on metadiscourse to outline specific verbal strategies for Ken to solicit feedback from patients, peers, clinical educators and clinical practitioners – for example (a) how to ask his clinical tutor for opportunities to stage his clinical skills acquisition: '*I would like to help insert a cannula. I've only watched it done once before. This time could I help set up, observe you and next time do it with your supervision?*'; and (b) how to seek constructive peer assessment and feedback in the clinical learning environment: '*Can you tell me what I did well on my history taking interview with Mary and what I might do differently next time to improve?*'. Rigour and skill in eliciting, understanding and providing feedback is a core professional necessity.

Karen then addresses professional and work-based systems. On ward rounds, Ken neither greets people nor makes himself known to nursing staff, particularly the Nurse Unit Manager (NUM), and he has difficulty gaining the attention of the residents. It is essential that he understand hospital ward structures and the parallel hierarchy in health professional staff, appreciating who can identify appropriate patients for him to see. If a clinician or patient appears busy, Karen suggests that he might set up a future time to return. '*I understand you're extremely busy right now. When would be a good time to talk?*' She confirms he understands that it is appropriate for him to introduce himself to senior colleagues.

Karen is also keen to explore Ken's daily interpersonal communication. She uses the CIF (Figure 5.2) to isolate three dimensions of culture and communication most impacting on Ken's performance of history taking with Mary. These are (a) a focus on task at the expense of building rapport, which affected his data collection; (b) politeness and formality patterns resulting in distancing behaviours and language; and (c) poor signalling of attentive listening.

His consultation with Mary McConnor indicated to Helen that Ken's communication style is perhaps affecting his engagement with clinical staff and his ability to gain consent from patients, reducing his independent learning opportunities. She explores this further by asking Ken if he noticed any change in Mary over the course of the interview. He comments, '*after a while I noticed she directed her answers to you not me and looked to you quite frequently... Yes, this has happened a couple of times previously.*' Karen takes this opportunity to focus on rapport building, politeness and formality patterns, and attentive listening. She explains that Mary's disengagement was a combination of these factors. First, continuing to call her Mrs McConnor was markedly *over*-polite, therefore distancing himself from the patient. Second, Ken did not recognise or respond to Mary's specific joke about the role of women in society: '*I noticed that she said that but I wasn't sure what she meant and I didn't think it was that important.*' Third, she explains that speaking rapidly to a patient who is unwell or lacking concentration may affect the patient's willingness to agree to talk. She stressed the importance of relationship building.

Karen provides Ken with concrete communication strategies. She advises Ken to (a) signpost groups of questions; (b) slow down; (c) summarise information collected during an interview to indicate attention and reassure the patient that he is absorbing information accurately; and (d) use a person's name, particularly when moving on to a new part of the history. He can also use a two-part response strategy, i.e. 'Respond + Move to related topic'. For example, in Mary's case, he might respond to her comments with: *'Yes, it's hard work being a mum'* (response) + *'Do you have any support?'* (move to social history). Frequently, challenging emotional information arises and the same strategy can help, e.g. on hearing about the recent death of a family member *'I'm sorry for your loss ...'* (response) + *'Was he ill before he died?'* (move to family medical history). Karen initiates a discussion about the medical and professional outcomes of poor rapport. In this case, important information was missed about Mary's family medical history and social situation. This impacted on Ken's conclusions about diagnosis and management.

During the discussion, Ken is leaning back casually, arm on the chair back, legs splayed directly towards Karen. When she comments on his posture, he replies, *'It's just the way I am, I always sit like this'*. Karen points out that clinicians, especially women, might find this unprofessional and that the casual posture could be interpreted as disinterested attitude by clinical staff and some patients. Ken looks taken aback. Karen is not sure whether Ken will try to address this issue and continues, *'I know I'm being quite direct, and maybe quite personal. But I do feel it's important you are aware of how this may be interpreted by others even if you choose not to change'*.

Finally, Karen asks Ken to repeat back three 'take home points'. What does he intend to practice? He is able to come up with only one practice point: *'I have to be more organised with questions.'* This is a useful take home point and Karen checks that he is clear about how he will do this. She encourages his participation in both tutorials and the wards, and asks Ken to request feedback about attentive listening from (a) a patient, (b) a peer, and, if possible, (c) a nurse, intern or registrar.

At a tutorial two weeks later Karen finds that Ken has asked a friend to observe him and give him feedback on whether or not he talks too fast or cuts off a patient or misses emotional or social content. Karen notes that Ken's questioning has slowed and he summarises information back to the patient. He reports introducing himself to nursing staff, has offered to help them and interns, resulting in additional clinical skills practice. She raises the issue of organizing questions and information to present clinical reasoning and suggests some strategies. Two months later, with repeated (weekly) feedback, Ken reports he is interviewing three patients a week, doing two examinations, he is accessing the hospital computer system to do follow-up study, and is presenting cases to a year 5 mentor. Karen notes that within the limits of his knowledge, Ken is beginning to link case information to his clinical judgements.

The above scenario has been unpacked in detail to illustrate ways in which the SCFF and CIF can be applied to (a) analyse a student's learning issues, and (b) structure the feedback conversation, both using a socio-cultural focus on skills development. Too often, it is assumed that the socio-cultural complexities of the learning environment are more challenging issues for international students. The second scenario shows how socio-cultural factors are equally at play in the learning and feedback processes of locally born students (not just those students of different ethnic and linguistic backgrounds).

Scenario 2: The 'over-confident' student

Learning context: Physiotherapy examination

Susan is a local final year mature-age graduate entry physiotherapy student who is being observed by Jess, an experienced physiotherapist, as she completes a physical examination on Ian, an elderly patient recovering from recent surgery. Susan appears confident and has good interpersonal skills, establishing rapport with Ian who is responding well to her approach. She keeps up a constant banter with both Ian and Jess, telling jokes and laughing at her previous experience with a patient with a similar condition. Jess feels uncomfortable as some of the comments are inappropriate and this approach is slowing down the physical examination itself. However, she avoids interrupting. Towards the end of the session, Jess sees Susan start to perform a technique that would be unsafe and abruptly intervenes, correcting Susan before allowing her to continue. Susan is clearly annoyed, arguing that she was going to stop before she was interrupted. She continues the rest of the exam in near silence.

Susan requests a meeting with Jess to discuss the 'debacle' and indicates that she is considering putting in a complaint about the 'inappropriate and unprofessional' feedback approach that was used.

Jess believes that Susan has misread the core roles of the professional learner/ educator relationship. Jess uses the SCFF to deconstruct the issues that require attention in this case and support her progressing a feedback conversation with Susan. In this conversation, it is revealed that Susan's *previous educational and professional experience* has established her high level of social and professional confidence. Susan states that she has always had excellent relationships with co-workers and employers in her workplaces. As a mature-age student with this experience, it is evident that Susan positions herself as a colleague with *a horizontal power distance* (or equal) relationship between herself and Jess. Susan's *learner expectation* is of a primarily 'friendly' and collegial relationship with her supervisor.

As in the previous case, the rationale for different feedback types and modes of delivery is discussed. Jess highlights that she is responsible for patient safety, regardless of the educational context, so her feedback to Susan on the unsafe aspect of her examination technique had been necessarily immediate and public. She comments that *pedagogical systems* for *appraisal and observation* in clinical settings differ from other contexts Susan has experienced. Jess makes four points: as a tutor, her judgement is based on relevant *professional standards and expectations*, which need to be an essential aspect of Susan's orientation to the *expected learning outcomes* of her new profession. Susan must be prepared to acknowledge and accept a hierarchy of expertise and appreciate that her own professional transactional knowledge will develop over time.

Cultural and communication dimensions in the CIF provide the basis for a discussion on communication factors impacting on Susan's approach to learning.

Jess compliments Susan on her willingness and capacity to take *the risk of raising* a difficult issue with her supervisor. This supports the development of a feedback conversation to clarify messages that may be new, complex and challenging to grasp or act upon. However, Susan's emotional reaction to the interruption by Jess made it difficult for her to absorb key messages. Jess clarifies the differences between what she observed Susan doing during the examination and the desired *professional standards and expectations*, suggesting communication strategies to support Susan's practice.

Jess highlights Susan's *interaction and communication style* with both her patient and herself as supervisor. Susan has been previously rewarded for a highly informal *register in communication* in other social contexts where it has never previously been identified as a problem. Her highly *personal* communication style with the patient, Ian, leads to mostly excellent *involvement* (rapport). Putting a patient at ease is an important focus of practice, and one that Susan recognises as valued. Joking is one strategy she consciously uses to build *solidarity* and support with both Ian and Jess. Susan tells Jess that she doesn't agree with the more distant *impersonal* manner of some physiotherapists.

These *values and attitudes* underlie the identity Susan wants as a practitioner and therefore her *communication style*. However, Jess observed 'over-familiarity' with the patients, risking another patient's confidentiality, and dangerously prioritising *relationship building over effective task completion*. In contrast to Ken, who is highly task-orientated and less attentive to building relationships, Susan compromises effective task completion (e.g. time management, gathering of patient information) to focus on relationship building through chatting and jokes.

Jess understands Susan needs knowledge of the boundaries and expectations of professional communication and professionally appropriate register. 'Making fun' of a patient encounter is not acceptable, and reference to a previous patient is clearly outside the boundary of professional practice. Susan needs to be able to create a safe and comfortable environment in which Ian and her other patients can communicate with her so that she can build her knowledge of their conditions and how to best select appropriate assessment and treatment strategies. Listening to a patient's verbal and nonverbal cues to learn more could be more clinically valuable than a highly verbal practitioner approach to a patient encounter. Jess asks Susan to discuss the outcomes of being highly verbal, taking into account both the 'pros and cons'. She then asks Susan to consider the possible outcomes of increased listening. A conversation takes place between them about the consequences of both communication strategies for physical examination and patient education. Jess tries to illustrate the ways that both these elements are necessary within the physiotherapy profession, and that attentive listening can also build rapport and good patient relationships.

Susan's choice to signal her discomfort with Jess's interruption via *non-verbal interactional communication* of marked change in volume, avoidance of eye contact and unnatural silence was not appropriate or acceptable. It affected Ian's comfort. It carried a number of implied and overt messages. Susan must understand that her verbal and non-verbal language (a) was misdirected, as she was using her interaction with Ian to communicate her anger to Jess; (b) indicated that she was not open to feedback; and (c) conveyed that Susan regarded patient safety to be less important than her patient's emotional comfort.

In terms of *pedagogical strategies,* Jess realised there may have been an alternative way of managing this 'crisis'. At the point where Ian's safety was at risk, she had a couple of options: to interrupt and advise as she did in this instance, or to ask for a short break in the exam to discuss some aspects of the assessment privately with Susan. Questioning Susan privately would allow her to think about the appropriateness of her technique and to choose an alternative strategy. This would allow Susan to maintain face and take time in a high stakes and pressured exam setting to think about a safe choice. It would also allow Jess to better appraise Susan's level of knowledge, to provide immediate feedback that is more specific to her learning needs, and potentially enable Susan to achieve her desired *learning outcomes.*

Summary and Conclusion

In this chapter, we have presented a framework for analysing and integrating into feedback the socio-cultural dimensions of work-based learning, with an emphasis on clinical contexts. We believe socio-cultural literacy to be a previously unconsidered dimension but nevertheless integral component of feedback. To every encounter the student and educator bring their socio-cultural experience and rules that govern how to interact within the educational and organisational contexts of learning. Providing and receiving feedback can be a fraught process for both parties involved. Supervisors at times mitigate difficult messages because they are socio-cultural in their basis rather than directly linked to content of the profession and because supervisors are concerned about negative impacts on learner self-esteem. We have attempted to make explicit strategies for deconstructing and realising the socio-cultural dimensions of their practice in feedback conversations. We have provided a framework for clinical educators to make explicit in their feedback the rules, practices and cultures of the health profession, including the discourse strategies for enabling learners to participate effectively in the feedback conversation and, by extension, acquire the professional skills of the clinic.

Expanding the workplace feedback conversation to include socio-cultural and communication components achieves a number of objectives; namely it:

1   Provides a basis for deconstructing areas of need and barriers to learning in work settings;
2   Empowers learners to develop sociocultural cognisance of their learning contexts, with enhanced capacity to evaluate their learning and performance;
3   Builds learner capacity to elicit feedback from a range of sources/participants in their learning environments;
4   Encourages learners to engage in conversations about their learning experiences and develop strategies sensitive to their learning contexts for supporting improvement in their performance; and
5   Supports teachers/supervisors to provide learners with clear examples of their own and others' behaviours and communication, evidence of performance to directly compare with the expectations and standards of their profession.

References

Billett, S. (2009) *Developing Agentic Professionals through Practice-based pedagogies: Final Report for ALTC Fellowship,* Strawberry Hills, N.S.W.: Australian Learning and Teaching Council. Online. Available HTTP: <http://www.altc.edu.au/resource-developing-agentic-professionals-griffith-2009> (accessed 8 September 2011).

Ende, J. (1983) 'Feedback in clinical medical education', *Journal of the American Medical Association,* 250(6): 777-81.

Ende, J., Pomerantz, A. and Erickson, F. (1995) 'Preceptors' strategies for correcting residents in an ambulatory care medicine setting: A qualitative analysis', Academic Medicine, 70(3): 224-9.

Haber, R. J. and Lingard, L. A. (2001) 'Learning oral presentation skills: A rhetorical analysis with pedagogical and professional implications', *Journal of General Internal Medicine,* 16: 308-14.

Hofstede, G. and Minkov, M. (2010) *Cultures and organizations: software of the mind,* 3rd edn, New York: McGraw-Hill.

Hyland, K. (2005) *Metadiscourse: Exploring interaction in writing,* London: Continuum.

Lave, J. and Wenger, E. (1991) *Situated Learning. Legitimate peripheral participation,* Cambridge: University of Cambridge Press.

Molloy, E., and Clarke, D. (2005) 'The positioning of physiotherapy students and clinical supervisors in feedback sessions', *Focus on Health Professional Education: A Multidisciplinary Journal,* 7: 79-90.

Moss, F. and McManus, I. C. (1992) 'The anxieties of new clinical students', *Medical Education,* 26(1), 17-20.

Nicol, D. and Macfarlane-Dick, D. (2006) 'Formative assessment and self-regulated learning: A model and seven good principles of feedback practice', *Studies in Higher Education,* 31(2): 199-218.

Norcini, J. and Burch, V. (2007). 'Workplace-based assessment as an educational tool: AMEE Guide No. 31', *Medical Teacher*, 29(9): 855-71.

Peräkylä, A. and Vehviläinen, S. (2003) 'Conversation analysis and the professional stocks of interactional knowledge', *Discourse and Society*, 14(6): 727-50.

Saedon, H., Saedon, M. H. M. and Aggarwal, S. P. (2009) 'Work-based assessment as an educational tool: AMEE Guide Supplement 31.3', *Medical Teacher*, 32: e369-e372.

Sharifian, F. (2003), 'On cultural conceptualisations', *Journal of Cognition and Culture*, 3(3): 188-207.

Thomas, J. (2000) *Meaning in Interaction: An Introduction to Pragmatics*, London; New York: Longman.

Trompenaars, A. and Hampden-Turner, C. (2010) *Riding the waves of culture: understanding cultural diversity in global business.* New York: McGraw-Hill.

Webb, G., Fawns, R. and Harré, R. (2009) 'Professional identities and communities of practice', in Delany, C. and Molloy, E. (eds), *Clinical Education in the Health Professions*, Chatswood, N.S.W.: Elsevier Australia.

Chapter 6

Trust and its role in facilitating dialogic feedback

David Carless

In this chapter, I seek to elaborate on new ways of thinking about feedback by exploring the role of trust in developing dialogic forms of feedback. Trust is an important but underexplored factor impacting on teaching, learning and assessment. Trust is of great relevance to feedback processes because of the relational, affective and emotional sides of feedback. Assessment and feedback experiences can arouse negative (e.g. anxiety or anger) or positive (e.g. pride or satisfaction) reactions. Trusting virtues such as empathy, tact and a genuine willingness to listen are ways in which positive feedback messages can flourish and more critical ones be softened. Trust needs to be accounted for because when it is absent, the prospects for learners' uptake of feedback are seriously constrained.

Three of the main limitations of existing feedback practice within modularized university systems are that feedback often comes relatively late in the process, is sometimes unidirectional transmission of information, and students find it difficult to act on the feedback they receive (Carless, 2006). A promising development elaborated in recent literature (e.g. Beaumont et al., 2011; Nicol, 2010), and underpinning the current chapter, is the notion of dialogic approaches to feedback. I define dialogic feedback as: interactive exchanges in which interpretations are shared, meanings negotiated and expectations clarified. Impacting on the extent to which such processes may be embedded in courses are relationships of trust between teachers and students, and between students themselves. Dialogic feedback is facilitated when teachers and students enter into trusting relationships in which there are ample opportunities for interaction about learning and around notions of quality.

The chapter is based on a case study of teaching at undergraduate level by a purposively selected award-winning teacher, chosen on the basis of his capacities to stimulate dialogic feedback processes. Practices in the teacher's repertoire which encouraged dialogic feedback included: a challenging interactive style of teaching which relied on extensive participation from all members of his classes; and peer feedback and self-evaluation of student oral presentations, one of the key learning activities in his classes. These practices were facilitated by the development of open and trusting course climates.

A single case is sufficient for current purposes because the aim is to theorize about practice and generate issues for further exploration. Although the case occurs within a university setting, it may also carry implications for other forms of professional education in which trust is likely to be a relevant dimension of feedback interactions. The focus of the chapter is mainly on the teacher as facilitator of dialogue. Other sources of feedback (see, for example, Chapters 10, 11 and 12 this volume) are, of course, equally worthwhile, but they were not the main focus of this particular case study.

A central element in the chapter is to show how trust facilitates dialogic feedback. Uptake of feedback is likely to be enhanced in a dialogic classroom in which all participants have sufficient confidence and faith in others to contribute ideas freely in an open, supportive atmosphere. The contribution to this volume lies in exploring key facets of trust; documenting how an award-winning teacher developed trust with participants; identifying key features facilitating dialogic feedback within trusting relationships; and charting some future directions for trust research.

Framework of trust, communication and feedback

The framework for the chapter is developed in three strands: the nature of trust; competence and communication trust; trust and feedback.

The nature of trust

For the purposes of this chapter, I use the definition of trust proposed by Tschannen-Moran (2004): one's willingness to be vulnerable to another based on an investment of faith that the other is open, reliable, honest, benevolent and competent. All these five features relate in some way to assessment and feedback in higher and professional education: openness and transparency in assessment procedures; reliability of judgments; honest feedback which identifies weaknesses as well as strengths; goodwill and generosity of spirit from the feedback provider; and the competence of others to provide useful feedback.

Trust is an important dynamic in various fields, including sociology, management, organizational theory and education. It is insufficiently discussed in relation to teaching, learning and assessment in higher and professional education; and when it is analyzed it is often a minor sub-theme rather than a topic of extended discussion. Developing relationships and trust with students impacts on student engagement with the learning process (Bryson and Hand, 2007). Trust is an important element of teacher-student relationships because it can prepare the ground for a transformative, dialogic learning environment (Curzon-Hobson, 2002). In a steadily expanding higher education sector, with limited time and space for the development of interpersonal relationships, trust may, however, be in short supply. Without trust, students may be unwilling to involve themselves fully in learning activities which may reveal their vulnerabilities, for example, when they open themselves to peer or teacher critique.

Competence trust and communication trust

There are a number of dimensions of trust and here I highlight the two most relevant to the current discussion: competence trust and communication trust. Competence trust or 'trust of capability' is an important aspect of trust (Reina and Reina, 2006) and denotes a person's ability to carry out a task efficiently and effectively. Trust in a party's competence creates an atmosphere conducive to the sharing of information and ideas. In relation to feedback, students need quality input from competent trustworthy sources, as well as potentially less refined feedback from peers.

Competence trust is mainly a facilitator for a further feature which is probably even more central to the current discussion of dialogic feedback: communication trust or the confidence that an interlocutor is sharing information transparently, and has one's best interests at heart. Communication trust, according to Reina and Reina (2006), includes willingness to share information, tell the truth, admit mistakes, maintain confidentiality, give and receive feedback, and speak with good purpose. Frequency of communication is also important in that trust is developed between participants through repeated interactions (Seligman, 1997).

Characteristics such as empathy and respect underpin communication trust. To build trust interlocutors listen to and empathize with others, as seeking to understand is one of the most important trust-builders because it communicates that you value the other person (Costa and Kallick, 1995). Empathy involves listening attentively and responding sensitively to the thoughts of others. Empathy is highly relevant for trust because it helps us to attribute motives, sympathize with them and perhaps tolerate deviations from expectations (Nooteboom, 2002). Students need to feel that their views are taken seriously if trust is to develop, thereby making risk-taking possible (Shady and Larson, 2010). Risk-taking for students may involve taking more responsibility and self-initiative than they are accustomed to contributing; and for teachers surrendering some control of content and process by opening up spaces in the curriculum for students to grow (Barnett, 2007a). My position is that such a pedagogy can most effectively be achieved within course climates in which there is mutual trust between participants. In this pedagogy of trust, teachers need to invest trust in students. When teachers lack trust in students they may rely mainly on an information-transmission mode of instruction because of a lack of confidence in the competence and willingness of students to make the most of opportunities afforded by more open-ended learning tasks. It takes trust to open up the learning environment to student initiative.

Trust and feedback

What does the literature on feedback in higher education say about issues related to trust? For formative feedback to flourish within a dialogic environment, it is necessary for students to be willing to reveal their own conceptions which may not be fully formed: in other words, to invest trust in the teacher. Conversely, 'faking good' (Gibbs, 2006, p. 26) occurs when students present themselves as knowing more than they actually do, as revealing their weaknesses or attempting something challenging may be perceived as risking lower grades or threats to self-esteem. Dialogue has most potential when students feel comfortable in being open about any partial understandings and do not try to conceal ignorance or hide mistakes.

Student response to feedback is also influenced by the relational aspect of their perceptions of the tutor giving the feedback (Orsmond, Merry and Reiling, 2005): for example, informants spoke of feeling comfortable with tutors who appeared approachable, but wary of those who they perceived as threatening, not open to alternative interpretations of assignment questions, or not to be trusted because of marks deemed to be awarded without adequate justification. Negative feedback experiences can threaten student self-esteem and identity (Crossman, 2007) and become a source of distrust and defensiveness. Empathetic feedback depends on relationships which are not easy to develop in conditions of large classes and heavy teacher workloads.

A useful strategy in the pedagogy of dialogic feedback is to involve students as assessors so that they develop an awareness of making judgments about quality, deepening their understanding of alternative ways of tackling a task, developing a more critical perspective on their own work and potentially learning from the work of their peers. For these potentials to be realized, students need to invest faith in their peers and allow their own work to be critiqued, i.e. placing themselves in a vulnerable state. A recent study by Beaumont et al. (2011) reports that some students saw peer feedback processes as constructive and motivational, whilst others were concerned about trust, competency and possible plagiarizing of their ideas. If students do not trust either the integrity or the competence of their classmates, they are less likely to commit themselves to the kind of peer interactions which have potential to develop their ability to self-assess and refine their notions of quality. Ways forward include the creation of course climates in which the giving and receiving of peer feedback is a regular aspect of teaching and learning processes (Boud, 2000; Liu and Carless, 2006).

A further relevant aspect to the interplay between feedback and trust is assessment task design. The possibilities for productive feedback provision are deeply affected by the number, timing and sequence of assessment tasks which students undertake. Task design is affected by trust and distrust (Carless, 2009). Sometimes more traditional assessment tasks, such as essays and examinations, are more readily trusted. An environment in which mistrust is prevalent may lead to more 'defensive' assessment, i.e. a task which protects the teacher from challenge or criticism. Conversely, space for the development of student authentic being is opened up when summative assessment is characterized by experiment and innovation, allowing students to embrace the challenge of risk, uncertainty and emotional response (Barnett, 2007b).

Summary of framework

To sum up, I have highlighted the relationship between various facets of trust and dialogic feedback. Competence trust and communication trust are viewed as facilitating factors for effective feedback processes. Recurring opportunities for communication characterized by openness and empathy create spaces for participants to demonstrate their trustworthiness. The interplay between trust and dialogic feedback represents a key aspect of an idealized view of learning as being risk-taking transformative adventure. Dialogic feedback is supported by openness, empathy, sensitivity and the development of course climates which support interactive teaching and learning environments. The challenge of developing trusting relationships in mass higher education underpins the need for a discussion of a pedagogy of trust.

The case study

The case study is now presented through three sub-sections which introduce the teacher, his courses and selected aspects of the student response. At the outset, I should acknowledge that the case represents something of an 'ideal' example involving a popular award-winner, teaching relatively small classes of elective students. I make no apology for that because the discussion of the case seeks to express possibilities and potentials, even hopefully to inspire.

The teacher

The teacher whose practice is discussed in this chapter is an award-winning teacher in the Faculty of Business, University of Hong Kong. He was one of the interviewees in a study on the feedback practices of ten distinguished teachers reported in Carless et al. (2011). From these ten interviews, he seemed to be most prepared to 'push the boundaries' of teaching, learning and assessment. A follow-up case study was subsequently undertaken, involving classroom observations and semi-structured interviews. Fifteen hours of classroom observations were conducted across two elective courses: Creativity and Business Innovation (class size: 20 students) and e-Business Transformation (class size: 35 students). Individual semi-structured interviews were also carried out with eleven students focusing on issues arising from the observations and the interviews with the teacher.

The teacher's philosophy of teaching is expressed as follows:

> *My basic philosophy is to motivate students to shift emphasis from memorizing and remembering to reflecting and understanding, as I believe that real education should entail a thoughtful understanding of why things happen as they do ... My reflections have led me to the belief that we need to shift our primary responsibility as educators from teaching content to generating knowledge and facilitating student learning through introspection and cognitive engagement with what they aim to learn ... Through such engagement, they would reach the*

requisite mental flow amenable to long-lasting predilection for learning as a process and not as an end in itself.

The courses and their assessments

The course outlines for both courses indicate a key requirement is for students to demonstrate effective skills in communicating their thoughts. Students are expected to communicate in writing through individual assignments and verbally by delivering oral presentations, and less formally through interaction in class and/or through the course blog.

The assignment tasks of a course are a critical factor influencing student learning habits and also the prospects for feedback which students can use while the course is in progress. The design of the assessment for both courses involved participation grades, individual written work and group projects. The weighting of the assessment is summarized in Figure 6.1.

Creativity and Business Innovation course

1. Case, Class and Blog Discussion	40%
2. Individual Written Case Assignment	30%
3. Term Project	30%

E-business transformation course

1. Class Contribution	30%
2. Case Presentation	20%
3. Written Case Analyses	20%
4. Design Project	30%

Figure 6.1 Course assessment types and weighting

The teacher is somewhat elusive about how participation or class contribution is measured and how the related marks are awarded. The teacher does have an educational rationale for this open-endedness in terms of the self-evaluative capacities he is seeking to develop:

> *It is important to put students in an assessing position because by doing that you let them understand the meaning of quality and you pass the responsibility to them to decide what is good and what is bad. Self-evaluation is about knowing the notion of quality. I intentionally leave it vague and don't put exact wording on its meaning, because quality is at the beginning of self-discovery.*

It seems that the teacher wants students to identify for themselves what quality participation should look like, and so refrains from prescribing tightly what students should achieve. Whilst this position is debatable, his expressed viewpoint is to challenge students to perform 'outside the box' and exceed expectations, rather than to conform to pre-set standards.

Selected student perspectives

The interviews with a range of students indicated a unanimously positive response to his teaching. Two examples of student comments:

> It's interesting and I learned a lot of things. The course is about creativity and innovation and it is quite different from the other courses we've taken at the university. Because most of the other courses are based on textbooks or fixed content, all you need to do is to memorize what you have learned, understand the concepts and then you can get good marks. But in this course, he focuses on our self-improvement. So the most difficult thing is that he always challenges you and pushes you to think. It is good because as a university student you need to upgrade your thinking.
>
> It's just wonderful. This course might be one of the courses that will benefit my whole life. It will have that kind of life-long enrichment. He is very good at engaging students in thinking. I have never met any teacher that can spark my curiosity and just keep it going like he does.

The assessment methods drew more mixed comments. Overall, the main positive elements were the variety of meaningful assessment tasks which prompted extended study over a period of time, and the focus on the process of learning which could generate critical thinking. Concerns were expressed about how participation was measured, fairness (some assigned cases or tasks were perceived as more difficult than others), and potential subjectivity in the teacher award of grades. Competence trust or confidence in the teacher seemed to be a factor in increasing student acceptance or tolerance of some of the ambiguities in the grading of the assessment task. In other words, the positive student response to the teacher seems to be a factor in supporting student acquiescence in the assessment processes (despite having some misgivings). I infer that innovative assessment is more likely to be accepted by students when they have confidence and faith in their teacher. Teachers may also find it useful to communicate with students the rationale for innovative assessment and how it can benefit their learning.

Key themes

I now analyze on the basis of the observational and interview data two key themes, the first focusing on the classroom atmosphere of the courses and how it helps to develop a climate conducive to dialogic feedback; and secondly, a discussion of a specific activity which promotes interactive dialogue. Within each theme, I bring out issues relevant to the interplay of trust and dialogic feedback.

Classroom atmosphere

Classroom atmosphere was a key theme in the data and below are two examples which provide a flavour of students' responses:

He is very successful in building an interactive relationship between himself and the students. He encourages you or even forces you to speak, so you build a kind of conversational dependency. I always have a better relationship with teachers whose class is more interactive. To build a relationship you have to have time and you have to have interaction. For some other classes, there is just a teacher standing and speaking, and students sitting there listening. At the end of the semester you don't know the teacher and the teacher doesn't know you, then how can you build trust or dependency on each other?

An environment and atmosphere has been created, so we seem to be more active in this class than in other courses. You just think you can make mistakes when you are talking in this course … In this class, everyone is very active and you won't think yourself strange if you are speaking out. Even if you don't say a lot at first, he will find ways to let you talk. He seldom says that something is right or wrong; he usually says it is interesting and it seems that your opinion will be appreciated. … You can really feel he is paying attention to what you are saying to him, it's a kind of respect. I think in this kind of course I am not afraid of losing face.

The first quotation emphasizes the importance of interaction in building trust. The student informant also mentions dependency, which relates to the idea of trust involving the mutual investment of faith. The second quotation also reiterates two themes alluded to earlier in the chapter: first, the perception that making mistakes or risk-taking is accepted; and second, the feeling that the teacher is really paying attention to what you are saying is an example of empathetic communication trust. By listening attentively and respectfully to an interlocutor one builds a relationship of trust and encourages the communication of ideas and thoughts. These ideas are not just limited responses which sometimes characterize classroom interaction, but more elaborated and possibly 'risky' forms of interaction.

Students were also asked about the teacher's feedback strategies and their perceived effectiveness. Students highlighted the verbal dialogic interaction in the class, for example:

Sometimes his feedback is like a catalyst to promote the process, to direct the discussion from one student to another. Often he was challenging people to think more. He will ask the same student many 'why' questions. It is feedback showing that the teacher is interested in your answer and wants to explore your answer more.

A salient point is that questioning is probably less threatening than evaluating.

Another student commented on how the atmosphere in class facilitated feedback between all class participants:

> *The whole intimacy of the course gives you an environment where you can give feedback more easily. One thing which creates intimacy is the interactive teaching in which every single person really gives something during the class.*

Several students also talked about the need to be alert and the need to prepare for the class, so that you would be ready to participate in the extended dialogues, for example:

> *Everyone is very active in the class which actually gives me motivation to participate. I would try to perform better. I would spend some time preparing before his class what questions he might ask. He has very high expectations, so I don't want to let him down. This is a kind of motivation to make me more hard-working because I want to live up to his expectations.*

These high expectations were not, of course, without drawbacks or challenges. Classroom observations did evidence occasional signs of student discomfort at presenting in front of the class, and opening oneself up to critique. One of the student informants commented on some feelings of stress, although she seemed to view them positively:

> *I feel stressful in class. I have to be awake every minute, every second, because he will seize every opportunity to ask why. Stressful in a good way, not in a bad way ... Being stressful in a good way pushes you further, you participate more and you push yourself to understand more what he is talking about.*

What she calls stressful might also be viewed as emotionally engaged. I interpret her words as carrying some resonance with Barnett's (2007a) vision of a higher education in which the student ventures into 'new places, strange places, anxiety-producing places' (p. 147).

I leave the final words of the section to the teacher himself:

> *I am a provocateur, bringing them into the arena ... and involving them cognitively and emotionally. It takes a while for them to get to know what you're doing and why, and then they're going to become more and more trusting.*

Dialogue through oral presentations

A particular feature of the teacher's practice is a large number of both formal (for assessment) and informal (as part of dialogic participation) oral presentations carried out by students in groups. These range from brief sharing lasting only a few minutes to more extended assessed presentations of projects. An example of the latter is an oral presentation activity which involves video-taped presentations. A major part of the teacher's stated rationale for the activity is that clear and effective oral presentations are an important part of success in the business field.

The activity is arranged as follows. First, students present on a self-selected topic within a general theme (e.g. a business innovation or a new product idea). Immediately at the end of the presentation, two short extracts lasting a few minutes are shown and presenters are invited to reflect on the strengths and weaknesses of their presentations. After the student has had the opportunity to share their own perceptions, other students and the teacher share ideas on how the presentation could be improved.

The teacher expressed the view that the video part of the activity is particularly useful because 'pictures don't lie' and students are able to focus on what they can see on the screen and reflect on it. He believes it is a useful process in getting students to analyze their presentation style and content. He also talked about the emotional impact of the challenge of reflecting on one's performance in front of a group of peers. He asserts that it is better for students to discover weaknesses in their presentation style in class rather than later in the workplace.

The majority of student informants were positive about the experience of participation in the video activity. A selection of student views:

> I think it is very useful because it was the first time that I could actually see myself presenting, and I could get useful feedback from my friends and the teacher. I saw myself on the video and I saw my mistakes, what I did well and what I must improve. I think it's good because it's like putting your mistakes right in front of your face.

> I think his purpose is to help us find a way to be convincing business presenters. By filming us, he got us to reflect on how to sell an idea or product. It's funny because trying to improve the way you present is not really related to innovation or creativity, but it's his way of doing things and it's really good.

> It is quite valuable. Basically I can see from other persons' perspective things about my presentation. I know that last time I did my presentation I was basically like a sales person. I kept pushing my ideas out, I spoke too fast, both in terms of the number of sentences and the quantity of ideas ... My presentation is focused on content, that means the analytical logic of the case, but I think my peers focus too much on the presentation style rather than the content. Sometimes their comments are quite superficial.

Most informants spoke positively about the peer feedback from their classmates, and the classroom atmosphere was a facilitating factor in this. In terms of limitations of the processes, some students referred to the superficiality of comments (as mentioned in the final quotation above) and a further stated drawback was that the activity consumes quite a lot of classroom time.

To sum up, students found the video activity useful in that it enabled them to reflect productively on their presentation style and performance. The interactive atmosphere of the classroom facilitated the sharing of honest peer and teacher feedback, and this was largely a product of the trusting relationships which had been developed. An important element of the activity is that through the interplay of student self-evaluation, peer feedback and teacher input it sharpens students' understanding of the notion of quality performance. In Carless (2013), I discuss how this activity enhances sustainable feedback – the ability of students to improve the quality of their work independently of the teacher.

Implications

The first implication is represented by a key theme of this volume, the desirability of feedback being dialogic rather than one-way transmission of information. Dialogic feedback refocuses largely unidirectional teacher comments at the end of a course towards feedback from teacher, peers and self-embedded within the curriculum. Through such processes, feedback has the potential to be more efficient and taken up more widely. Dialogic feedback is facilitated by relation-ships of trust in which classroom participants value the views of others, respond empathetically and co-construct classroom atmospheres in which students can feel free to take risks.

One of the contributions of the chapter is to analyze in detail the role of trust in the implementation of these dialogic feedback processes. Communication trust is a facilitating factor for the development of an atmosphere that fosters engagement, risk-taking and a willingness to take part in sustained and challenging dialogues around both subject matter and the learning process. In the case study, dialogic feedback was facilitated by expectations and enactment of a high degree of student participation, and an empathetic teacher response which made clear that student views were valued and would be addressed. Communication trust reinforces the message that feedback is a social and relational process in which classroom atmosphere, expectations and social dynamics between participants are paramount.

Competence trust relates to the confidence that the students developed in the teacher to arrange both classroom activities and the course assessment. His skilful handling of interaction in the classroom facilitated learning activities, such as the oral presentations with embedded self and peer critique. The innovative assessment task design focused on maximizing productive student learning, rather than a more traditional focus on reliability of grades. Competence trust in the teacher seemed to be a factor in student tolerance of limitations to the reliability and fairness of the assessment procedures.

Table 6.1 summarizes some features of the case which supported the devel-opment of dialogic feedback and trusting relationships. These features represent ways in which teachers can develop an interactive atmosphere in which sustained dialogue can occur.

Table 6.1 Features facilitating dialogic feedback within trusting relationships

Feature	Evidence from the case
Classroom atmosphere	Intimate class environment; speaking out is normalized.
Relationship building	Frequent interaction as path to co-dependency.
Establishing dialogue	All students are required to contribute; every individual gives something.
Promoting student self-evaluation	Sharing of responsibility of evaluation. Student reflections on oral presentations; use of peer feedback.
Establishing high expectations	Expectations are high and students are pushed to fulfil their potential. 'I don't want to let him down'.
Inviting elaboration	'He will ask the same student many "why" questions'.
Responding positively and non-judgmentally	Students feel they can task risks or make mistakes. 'He seldom says that something is right or wrong, he usually says it is interesting'.
Showing empathy	Opinions are valued and appreciated (although some critique was robust).
Listening attentively and valuing the ideas of others	'You can really feel he is paying attention to what you are saying'.
Student faith in the teacher	Competence of teacher established. Students have faith in his handling of teaching, learning and assessment.

Conclusion

In this chapter, I have highlighted the role of trust as an important but under-explored dimension of feedback. Trust is an important dimension of feedback because without it, students may not want to confront threats to face or the emotions implicit in peer and teacher critique. I have emphasized the role of open communication in trust and illustrated it through a discussion of the classroom atmosphere and a specific pedagogic activity in a case study of an award-winning teacher.

This chapter has focused on the role of trust in relation to feedback, whilst in an earlier publication (Carless, 2009) I focused on trust in relation to assessment reform. In terms of future directions, I intend to review the impact on trust relationships from a wider perspective of a pedagogy of trust. Issues to be addressed include: caring relationships between participants; empowerment and risk-taking; pedagogic tact; collaborative learning and student engagement.

References

Barnett, R. (2007a) *A will to learn: Being a student in an age of uncertainty.* Maidenhead: SRHE and Open University Press.

Barnett, R. (2007b) 'Assessment in higher education: An impossible mission?', in Boud, D. and Falchikov, N. (eds), *Rethinking Assessment in Higher Education: Learning for the Longer Term* (pp. 29-40). London: Routledge.

Beaumont, C., O'Doherty, M. and Shannon, L. (2011) 'Reconceptualising assessment feedback: A key to improving student learning?', *Studies in Higher Education,* 26(6): 671-87.

Boud, D. (2000) 'Sustainable assessment: Rethinking assessment for the learning society', *Studies in Continuing Education,* 22(2): 151-67.

Bryson, C. and Hand, L. (2007) 'The role of engagement in inspiring teaching and learning', *Innovations in Education and Teaching International,* 44(4): 349-62.

Carless, D. (2006) 'Differing perceptions in the feedback process', *Studies in Higher Education,* 31(2): 219-33.

Carless, D. (2009) 'Trust, distrust and their impact on assessment reform', *Assessment and Evaluation in Higher Education,* 34(1): 79-89.

Carless, D. (2013, forthcoming) 'Sustainable feedback and the development of student self-evaluative capacities', in Merry, S., Price, M., Carless, D. ans Taras, M. (eds), *Reconceptualising feedback in higher education.* London: Routledge.

Carless, D., Salter, D., Yang, M. and Lam, J. (2011) 'Developing sustainable feedback practices', *Studies in Higher Education,* 36(4): 395-407.

Costa, A. L. and Kallick, B. (1995) 'Teams build assessment – and assessment builds teams', in Costa, A. L. and Kallick, B. (eds), *Assessment in the Learning Organization: Shifting the Paradigm* (pp. 141-152). Alexandria, VA: Association for Supervision and Curriculum Development.

Crossman, J. (2007) 'The role of relationships and emotions in student perceptions of learning and assessment', *Higher education research and development,* 26(3): 313-27.

Curzon-Hobson, A. (2002) 'A pedagogy of trust in higher education', *Teaching in Higher Education,* 7(3): 265-76.

Gibbs, G. (2006) 'How assessment frames student learning', in Bryan, C. and Clegg, K. (eds), *Innovative Assessment in Higher Education* (pp. 23-36). London: Routledge.

Liu, N. F., and Carless, D. (2006) 'Peer feedback: The learning element of peer assessment', *Teaching in Higher Education,* 11(3): 279-90.

Nicol, D. (2010) 'From monologue to dialogue: Improving written feedback in mass higher education', *Assessment and Evaluation in Higher Education*, 35(5): 501-17.

Nooteboom, B. (2002) *Trust: Forms, foundations, functions, failures and figures.* Cheltenham: Edward Elgar.

Orsmond, P., Merry, S. and Reiling, K. (2005) 'Biology students' utilization of tutors' formative feedback: a qualitative interview study', *Assessment and Evaluation in Higher Education*, 30:369-86.

Reina, D. S., and Reina, M. L. (2006) *Trust and betrayal in the workplace: Building effective relationships in your organization.* San Francisco: Berrett-Koehler.

Seligman, A. B. (1997) *The problem of trust.* Princeton, NJ: Princeton University Press.

Shady, S. L. H. and Larson, M. (2010) 'Tolerance, empathy or inclusion? Insights from Martin Buber', *Educational Theory*, 60(1): 81-96.

Tschannen-Moran, M. (2004) *Trust matters: Leadership for successful schools.* San Francisco: Jossey Bass.

Chapter 7

Written feedback
What is it good for and how can we do it well?

Brian Jolly
David Boud

> *Mass higher education is squeezing out dialogue with the result that written feedback, which is essentially a one-way communication, often has to carry almost all the burden of teacher–student interaction.*
> (Nicol, 2010, p. 501)

Almost all students and teachers spend a vast amount of time writing. Paradoxically, in the age of electronic media, writing, emails or 'texting' has replaced many other forms of communication, so when the opportunity arises to give or receive feedback there is a high likelihood that it will be delivered in written form.

There are great differences in what and how we write. For example, as young researchers, we might spend a week or two blitzing out a long rambling article. Then, in the struggle to communicate to others, over the following many months, we hone the paper into something that somebody else would like to read, using many self-feedback loops. This type of auto-feedback forms the major part of most academics' experience of feedback. Finally when we ran out of our own resources, or when our writing showed visible improvement, we sent it to someone else for judgement or formal feedback. Sometimes that person was the editor of the intended journal, and sometimes it was just a colleague. Either way, there was usually a long wait, and the results were altogether unpredictable.

With all this writing being done, and with the amount of self-feedback that we generate, one might think that:

a)   a lot of feedback to others gets delivered via writing;
b)   guidance about how to give written feedback is pretty well formulated;
c)   this guidance is underpinned by substantive research on written feedback.

Only the first of these statements seems to be true (see Nicol, 2010). But research on written feedback as such is hard to come by. In a recent literature search of *PsychInfo*, the vast database on things psychological and educational, only 36 articles were found with the words 'written feedback' in the title, and in at least 25 per cent of these the advice given was about feedback in non-written modalities, such as oral debriefing. The word feedback alone yielded 39,000 hits. This strongly suggests that how feedback is given is not often made explicit in articles on this topic, or perhaps written feedback is so ubiquitous that it is just assumed that all feedback is written!

Even option (a) is not a consistent feature, especially in professional disciplines. For example, in the simulated and clinical learning environments now used extensively in health-related disciplines, the vast majority of feedback is given verbally, usually in small group settings, with contributions from peers and consumers as well as teachers (See Chapters 10, 11 and 12).

That said, providing written feedback on students' work is still one of the most common practices in most academic programs. In addition, written feedback is often given about tasks and activities that are not themselves written, such as interviews, observations and procedures, student-client encounters, and staff-student interactions. Unlike face-to-face activities in work-based placements, written feedback often has little immediacy and the chances for it to be misunderstood are high. There is also considerable evidence that it may not be taken up by learners to improve their performance (Kluger and DeNisi, 1996).

What is written feedback?

Written feedback is information about student performance conveyed by prose – through email, letters, reports, notes on documents, and other means of production. It also includes information given using pre-designed rating schedules, forms or 'score sheets' that might contain a tick in a box against a particular criterion or characteristic to indicate whether the work being assessed has that attribute. It also incorporates model outputs, given after assignments are submitted, to indicate what the constituents of an appropriate completed assignment might be.

As heralded by the somewhat pessimistic quotation from Nicol (2010) at the head of this chapter, in academia most feedback, written or otherwise, tends to be made in a teacher to student mode. In many disciplines it is effectively 'one-way traffic', that is, it is mere information; it does not have the kind of follow-up or monitoring that would turn it into feedback. Students rarely have an opportunity to 'answer back' or even to respond in any way. And yet some of the best things we have written and published have come from debating with editors and reviewers the information we got. Sometimes that reasoning process convinces us that they are right; sometimes we can avoid some changes by convincing them that we are right; and sometimes it just gives us a chance to reformulate the work into a more acceptable framework – a kind of academic 'entente cordiale' is reached. However, the predominantly 'one-way' feedback model in higher education shares the same disadvantages as one-way road traffic management. Such systems are easily blocked or held up by extraneous events, resulting in multiple bottle-necks, because there is no flexibility to alter the route. The learner is basically hemmed in to follow a certain itinerary until the next staging post is reached.

The one-way traffic system of feedback contributes to another feature of our academic work that is generally not available to students: students do not normally engage in the iterative nature of academic work unless they are failing, and are forced to resubmit work or complete an equivalent task again. Such privilege is also usually available only to masters and doctoral students. When teachers are working towards a rewarding event, such as a publication or a good teaching session, this usually allows for an iterative, that is, genuine feedback process. But for most students this opportunity – for example, when receiving marks for an end of unit assignment – does not occur. The assignment will not be done again, there is just one shot, and a mark is given.

So academics' research work is largely the result of very large amounts of feedback, both written and verbal, given over an extended timeframe. By contrast, students' work is usually feedback-light or feedback-free. Perhaps we should not be surprised when the work looks half-baked?

Nonetheless, there are academic and vocational disciplines in which the two-way 'conversation' is a valued methodology: some humanities programs, art, graphic design and media studies and architecture courses. Most of these courses get high ratings from students on the value of 'feedback' as part of the Good Teaching Scale of the course experience questionnaire (Graduate Careers Australia 2012). But in other areas, especially professional courses such as medicine and engineering, students have rarely been given the chance to iteratively work towards a goal. This lack of opportunity for students to respond may account for many of the studies in which 'feedback' has been shown to be ineffective, that is, no change results (Carless et al., 2011).

This chapter explores how opportunities for dialogue and iteration can be maximised within a written feedback model. It builds on the view that feedback is a process – a cycle – not simply the provision of information and judgement, that feedback from multiple sources needs to be considered, and that learners need to build the capacity to effectively seek and utilise information from others, usually by having their reconstructions become the object of further feedback. It conceptualises the process as ideally a learner-managed, or at least a learner-engaged, activity and suggests that there are windows of opportunity during which comments from others are useful, can be acted on, and the feedback loop closed.

Why is written feedback important?

Written feedback is important because it has unique characteristics. First, written feedback is usually, or can easily be made, private. Although this might seem strange in many academic contexts, some research suggests that, even when receiving praise, two-thirds of adolescent students prefer this to be done quietly and privately (Sharp, 1985). Written information is also explicit and tangible and, as distinct from information delivered verbally, can be made to be enduring through paper or electronic storage. Consequently, unlike real-time verbal feedback, written feedback is traceable. It is quite feasible to know who gave it, when, to whom and under what circumstances, and its reported content can therefore be verified. This is important for some contexts, especially those involving registration of practitioners or when academic progress decisions hinge upon consideration of a student's history.

Written feedback is helpful when a response from the recipient is not expected or needed immediately, or when the provider of the feedback hopes for a considered response and will follow this up. The 'pause' afforded by written feedback may also be valuable when learning episodes are infused by high emotion – for example, a learner's role in an emergency clinical scenario when there has been a poor outcome for the patient. The recipient may not have the 'head space' to deal with feedback about their performance. Likewise the feedback provider may recognise that they are not in an ideal space for considered judgement, and may elect to frame the feedback at a time when they can offer better clarity and distanced judgement.

Most importantly, written feedback is useful when further work might be appropriate that would itself take written forms, or when the complexity of the task might require a set of issues to be dealt with. It can be accessed on multiple occasions when needed. For example, feedback to educational institutions from regulatory, accrediting or quality assurance bodies is almost always given in writing even if a prior comprehensive verbal report has been delivered. This type of arrangement would be useful to learners when they need to refer back easily to what has been recorded.

There are modes in which verbal feedback can be made to operate like written feedback. For example, comments on audio or video can be a quick way of storing feedback that would otherwise be delivered 'live' and subsequently be lost (Kneebone et al., 2008). This enables oral feedback to be used in similar ways to written feedback, with traceable qualities, but the initial input may not be as considered as its written equivalent, perhaps because it is more difficult to scan, identify and edit key features from audio than it is from text (Lunt and Curran, 2010).

In written feedback it is possible to make clear that the information is addressed to an individual or specific group (such as a student project group or a course design team). This obviates or reduces the problem that in a social setting feedback can be misappropriated, socially adumbrated or deflected onto others. As Hattie and Timperley (2007) state:

> *When delivered in groups, the feedback messages may be confounded by the perceptions of relevance to oneself or to other group members. For example, a student may interpret the feedback as pertaining to him or her, or may interpret it as relating to the group as a whole or to other individuals in the group. In these latter two situations, it is likely to be diluted or to be perceived as irrelevant to the individual student's performance.*

(p. 92)

Moreover, these authors further point out (p. 97) that praise delivered publicly can be perceived negatively by some students if it is delivered in the presence of a peer group that does not value achievement or has group values that inhibit individual praise.

Taken together with the specific characteristics of written feedback, ideas about different purposes of feedback and how these purposes can best be addressed can help to fortify and maximise the potential of written feedback. Here we will consider some of these principles.

When is written feedback inadvisable?

There are clearly situations in which written feedback would not be appropriate. One of these is in situations in which there is a complex task being learnt (either real or in simulation mode), in a position of high cognitive load (Chandler and Sweller, 1991; van Merrienboer and Sweller, 2005) or urgency. In such situations information will need to be delivered 'in the moment' to encourage or discourage a course of action. This type of information would typically be oral, or pre-programmed within a computer mediated response – for example, 'are you sure you want to do that now?'; 'will engaging the motor at this stage endanger anyone?'.

Similarly when simulated activities are being used (especially team-based ones), guidance about and modifications to a learner's course of action may need to be delivered very quickly, and aurally or visually with simple statements because other learners are involved, or the task needs to be kept on track to ensure success. The information in such situations must be both timely and readily assimilated without delay: much like the kind of information you need when learning a psychomotor skill, like suturing (start in the middle!) or riding a bike (keep pedalling!). In such situations immediate oral information will be much more useful to the learner and may speed up good outcomes (Fiorella et al., 2012). This is not to say that written feedback provided at the end of the psychomotor task would become redundant. It may have considerable value in reinforcing the cues or messages raised during the *in situ* performance.

Models of feedback

There are a number of models for giving good feedback, many of these arising from language teaching, management theory and clinical training, and they include extensive discussion of the structure of the feedback, how it should be delivered and by whom (see Pendleton et al., 2003; Hargie et al., 2010; Boud and Molloy, 2012). However most of these models operate in the complex, often public, face-to-face environment associated with such educational programs. They tend to operate from a perspective that the teacher (who may be an academic, educator, doctor, nurse, lawyer, manager) knows best. They contain elements that can be applied to written feedback, for example most of these features emphasise the notion that, for feedback to be effective, it must be conveyed in an environment in which the learner feels safe.

However, one of the significant characteristics of written feedback is that while it may be generated by a teacher, the learner may 'receive' it in a wide variety of settings outside of the control of the teacher; as SMS on the phone, to read on the bus, at home, or in a café, or as emails in all of those and other locations, where no support is available. This might be of concern if the focus was on highlighting deficits, and did not contain messages about how to improve subsequent tasks. Or, at worst, was person-focused and expressed in a tone that positioned subsequent improvement as unlikely; for example 'you don't seem to have what it takes to be an academic; try an applied field' – which, incidentally, was a piece of feedback given to one of the authors of this chapter on graduation.

We suggest that in written feedback, safety for the learner still needs to be created by the text and its tone. Because this process is essentially private it can do this well, but for the same reason it is easy to abuse. Keeping a friendly but distanced perspective, not engaging in negative person-focused feedback, and giving lots of supportive encouragement are three ways to do this.

In the models we describe below we recognise a number of features of research on feedback. First, research on feedback is not as voluminous as might be expected, given its central role in learning (see Sadler, 2010). Notwithstanding extensive reviews by e.g. Hattie and Timperley (2007) and Shute (2008), the assumption seems to be that writing is so common that nobody needs to develop special styles of delivery when writing feedback. Second, there are a number of articles that discuss principles of feedback, but they are not always research-based nor commonly worked through in their implications for communication through text.

Third, writers on feedback have used a variety of different theoretical perspectives: some overlap; some complement each other; some do and some don't recognise the need for 'dialogue' between student and teacher, and so on. There are research findings that may be useful, but they cover a wide variety of issues, such as the value of grades versus comments (Butler, 1988), the actual content of feedback given by lectures/teachers versus the content preferred by students (Ferguson, 2011), and so on. It is very difficult to discern fundamental broad principles at work here, probably also because disciplinary codes make different assumptions about how feedback works, and what is important in guiding good practice for feedback.

In the next section we explore the characteristics of written feedback in terms of some principles that guide what to give feedback on; how to give it; the best ways in which to use written as opposed to other types of feedback; and from whom should feedback come? In doing this we draw on general advice about feedback, and contextualise it for the written form, as many authors on feedback are equivocal about the mode of feedback for which their writing is useful. We start with a number of perspectives on feedback that seem to be useful because they include the notion that students should be able (through dialogue or prompting) to *respond* to feedback.

What to give feedback on: Hattie's notion of levels of operation (foci) of feedback

In two major works (Hattie and Timperley, 2007; Hattie 2009) that meld considerably with other reviews (Shute, 2008; Kluger and DeNisi, 1996, 1998), Hattie and co-workers have shown that the extent to which feedback effectively serves to reduce the gap between current and desired performance is partly dependent on the level at which the feedback operates. This is because there are different ways that students can respond when attempting to deal with feedback. These ways include

- increasing effort
- tackling more challenging tasks
- increasing their ability to detect the need for and deliver modifications to work
- changing strategies to deal with the work
- doing more groundwork before starting a task, and so on.

In Hattie's model he proposes that feedback can be directed at four different levels of operation of the student and that, essentially, feedback will be ineffective if directed at an inappropriate level. The responses that students develop and their efficacy will be dependent on the focus and type of feedback they get. If the focus is inappropriate to the needs of the student and/or the teacher, the feedback may be ineffective, because the student is unable to transform the information into action where it is needed most, and thus make it into 'real feedback'. A simple but regrettable example of this is the frequent use of the humiliation of learners in the health professions (see Lempp and Seale, 2004; Seabrook, 2004). Here, feedback is frequently delivered at the 'personal' level (see below) when results are really needed at the 'task' or 'process' level.

Hattie also uses a set of three questions that can be mobilised synergistically at each of the four levels. These are: 'Where is the student going?' (goal), 'How is the student going?' (performance in relation to the goal), and 'Where to next?' (further steps to achieve the goal, or goal redefinition).

The following points are essentially a digest of the Hattie model. (Further information can be found in Hattie and Timperley, 2007; Hattie, 2009; and Shute, 2008).

The four levels of feedback are:

a)   Feedback that is task focused (FT)
     This includes feedback about how well a task has been done. This includes identifying when statements are incorrect or contestable, and suggesting that more or different information is necessary to complete the task or do it better. In the studies reviewed by Hattie this type of feedback was most common. Hattie suggests that task focused feedback is more powerful when

it is about faulty interpretations, not lack of information. For example, identifying that a student 'does not know enough anatomy to understand this patient's problem', or 'enough quantum mechanics to appreciate the particle theory of light', requires the student to go away and learn more. On the other hand, pointing out that the student has identified the femoral artery as the femoral vein, and the consequences of this, might be much more useful to the student. If students lack necessary knowledge, further instruction or study may be more powerful than more feedback-type information.

However, feedback at the task level does not always generalise to other tasks. Explanatory comments can lead to more interest and motivational gains than simply giving marks or grades alone. Surprisingly, and of considerable practical significance, if grades are given and these are supplemented by comments, the positive impact of the comments on performance disappears (see Butler, 1988). This effect is more widely discussed by Hattie and Timperley (2007).

b)   Feedback that is process focused (FP)

Here feedback is addressed to the processes used when completing tasks or to those used to make connections across tasks to broaden or expand tasks into new areas. This focus attempts to assist the learner to create meaning and relates to the connections between concepts, to how students' cognitive processes are being developed, and to their application to other more difficult or untried tasks. One mode of process focused feedback tackles students' strategies for error detection, which can range from finding a different way to express an issue to self-diagnosis by the learners of their misunderstanding. According to Hattie, feedback at the process level can be more effective than at the task level for enhancing deeper learning. For example, asking students to explain to themselves or a peer how they arrived at an answer will sometimes trigger a realisation that they have left out a stage, or used the wrong terminology.

c)   Self-regulation focused feedback (FR)

One of the more interesting elements of Hattie's foci, because it speaks to the need for feedback to be a two-way process and one that, under the right circumstances, should originate within the learner, is the use of feedback for the student's self-regulation. In this context self-regulation includes the way students 'monitor, direct, and regulate actions toward the learning goal. It implies autonomy, self-control, self-direction, and self-discipline.' (Hattie and Timperley, 2007, p. 93). Hattie and Timperley identify that 'less effective learners have minimal self-regulation strategies, and they depend much more on external factors (such as the teacher or the task) for feedback' (p. 94). Moreover, given that two-way dialogic feedback between teacher and student is so undervalued in much of education, the fact that students 'rarely seek or incorporate feedback in ways that will enhance their future learning or self-regulation strategies' (p. 94) should not be surprising.

Self-regulation focused feedback has at least six elements that mediate the effectiveness of feedback. They are:

i. The capacity to create 'internal' feedback

This includes feedback directed at encouraging the student to monitor their engagement with work and how they are going. It focuses on the type of outcomes required and the attributes of effective cognitive strategies required to meet them. This is the first step in self-regulation. For example, exhorting a student to read 3 or 4 paragraphs of their text and asking themselves questions about coherence and phrasing rather than sentence construction and vocabulary, and promoting the idea that the intended meaning should drive the grammar and syntax.

ii. The ability to self-assess

This is the major powerhouse of self-regulation in Hattie and Timperley's model. It involves two sub-elements. First, cognitive activities where students constantly review and evaluate their skills, their need for more knowledge about a topic, the way they are thinking about it, and how they will identify missed opportunities. Second, mental strategies to plan tasks, correct errors, and generally fix things up in work. Put together, these two sub-components deliver strengths in evaluating understanding, both in relation to curricular goals and in judging performance against that of peers. Such activities also provide maintenance to students' cognitive 'engines' throughout all this activity.

iii. The student's willingness to invest effort into seeking and dealing with feedback information

Students seem to have a cost-benefit approach to using feedback appropriately. If the balance of the effort against other factors such as potential loss of face, or the difficulty of interpreting feedback, is not seen by the student to result in a positive outcome, feedback will not be sought. The easier feedback is to assimilate, and the less it 'costs' the student to deal with, the more likely the feedback is to produce change.

iv. The degree of confidence or certainty in the correctness of the response

Feedback has its most potent effect when a learner expects a task to have been done correctly and it turns out not to be so. If the learner has low confidence in what they have done, and is given negative feedback about it, this feedback can be ignored. When this happens, additional education and/or direct information is more effective than more feedback on the same topic – a type of 'clear the decks and let's start again' approach.

v. The attributions about success or failure

Students' views about what caused the success or failure will have a major impact on the effectiveness of the feedback. One determinant of the capacity of students to inappropriately attribute their performance to external rather than internal factors is the degree of clarity of the feedback. When it is unclear, and does not specify the basis on which students have met with success, or lack of it, feedback can aggravate poor outcomes and increase uncertainty about how to approach the task again. Conversely, feedback that identifies the students' own efforts as the contributor to performance can increase commitment and level of outcomes.

For example, the statement:

'In my view, your recent interest in conversing with local Italians for your project, seems to have made a dramatic improvement in your pronunciation of Italian double consonants, like the "zz" in Pizza, and the "rr" in "terrible"'

directly attributes success to learner motivation, engagement and activity.

vi. The level of proficiency at seeking help
In general, getting hints about work rather than answers to the tasks posed is more effective in focusing on the self-regulation dimension of approaches to work. Getting 'the answer' that can be reproduced to save time is feedback, at best, only at the task or process level. Having an open submission day or hour for feedback on drafts by students is one way of encouraging weaker students to seek help. Giving written feedback to students on their pre-submitted opening paragraphs, or a draft of the essay plan, will be more appropriate than reading the essay when it's finished, if the goal is to help students self-regulate better. Even so, getting hints from the teacher will be seen by some students as socially embarrassing (and feedback from a peer potentially more so). Work on feedback in the socio-professional environment would tend to support this view. 'Hints' are sometimes used to modify feedback from serious confrontation to a kinder gentler approach, so called 'vanishing feedback' (see Arluke, 1980; Ende, 1983; Balmer et al., 2010).

d) While these six elements of self-regulation clearly overlap, and not all will apply to any one task undertaken by students, they give a useful and rich framework for addressing this key facet of feedback.

Person (self) focused feedback. (FS)
The final focus of Hattie's framework concerns feedback given about personal attributes.

The key difference between self-regulation and person focused feedback is that self-regulation feedback includes information about the student's capacity to apply a metacognitive view of their task-related efforts, skills and intellectual deployment. Person focused feedback is directed at personal attributes, such as understanding, intelligence and ability. It usually contains little or no task-related information. Examples of person focused statements are: 'You did a great job'; 'You are so clever'; 'You have a very interesting approach to things'. For this reason person focused feedback is usually ineffective: it doesn't include information on matters that learners can see that they can change.

Meta-analyses have shown that such praise on its own, while highly valued by many students, does not translate into more engagement with, or commitment to, learning goals, does not promote self-efficacy, nor lead to greater understanding about learning tasks. The effects of person focused feedback are usually too dispersed in relation to usable content (task, process or self-regulation information) to be effective.

However, praise directed to the person sometimes can be a vehicle for information on process issues. This would involve comments on effort, self-monitoring, engagement, or on cognitive operations relating to the task and its performance (e.g. 'You are a really stylish writer, because the metaphor you used to sum up your explanation was quite unique, and worked really well'). So, although person focused feedback is not generally recommended, when also accompanied by rationales and highlighting of processes (process or self-regulatory focus) it can be a useful route to more effective modes. Both self-regulation and person focused feedback are directed at the personal attributes of the learner. They stem from teachers' perceptions and tend to be normatively judge-mental. Nevertheless, person focused feedback may also be used to build trust between the learner and a supervising professional (see Iedema et al., 2010). Written person focused statements (notes and emails) may also carry more weight than 'off the cuff' comments. They can also set better defined challenges or limits to the learners' activities – for example, 'I am impressed by your capacity to develop a management plan for this type of patient, but just check in with me briefly before prescribing this drug again: we need to ensure you have a complete grasp of the side effects and contra indications'.

Finally positive written feedback comments can also contribute usefully to students' portfolios.

These four levels of Hattie and Timperley's model have been further elaborated in a diagrammatic model by Hattie and Gan (2011).

How to give and how not to give feedback

a) Rorty's notion of final vocabulary

We have drawn attention elsewhere to the idea that information is too often written in a form that uses language that is 'final' and hence leaves the learner with effectively nowhere to go (Boud, 1995). Such 'final vocabulary' (from Rorty, 1989) will describe the work as 'good' or 'poor', or use phrases such as 'you've missed the point' or 'excellent, well done!'. Rorty ascribes this very common usage to the need for humans to justify their actions in simple and 'non-negotiable' terms: 'right, good, let's get on with it then!'. This leaves no room for manoeuvre and positions feedback as a one-way process in which an authority pronounces on another less powerful person. The avoidance of final vocabulary is also important in feedback for other reasons. First, it is usually without substantive content and lacks direction. It says nothing about what the learner might do in further work. Second, it can easily be misread as the giver of information making comments about the person, rather than the work being considered, because it is not grounded in the specifics of that work. Third, it inhibits the possibility of dialogue. It closes discussion rather than opening it up.

It is a salutary experience trying to exclude final vocabulary from a piece of feedback. We have found that it is easier to write the words 'good' 'poor' 'excellent' and so on, than to explore the reasons why these epithets have been used. Rephrasing statements as questions to the learner is a useful way of avoiding the finality of some statements, e.g. 'The level of detail is poor' can be rewritten as 'What missing details could usefully be included?'; 'You have identified three factors contributing to social unrest but what others are there? Have you fully justified each of the ones you included?'. Doing likewise with all other instances usually results in a set of rich and rewarding prompts to the learner.

b) The notion of nurturing of the learner

The use of rich, non-final vocabulary is all part of the process of nurturing the learner. However there is evidence that feedback can be ineffective or even damaging (Hattie, 2009; Kluger and DeNisi, 1998; Archer, 2010), as well as having a positive impact. As we suggested earlier, most damaging, or at least alarming, feedback seems to be delivered in face-to-face settings (Seabrook, 2004; Lempp and Seale, 2004). But in the health care environment over the last twenty years alternative approaches to appropriate delivery of feedback have been strategically created to take the emotional heat out of the feedback environment (see Pendleton et al., 2003), and we can incorporate some of these ideas to make written feedback more learner-centered. For example, in written feedback start with a summary of what you think the writer or producer of the work is trying to achieve (irrespective of the brief or task given); indulge their space! Then find some positive attributes of the work to showcase. We find it helpful sometimes to repeat back to the learner the phraseology that they have used while at the same time offering a positive comment. Then, identify one to four major issues with the work and discuss each in turn, asking the student appropriate questions within the comments.

Nurturing the learner is usually done by teachers, so it is salient to consider what exactly teachers do, habitually, in the feedback process. Below we consider this question and contrast it with what students want.

c) Research on what teachers do

Educational research is peppered with articles that suggest that teachers are not very astute at accurately identifying things that they do with students, or things that they don't do. Most teachers say they give students lots of feedback, but most students do not agree with this statement. In a study of written feedback given by English language teachers on students' written work, Lee (2009) identified ten 'mismatches' between what teachers said they knew about feedback and what they gave back to students. Two of these resonate with common practice in higher education, especially in professional areas. Her Mismatch 6 states: 'Teachers respond mainly to weaknesses in student writing although they know that feedback should cover both strengths and weaknesses' (p. 17). She found that nearly 92 per cent of feedback identified errors, but only 8 per cent mentioned other aspects like a critique of the meaning of the text or positive feedback about what was written. Her Mismatch 7 identified that teachers' written feedback did not allow students much jurisdiction over their capacity to correct their own work. Quoting from an interview with a teacher, Lee states: 'all they have to do is just to rewrite the essay by correcting mistakes; students are not required to assess themselves or to assess each other. Since direct correction is provided to the majority of errors, students' role in correcting mistakes in their writing is minimal; often they do not even have to think because correct answers have been given by the teachers' (p. 17). In Lee's study, teachers did this even though they believed that students should learn to take greater responsibility for their learning.

d) Research on what students want

What students say they want might not be the same as what they need. The absence of dialogue between teachers and students often leads to mismatched expectations, irrespective of whether we approve of what they want or not. There is considerable merit in presenting feedback as subjective reactions rather than as the voice of authority that some students seem to want. This implies the need for better dialogue.

Clearly, students need to develop insight into the quality of their own work, to enable a meaningful dialogue between tutor and student. One approach to this involves students presenting work plans or drafts in the classroom. Peers (and perhaps the tutor) review the draft before it is written up. This has been found to generate experience of working as a team and to promote students' success (Lilly et al., 2010, p. 36). In this study students also identified that feedback frequently lacked clarity due to unclear handwriting. (Lilly et al., 2010, p. 37). It would not seem unreasonable to expect all teachers to deliver their feedback in typed mode; the options are huge: SMS text, email; 'Word' documents sent as attachments or text inserted into documents; using editing and review facilities within pdf and 'Word' files, etc. For example, this paragraph is being written now by a two-finger typist, who can still type faster than he can construct sentences, so there seems to be no good excuse for feedback delivered by handwriting, quite apart from the utility of spelling and grammar checkers.

When the content of feedback relates to a particular aspect of a written text, the tempting approach is to deliver this information in writing physically on the students' work. However there is debate about how best to do this and whether writing directly over students' text is disrespectful. We prefer to use comment boxes rather than the track changes option which is the electronic version of the 'red pen' effect. A comment box to the side of the text appears to infringe less on students' work, leaving it up to them to modify the text, and it promotes the use of dialogue if it contains questions rather than statements. Most things that you would use in track changes can be just as well delivered in the comment box. Inserting urls as reference points for students is also not too invasive.

In the quote at the start of this chapter Nicol (2010) foreshadowed the disenfranchisement of students in the feedback process. In that article Nicol synthesizes research on written feedback. He makes several suggestions for ways in which feedback can be made more 'dialogic'. These include (p. 512-3):

Written feedback comments should be:
- *Understandable*: expressed in a language that students will understand.
- *Selective*: commenting in reasonable detail on two or three things that the student can do something about.
- *Specific*: pointing to instances in the student's submission where the feedback applies.
- *Timely*: provided in time to improve the next assignment.
- *Contextualised*: framed with reference to the learning outcomes and/or assessment criteria.
- *Non-judgemental*: descriptive rather than evaluative, focused on learning goals, not just performance goals.
- *Balanced*: pointing out the positive as well as areas in need of improvement.
- *Forward-looking*: suggesting how students might improve subsequent assignments.
- *Transferable*: focused on processes, skills and self-regulatory processes, not just on knowledge content.
- *Personal*: referring to what is already known about the student and her or his previous work.

Several researchers have identified that students perceive feedback disdainfully if it does not provide information that they regard as helpful, if they find it too impersonal (although one study found the opposite), and if it is too generic and/or vague to guide future work. So, do teachers have a 'well-rehearsed script' that learners discern (and therefore interpret as impersonal)? A study by Huxham (2007) in a biological sciences course found that students, having taken assessments using short answer questions, and been given experience of two modes of feedback, much preferred individual comments on their work to model answers. However, when given a subsequent examination, in which some content areas had previously received model answer feedback while others had received personal feedback, students performed substantially better on the questions relating to content in which they had previously received model answer feedback. These results are consistent with the Hattie and Timperley assertion that feedback focused on the task, rather than the self, is generally more effective. It would be expected that model answers might be more task focused while personal feedback might involve more comment on personal characteristics as well as some task elements.

In a study of the views of over 500 student teachers on what they would like to see in their feedback, Ferguson (2011) found that the top-rated elements were brief comments throughout an assignment, and a written summary from the assessor at some point on the task. It also found that comments should relate to students' work rather than reiteration of marking schemes or assessment criteria. Students felt that a balance between critical comments and supportive encouragement was crucial to maintaining their motivation and building confidence.

Bloxham recently reinvigorated the debate around student involvement in their own assessments processes, their role in 'self-assessment', and the potential of dialogic feedback (Bloxham, 2009; Beaumont et al., 2011). In the health professions 'involvement' can be manifested in different ways and developing professionals who can 'understand the standard they are aiming for and can judge and change their own performance in relation to that standard, i.e. self-regulation' (Bloxham 2009, p. 218), is certainly a goal of most vocational courses and echoes Hattie's call to pay attention to self-regulatory processes in feedback. The logical extension of this, in written feedback, is to encourage or require students to use assessment criteria to judge peers' work (Bloxham and West, 2004), and also to emphasise self-regulation features, such as time on task, diligence, honesty, research thoroughness, and similar characteristics in that process. However the establishment of dialogue between student and assessor in written format is challenging (Bloxham and Campbell, 2010). These authors suggest that the tacit knowledge needed in professional work may only be developed effectively through frequent interaction with communities of practice (Lave and Wenger, 1991) and would involve considerable 'observation, imitation, participation and dialogue' (p. 292). However they also describe the use of interactive cover sheets on written assignments that allow students to identify particular aspects of their work on which they would like feedback, and receive comments targeted to those needs. Carless et al. (2011) suggest that a good proportion of assignments should be two-stage ones, in which the first stage involves feedback both on achievement and on 'gaps' that could be filled before the second stage is completed. The implication of this is that more diverse and voluminous assessment instruments such as portfolios should not be used as a once-off summative assessment, but should be supported by iterative written dialogue between student and faculty as students build up the quality of their work over time.

Another strategy to foster dialogue is to post drafts of work on-line for comment by other students and teachers. Assessed contributions to blogs have also been suggested as mechanisms to stimulate self-regulation and dialogic feedback. Feedback of this kind requires assessments with more than one stage, so that not only do students have a chance to improve, they can also demonstrate that improvement. As one of the professors in the Carless et al. study described:

> I've tried to explain to students my approach. Some of the students accepted it and some of them didn't. They think getting a high mark is the main priority ... Many of my students would complain that I pose too many questions without giving them answers. But my strategy is that the same question has to be asked twice, so students can realize what they have learnt.
>
> (Carless et al., 2011, p. 403)

Effectively, their argument is that sustainable feedback needs to be based around assessments that engage students over time, and that time be used to generate feedback from multiple sources, which is then integrated by students to improve their performance on sequential stages of assignments.

One way of engaging students is through other students. And it is clear in the examples above that other students may have a useful role in written feedback. In the next section we pose questions around who should or could deliver good quality written feedback.

Who should give feedback?

In many professions there has been a recent expansion of attention on workplace-based learning and assessment (Newton et al., 2009; Wilkinson et al., 2008; Keating et al., 2009) and how written feedback can be tied to workplace activities. Some professions in Australia have been very successful in designing and agreeing common instruments to use, within the profession, across different teaching institutions (e.g. Dalton et al., 2011; McAllister et al., 2010; Kirk and Jolly, 2007) so that workplace teaching environments can share a common tool no matter which institution students come from and who is assessing them. A common thread across these developments is that virtually all the instruments used to capture the student's or trainee's performance entail written feedback on strengths and weaknesses and, most importantly, a discussion about these between assessor and student. The assessments also potentially broaden the range of 'assessors' or feedback givers that can legitimately contribute to the student's development as a working professional.

In a review of some of this work Crossley and Jolly (2012) identify a number of principles pertaining to the usefulness or feasibility of such assessments, and their efficacy as feedback, of which three are relevant here:

i)   The response scales for the judgements about students/trainees' performance that form the basis for the feedback given, need to be aligned to the 'reality-map' or everyday world of the feedback giver.

      They found that different instruments used for assessment and feedback typically focused on three different areas or domains of activity, similar to those identified by Hattie and Timperley (2007). These were, first, 'outcome level' – equivalent to Hattie's task focus. The second was 'structural level', the relatively stable characteristics, or traits, of the professional – similar to Hattie's self-regulation focus. And the third was a 'process' level – generally congruent with the Hattie notion of process. From this analysis it became clear that many tools used for workplace-based feedback are not clear enough about which level of operation they are aimed at. Moreover, workplace-based tutors have difficulty operating along dimensions that reflect 'academic' criteria, or they may not be fully familiar with academic tasks that the students might be completing. So anchoring judgements around students' developmental or graded achievements, such as 'performs above expectations' or 'distinction' respectively, will not necessarily be meaningful to the professional. Although these descriptors might be salient to the students' needs, they are not easily used as a frame of reference by workplace assessors. Dimensions related to work activities, such as degree of supervision required or the students' preparedness for independent practice, will be more successful. They will also be more easily interpreted by students, and more useful in encouraging them to operate within their limitations in the workplace. In addition, workplace assessment tools that include items pitched at the behavioural level (i.e. 'establishes eye contact during the communication encounter' or 'seeks informed consent prior to treatment') can help in the provision of feedback, and can help the learner understand the 'goals' or target performance.

ii) Asking for judgements about the practical or clinical adequacy of observed tasks will be more effective for both student and teacher than merely scoring the minutiae of the observations.

      Students may need teachers to interpret their elemental observations of the student at work back to them. These integrative interpretations or judgements, allied to specific examples of success or need for improvement, allow students to strive for a better performance and to know how to get there.

iii) Not all workplace tutors and not all academic teachers are well placed to assess and/or give feedback on every outcome of the curriculum. Some assessors do not see the students often enough, and this applies as much to academics as to workplace-based tutors. Other assessors see only a few students, or engage with only a small sub-set of students' activities, probably not enough to substantiate or underpin accurate and well-informed judgements. Peers frequently see more of the students' day-to-day clinical activities than teachers do, yet quite often we take tutors' views about students at face value without asking what their experience of the student is. Feedback given based on limited exposure could be very misleading. Feedback should be given by the person who is in the best place to give it, for the purpose, focus, and type of feedback required. This has important implications for who gives or 'manages' this feedback. The task or activity at the focus of feedback could entail feedback managed by the teacher, by peers, by the student, or by any combination of these.

Conclusion

Clearly, written feedback will continue to have an important role to play in all contexts. However, we have seen that it is often much more valuable when clearly focused at the appropriate level for the occasion, is related to what the learner is going to do, involves a two-way interchange and enlists other parties. Like all modes of feedback, engagement by the learner in the activity, and subsequent use of the information gained in future work, is vital.

In giving written feedback we need to answer several questions.

- What have we given feedback on?
    o The task?
    o The process?
    o The student's self-regulation?
    o The student's personal qualities?
- Who is best placed to give feedback on each of these areas?
  Have we framed the feedback in ways that help the student?
  Have we followed up? Is the feedback really feedback or just an outpouring of information?

References

Archer, J. C. (2010) 'State of the science in health professional education: effective feedback', *Medical Education*, 44:101-8.

Arluke, A. (1980) 'Roundsmanship: inherent control on a medical teaching ward', *Social Science & Medicine. Part A, Medical Sociology*, 14A:297-302.

Balmer, D. F., Master, C. L., Richards, B. F., Serwint, J. R. and Giardino, A. P. (2010) 'An ethnographic study of attending rounds in general paediatrics: understanding the ritual', *Medical Education*, 44:1105-16.

Beaumont, C., O'Doherty, M. and Shannon, L. (2011) 'Reconceptualising assessment feedback: a key to improving student learning?', *Studies in Higher Education*, 36:671-87.

Bloxham, S. and West, A. (2004) 'Understanding the rules of the game: marking peer assessment as a medium for developing students' conceptions of assessment', *Assessment & Evaluation in Higher Education*, 29:721-33.

Bloxham, S. (2009) 'Marking and moderation in the UK: false assumptions and wasted resources', *Assessment & Evaluation in Higher Education*, 34:209-22.

Bloxham, S. and Campbell, L. (2010) 'Generating dialogue in assessment feedback: exploring the use of interactive cover sheets', *Assessment & Evaluation in Higher Education*, 34:291-300.

Boud, D. (1995) 'Assessment and Learning: Contradictory or Complementary?', in Knight, P. (ed.) *Assessment for Learning in Higher Education*, London: Kogan Page.

Boud, D. and Molloy, E. (2012) 'Rethinking models of feedback: the challenge of design', *Assessment and Evaluation in Higher Education* DOI:10.1080/0260293 8.2012.691462.

Butler, R. (1988) 'Enhancing and undermining intrinsic motivation; the effects of task-involving and ego-involving evaluation on interest and performance', *British Journal of Educational Psychology*, 58:1-14.

Carless, D., Salter, D., Yang, M. and Lam, J. (2011) 'Developing sustainable feedback practices', *Studies in Higher Education*, 36: 395-407.

Chandler, P., and Sweller, J. (1991) 'Cognitive load theory and the format of instruction', *Cognition and Instruction*, 8:293-332.

Crossley, J. and Jolly, B. (2012) 'Making sense of work-based assessment: ask the right questions, in the right way, about the right things, of the right people', *Medical Education*, 46:28-37.

Dalton, M., Davidson, M. and Keating, J. (2011) 'The assessment of physiotherapy practice is a valid measure of competence of physiotherapy students: a cross sectional study with Rasch analysis', *Journal of Physiotherapy*, 57:239-46.

Ende, J. (1983) 'Feedback in medical education', *Journal of the American Medical Association*, 250:777-81.

Ferguson, P. (2011) 'Student perceptions of quality feedback in teacher education', *Assessment & Evaluation in Higher Education*, 36:51-62.

Fiorella, L., Vogel-Walcutt, JJ. and Schatz, S. (2012) 'Applying the modality principle to real-time feedback and the acquisition of higher-order cognitive skills', *Educational Technology Research And Development*, 60: 223-38.

Graduate Careers Australia (2012) 'Data from the Course Experience Questionnaire 2010'. Online. Available at <http://www.graduatecareers.com.au/wp-content/uploads/2012/01/gca002524.pdf> (accessed 12 May 2012).

Hargie, O., Boohan, M., McCoy, M. and Murphy, P. (2010) 'Current trends in communication skills training in UK schools of medicine', *Medical Teacher*, 32:385-91.

Hattie, J. (2009) *Visible learning: A synthesis of 800+ meta-analyses on achievement.* Oxford: Routledge.

Hattie, J. and Gan, M. (2011) 'Instruction based on feedback', in Meyer, R. E. and Alexander, P. A. (eds) *Handbook of Research on Learning and Instruction*, New York: Routledge.

Hattie, J. and Timperley, H. (2007) 'The power of feedback', *Review of Educational Research*, 77:81-112.

Huxham, M. (2007) 'Fast and effective feedback: are model answers the answer?', *Assessment & Evaluation in Higher Education*, 32:601-11.

Iedema, R., Brownhill, S., Haines, M., Lancashire, B., Shaw, T. and Street, J. (2010) '"Hands on, hands off": a model of clinical supervision that recognises trainees' need for support and independence', *Australian Health Review*, 34:286-91.

Keating, J., Dalton, M. and Davidson, M. (2009) 'Assessment in clinical education', in Delaney, C. and Molloy, E. (eds) *Clinical Education in the Health Professions*, Sydney: Elsevier.

Kirk, P. and Jolly, B. C. (2007) 'Exploring the use of a portfolio as an assessment process: a narrative review of the literature and indications for best usage in occupational therapy (OT) education', *Focus on Health Professional Education: A multi-disciplinary journal*, 9:44-57.

Kluger, A. N. and DeNisi, A. (1996) 'The effects of feedback interventions on performance: A historical review, a meta-analysis, and a preliminary feedback intervention theory', *Psychological Bulletin*, 119:254-84.

Kluger, A. N. and DeNisi, A. (1998) 'Feedback interventions: Toward the understanding of a double-edged sword', *Current Directions in Psychological Science*, 7:67-72.

Kneebone, R., Bello, F., Nestel, D., Mooney, N., Codling, A., Yadollahi, F., Tierney, T., Wilcockson, D. and Darzi, A. (2008) 'Learner-centred feedback using remote assessment of clinical procedures', *Medical Teacher*, 30:795-801.

Lave, J. and Wenger, E. (1991) *Situated learning: Legitimate peripheral participation*, Cambridge, Eng.: Cambridge University Press.

Lee, I. (2009) 'Ten mismatches between teachers' beliefs and written feedback practice', *English Language Teaching Journal*, 63:13-22.

Lempp, H. and Seale, C. (2004) 'The hidden curriculum in undergraduate medical education: qualitative study of medical students' perceptions of teaching', *BMJ*, 329:770-3.

Lilly, J., Richter, U. M. and Rivera-Macias, B. (2010) 'Using feedback to promote learning: student and tutor perspectives', *Practitioner research in higher education*, 4: 30-40.

Lunt, T. and Curran, J. (2010) '"Are you listening please?" The advantages of electronic audio feedback compared to written feedback', *Assessment & Evaluation in Higher Education*, 35:759-69.

McAllister, S. M., Lincoln, M., Ferguson, A. and McAllister, L. (2010) 'Dilemmas in assessing performance on fieldwork education placements', in McAllister, L., Paterson, M., Higgs, J. and Bithell, C. (eds), *Innovations in allied health fieldwork education: A critical appraisal*, Rotterdam, The Netherlands: Sense Publishers.

Newton, J. M., Billet, S., Jolly, B. C., Ockerby, C. M. and Cross, W. (2009) 'Lost in translation: Barriers to learning in health professional clinical education', *Learning in Health and Social Care*, 8:315-27.

Nicol, D. (2010) 'From monologue to dialogue: improving written feedback processes in mass higher education', *Assessment & Evaluation in Higher Education*, 35:501-17.

Pendleton, D., Schofield, T., Tate, P. and Havelock, P. (2003) *The New Consultation*, Oxford: Oxford University Press.

Rorty, R. (1989) *Contingency, irony, and solidarity*, Cambridge UK: University of Cambridge Press.

Sadler, D. R. (2010) 'Beyond feedback: developing student capability in complex appraisal', *Assessment & Evaluation in Higher Education*, 35:535-50.

Seabrook, M. A. (2004) 'Clinical students' initial reports of the educational climate in a single medical school', *Medical Education*, 38:659-69.

Sharp, P. (1985) 'Behaviour modification in the secondary school: A survey of students' attitudes to rewards and praise', *Behavioral Approaches with Children*, 9:109-12.

Shute, V. J. (2008) 'Focus on formative feedback'. *Review of Educational Research*, 78:153-89.

van Merrienboer, J. J. G. and Sweller, J. (2005) 'Cognitive load theory and complex learning: Recent developments and future directions', *Educational Psychology Review*, 17:147-77.

Wilkinson, J. R., Crossley, J. G. M., Wragg, A., Mills, P., Cowan, G. and Wade, W. (2008) 'Implementing workplace-based assessment across the medical specialties in the United Kingdom', *Medical Education*, 42:364-73.

Chapter 8

Feedback in the digital environment

Brett Williams
Ted Brown
Robyn Benson

Recent rapid advances in learning technologies do not change the fundamental nature of feedback in learning and assessment, but they markedly increase the ways in which students may receive comments about their performance, and give feedback to others. The emergence and continuing evolution of internet applications that facilitate interaction between users, and interaction with course-related content, extend the boundaries of how both synchronous (real-time) and asynchronous (delayed-time) feedback can be implemented and provided. These developments offer a range of non-traditional approaches to feedback for educators to consider, along with accompanying opportunities and challenges.

Although digital technologies are not confined to applications available via the World Wide Web (WWW), web-based teaching has been a major focus of digital learning environments. The potential for digital technologies to facilitate student-centred and peer learning spaces where students engage in real-world tasks and student and teacher roles become blurred were identified in the early years of web-based teaching (Siegel and Kirkley, 1997). These features have become even more relevant to teaching and learning as the characteristics of recent internet applications have expanded across the higher and professional education sectors.

We begin by outlining some theoretical perspectives that have particular relevance for implementing and supporting the feedback process. We then summarise some of the key aspects of internet technologies for learning and assessment, from 'first generation' technologies which provided the fundamental capacities of the internet that allow interaction between users and with content (Benson and Brack, 2010), to the development of Web 2.0 software that supports group interaction such as blogs, wikis, immersive virtual worlds and other social networking applications. Since recent literature primarily focuses on Web 2.0 applications, we will concentrate our attention on this generation, addressing the implications of Web 2.0 for feedback and highlighting some opportunities and challenges. Finally, we explore the potential of these developments for the practical application of feedback in digital environments for supporting effective learning communities, particularly given the egalitarian nature of interaction in these contexts.

Theoretical framework

Since the early 1990s, theoretical perspectives based on cognitive psychology have dominated the educational technology literature. These focus on learning as the construction of meaning by students and therefore on the importance of active involvement by the learner in authentic learning tasks (e.g. Duffy and Jonassen, 1992; Grabinger, 1996). This emphasis has implications for both the content of feedback and the activity of students in receiving and giving it. While the initial focus was on the construction of meaning by individual students, developments in social software have foregrounded the idea of social constructivism (Vygotsky, 1978) to explain how students learn, with potential for social learning tasks and feedback.

Holmes and Gardner (2006) extended this concept to communal constructivism, to reflect the 'hugely magnified opportunities for communal support for learning – and, most importantly, for providing a medium to store and make available the knowledge created by the learners' (p. 85) through the one-to-one, one-to-many and many-to-many opportunities for interaction and feedback made available by e-learning environments. This draws on the concept of communities of practice where groups of people 'deepen their knowledge and expertise ... by interacting on an ongoing basis' (Wenger, McDermott and Snyder, 2002, p. 4). Siemens (2005) introduced the term 'connectivism' where learning is seen as 'a process of building networks of information, contacts, and resources that are applied to real problems', relying on 'the ubiquity of networked connections between people, digital artifacts, and content, which would have been inconceivable ... were the World Wide Web not available to mediate the process' (Anderson and Dron, 2011, p. 87).

These ideas highlight the multi-dimensional nature of feedback in e-learning environments, extending beyond the roles of individual teacher and learner to include potential contributions from student peers, other people and resources in exchanges that may be recorded, built upon, extended, revised and updated. This challenges the concept of a hierarchical 'power' relationship between educator and student in providing and receiving feedback. It also raises the issue of *transactional control* in the use of social software (Dron, 2007) where the potential for collaborative engagement in building knowledge, and integrating feedback as part of this engagement, may be restricted by teacher control. The concept of *transactional control* is related to, but different from, transactional distance theory (Moore, 2007). It suggests that when there is separation between teacher and learners (as in most e-learning environments), there is transactional distance that needs to be bridged by a balance of structure and dialogue appropriate to the autonomy of the learners. *Transactional distance and control* are useful notions for managing feedback in digital environments because they provide a way of taking into consideration the nature of the particular setting (including Web 2.0 environments).

We now outline the main generational characteristics of internet technologies themselves, relating them to generational characteristics of users (students, educators and others). These factors have been an important focus of discussion about the potential use of the internet for learning that therefore has implications for the feedback process.

Generational factors: internet technologies and users

Tim Berners-Lee commenced development of the WWW in 1989, but the internet did not become widely accessible until the Mosaic web browser became available in 1993 (Richardson, 2009). The first generation of web applications was characterised by static, non-interactive websites and proprietary rather than open source applications before the dot-com collapse in 2001 marked the beginning of the development of social software (Web 2.0) (O'Reilly, 2005). Users have also been classified in terms of generational characteristics related to their different experiences and exposure to the application of internet technologies. A generation is viewed as the average interval of time between the birth of parents and the birth of their children. This would also influence the type and mode of feedback students from each generation would typically be conversant with, expect and assimilate.

Baby Boomers were born between 1946 and 1964 while *Generation X* (also referred to as *Baby Busters* or *Post Boomers*) generally includes individuals born in the mid-1960s up through the early 1980s (Zemke, Raines and Filipczak, 2000). *Generation Y*, also referred to as the *Millennial Generation, Millennials,* or the *dot.com generation,* are individuals born between 1982 and 1994 (Howe and Strauss, 2000). They may be considered different from the previous generation in their familiarity with communications, media and digital technologies and the regularity with which they use them. The media and technology era accompanying Generation X and Y was the *PC Era – 1980-1990,* which preceded the availability of the World Wide Web (see Figure 8.1). *Generation Z* or the *net generation* is the term coined for the group of people born between the early 1990s and early 2000s (McCrindle, 2006) and consists almost exclusively of the children of *Generation X. Generation Z* is highly connected and networked with many of this cohort having experienced a lifelong use of information and communications technologies, including the World Wide Web, text messaging, mp3 players, Twitter, Facebook, MySpace, Skype, mobile devices and YouTube (see Figure 8.1).

While the 'generational approach' provides one framework to view each decade of the interaction between technology and feedback, it is not the only way. Kennedy et al. (2007) argued that 'such generalised assumptions ignore the possibility that current students and teachers might have a more complex mix of skills and experiences with new technologies' (p. 518), finding in their final report of a major Australian study on the net generation 'little evidence that technology usage patterns can be explained primarily on the basis of broad generational differences' (Kennedy et al., 2007, p. 5). The assumption that all Generation Y and Z students have familiarity and sophistication

PC ERA	WEB 1.0 ERA	WEB 2.0 ERA
1980 → 1990	1990 → 2000	2000 → 2010
• Desktop computers	• Desktops, laptops	• Laptops, tablets
- Email (emerging)	- WWW (dial-up); email/ listservs /attachments; MS Windows; Java; Adobe; databases; search engines	- WWW (broadband, wireless); social software incl. multimedia (wikis, blogs, social networking, podcasts, virtual worlds, Google Applications, YouTube, etc.); Skype
• Telephone		
- Voicemail, mobile, audiographics		
	- LMSs (incl chat, discussion, quizzes, assignment dropbox)	- LMSs with collaborative tools
• Audio		• Smartphones
- Cassettes, Walkmans	• Telephone	- WWW; SMS; images; video microblogging (Twitter)
• Video	- Mobile, SMS, conferencing	
- Cassettes, VCRs	• Audio/video/multi-media	• Other mobile devices
	- CDs, DVDs, videoconferencing	- mp3 players, PDAs, clickers, etc.

Media and Technology Feedback Time Line →

Feedback in PC ERA	Feedback in WEB 1.0 ERA	Feedback in WEB 2.0 ERA
• Increased speed and flexibility (synchronous, asynchronous, anywhere)	• Improved individual feedback (e.g., dropbox, attachments, tracked changes)	• Feedback increasingly communal/networked (access to people and resources)
• Mostly individual except for audiographics (distance education)	• Group feedback (discussion, chat)	• Integrated as part of authentic, timely, immersive group tasks
	• Authentic feedback – individual (e.g., multimedia) and group (e.g., role plays)	• Flexible, audiovisual feedback (e.g., podcasts, frequently authentic [e.g., visual])
• Feedback recorded for later reference (e.g., email, audio)	• Automated feedback (quizzes, multimedia)	• Egalitarian or easy access to experts
	• Provision for repeated attempts and recorded feedback	• Other automated options (e.g., clickers)

Figure 8.1 Illustrates the progressive convergence of media and technologies into digital forms, including the emergence of learning management systems (LMSs) (e.g., Blackboard™, MOODLE™) which support various kinds of feedback, and the increasing movement from individual to social, communal and networked feedback, along with greater capacity for authenticity and democratic control

with using and applying internet technologies is flawed. It is still important to consider the characteristics of particular groups of users (educators and students), and ways of supporting learners, when planning feedback in digital environments.

The next section will provide an overview of specific types of technology applications that can be used to provide feedback in educational and professional contexts.

Implementing feedback in digital environments

To consider the potential for implementing feedback in digital environments, this section examines examples of web-based feedback studies that have been undertaken in Web 2.0 settings. Specifically, the section will consider the following digital applications: ePortfolios, mobile learning, internet videoconferencing, Facebook, wikis/blogs, and student response systems (also referred to as 'clickers'). The landscape of digital environments is rapidly changing from general convenience to near-ubiquitous reliance. Demands on universities and educators are changing, as are students' expectations of feedback methods. Increasingly, educators are utilising Web 2.0 applications in their day-to-day teaching and learning activities, raising issues relating to social and communal constructivism, and connectivism, as they design learning environments. While there may be a wealth of literature on feedback for traditional face-to-face (f2f) teaching settings, the same cannot yet be said for digital environments using social software.

The surge in technological advancements and Web 2.0 social applications (Facebook, Flickr, MySpace, wikis, blogs, etc.) has had direct implications for *giving* and *receiving* feedback in the education context, partially due to the social flexibility that Web 2.0 digital applications provide compared with traditional f2f environments. Smits, Boon, Sluijsmans and van Gog (2008) highlight the challenges for educators using web-designed courses in determining 'what constitutes appropriate feedback for individual students at different moments in their learning trajectory' (p. 3). Web 2.0 brings a range of advantages to higher and professional education settings that, in addition to social interaction, include simplicity, openness, flexibility, increased capacity for peer-learning, and creative expression (Gray, Thompson, Sheard, Clerehan and Hamilton, 2010). Web 2.0 applications allow users to be content creators, contributors, revisers and generators of information at any time – involving authoring, tagging (e.g. bookmarking), editing, and/or mashing (e.g. combining features from different websites). In turn, this provides opportunities for a variety of feedback to be provided from multiple sources.

Feedback in digital environments

Vickery and Lake (2005) refer to the problematic aspects of providing effective feedback when teaching and learning take place in a digital environment. One challenge is that most strategies for improving feedback in higher education and professional education contexts are not necessarily able to accommodate the uniqueness and rapidly changing nature of digital environments (Duffy and O'Neill, 2003). However, the use of digital learning environments has made it easier to provide continuous, faster, practical feedback compared to f2f contexts, for example, in the use of online formative quizzes. Other benefits include provision for internationalisation of curricula, anonymity, and economies of time which are generally more cost-effective, particularly for distance education students (Neighbours et al., 2010). Moreover, digital learning management systems (LMSs) are able to track students' individual, group and peer-based performance more easily and accurately. Despite these advantages, little empirical evidence has been reported about student feedback within digital environments (Gao and Lehman, 2003).

Feedback provides learners with an ability to compare actual performance with some form of expected performance while at the same time reducing cumulative error (Gao and Lehman, 2003). This is true in both f2f and digital environments. Web 2.0 applications may be used to manage the timing of feedback, including both immediate (synchronous) feedback (e.g. audience response systems [clickers], internet videoconferencing) and delayed (asynchronous) feedback (e.g. wikis, blogs). In a qualitative study examining the use of a Web 2.0 constructivist professional development program for college teachers, Archambault, Wetzel, Foulger and Williams (2010) found that educators felt that the use of Web 2.0 tools in their pedagogy had a positive impact on their ability to give more effective feedback to students. One such example was the use of Google applications with better peer-to-peer feedback opportunities. They also found that because Web 2.0 provided greater access and flexibility, teachers were able to provide much faster and more sustained feedback crucial to students' ongoing learning.

While the integration of Web 2.0 provides educators with many options for improving the authentic and engaging nature of learning, it is also fraught with negative outcomes unless the use of the technology is clearly driven by appropriate pedagogical aims. The following sub-sections will focus on the uses of peer learning since digital environments provide greater flexibility in promoting these activities. Because of their social nature, the majority of Web 2.0 environments inherently use some form of peer learning. The use of feedback in ePortfolios, mobile learning internet videoconferencing, Facebook, wikis/blogs and clickers will be discussed. This will be followed by a comment on feedback through access to resources.

ePortfolios

The use of portfolio-based assessment in higher education settings has grown rapidly in areas such as Arts, Business, Engineering, Teaching, Architecture, Nursing, and Medicine, and can play a valuable role in implementing feedback strategies (Lambert and Corrin, 2007). Advances in digital technologies have allowed ePortfolios (such as PebblePad and Mahara) to be used to promote student reflection, mutual learning, collaboration, peer feedback and the capacity to demonstrate the achievement of identified learning outcomes (Chang, Tseng, Chou and Chen, 2011). Integration of social networking tools such as blogs, wikis and Flickr into ePortfolios can increase students' learning experiences through social learning (Beresford and Cobham, 2010).

Lambert and Corrin (2007) and Tang, Lai, Arthur and Leung (1999) both assert that ePortfolio feedback provides students with rich multi-textured learning opportunities with the capacity to develop high-level cognitive attributes such as reflection, self-discovery, critical thinking, and the application of new knowledge. The benefits of paper-based and online portfolios are well documented. However, there are limitations to both approaches. For example, they are resource-intensive to generate and time-consuming to assess, which has obvious ramifications for large class sizes (Biggs and Tang, 2007). Other challenges include issues surrounding student equity, ownership of the work, and the potential risk of plagiarism (Biggs and Tang, 2007).

ePortfolios are able to provide both formative feedback *for* learning and summative feedback *of* learning (Chen and Chen, 2009). Information collected in the ePortfolio allows students and educators to make appropriate learning adjustments, depending on the form of feedback required. For example, ePortfolios used in capstone courses can be used to inform progress over and between academic semesters. Similarly, teaching staff addressing formative feedback within the portfolio can amend their teaching strategies if required (Chen and Chen, 2009). In this way, the ePortfolio has the capacity to act as the teaching agent in recording the learning processes, progress, attendance, level of peer engagement, and provision for learners to become more self-examining of their learning outcomes.

Mobile Learning and Internet Videoconferencing

Mobile devices are changing rapidly and can now be seamlessly integrated with social software. Mobile learning or m-learning uses portable mobile devices, such as Smartphones, and personal digital assistants (PDAs). These can be used in work-based settings (e.g. while students are on placements in hospitals, clinics, small businesses, community agencies and schools, etc.) and can be used at any time using wireless networks. Mobile learning devices allow teaching staff to provide students with timely feedback and monitor progress remotely, given their networking capabilities (Coulby, Hennessey, Davies and Fuller, 2011). They are now frequently used to provide feedback and summative results. Cochrane (2008) used a qualitative action research method to investigate the use of mobile learning devices within several university courses in landscape design and contemporary music in New Zealand. Using a range of Smartphones (iPhone, Sonyericsson and Nokia) students were required to participate in blogging and ePortfolio development. Findings from this study indicated that 'mobile' students now expected tutor feedback virtually anytime and anywhere. While their feedback demands increased, general findings suggested that the use of Smartphones for blogging activities was quite time-consuming due to the small screens and keypads. In another pilot study using mixed methods, Coulby et al. (2011) investigated final year medical students' ability to perform competency-based assessments via a PDA during their clinical placements in hospitals. Not only did students feel they had clearer learning direction while on placements because of the PDAs, but positive views were held regarding the immediacy and relevance of the feedback provided by peers, preceptors and faculty staff.

Internet videoconferencing (such as Marratech and Elluminate) is another educational application that can be used for synchronous feedback in both f2f and off-campus settings, often overcoming the tyranny of distance that frequently occurs in off-campus, blended courses, or when students undertake professional placements. Placements are recognised as rich learning environments for students as they provide important contextualised learning opportunities, and internet videoconferencing can offer an important link in reducing the theory practice gap and offering formative feedback (Yonge, Myrick and Ferguson, 2011), not easily achievable by traditional means.

This 'merging' of geographic borders by providing education and communication regardless of physical locations is demonstrated in the descriptive study by Waddell, Tronsgard, Smith and Smith (1999), where they successfully offered a short course using case studies to undergraduate nursing students from England and the United States. The integrated use of internet videoconferencing in this study produced high levels of student enthusiasm, improved feedback and learner satisfaction (Waddell et al., 1999).

Facebook

Facebook is the world's most popular social networking service that allows users to generate personal profiles, allowing others to view and add to profile updates. Recently, a number of studies have investigated the use of Facebook for providing feedback. McCarthy (2010) explored the use of Facebook in a blended Architecture program at the University of Adelaide, and found that it provided important and rewarding feedback for students. In particular, Facebook provided a *social connectedness* while, at the same time, freedom for students to generate academic connections with other students, and opportunities to undertake peer critiques. Charlton, Devlin and Drummond (2009) reported another Facebook study involving Engineering students from Newcastle and Durham Universities, where Facebook was used as a medium for student work, submission of assignments and email. Preliminary attitudinal evidence results suggested that Facebook provided positive student satisfaction scores in communication, collaboration and feedback.

An exploratory study by Wang, Woo, Quek, Yang and Liu (2012) examined the use of Facebook in conjunction with a learning management system involving undergraduate and postgraduate Education students in Singapore. Findings indicated that Facebook provided effective communication, collaboration and feedback for students, though several postgraduate students felt that Facebook was not good for formal learning activities. Li and Pitts (2009) explored the use of Facebook as a replacement to traditional student consultations. Academic staff involved in the study offered additional virtual office hours using Facebook, where students could simply log into Facebook and chat synchronously with staff. Overall, the study produced positive results improving students' satisfaction levels, and improved feedback opportunities with academic staff members. Areas for further investigation include possible privacy issues (some universities prohibit staff using Facebook for teaching purposes), cultural barriers and identity management of student/faculty relationships on Facebook.

Wikis

Wikipedia is the best-known example of a wiki (Boulos, Maramba and Wheeler, 2006). Wikis provide a space where information can be created, shared, revised, corrected and updated by anyone at any time through the internet. The key feature of wikis used for educational purposes is that they provide students with the capacity to author a shared document, allowing them to write, edit and rewrite material together. Hence, wikis are now embraced as a means of providing peer-based, collaborative learning opportunities (Parker and Chao, 2007). The collaborative features of wikis provide an environment where the opportunities for social and communal co-construction of knowledge and establishment of a community of practice are facilitated (Su and Beaumont, 2010). This is achieved through direct peer feedback that is an integral part of interaction within the community.

Wikis have been shown to be effective in promoting peer feedback through their capacity to provide cooperative learning opportunities (Xiao and Lucking, 2008). In a quasi-experimental design using a cohort of undergraduate education students, Xiao and Lucking (2008) found that the wiki platform provided a high level of student satisfaction. In addition, the majority of students felt that peer feedback was an important facet of their education, and was also seen as an effective approach in improving their critical thinking and reasoning skills. Su and Beaumont (2010), using a combination of interviews and self-report measures, also found wikis to be effective in promoting student collaboration, peer feedback, quicker feedback and learning confidence. An emergent theme from the study was bi-directional feedback gained though the wiki, in particular constructive feedback on essay formatting, structure, spelling and grammar. An important finding from the peer feedback was that students were able to learn from each other's mistakes, given the community of practice generated in the wiki space.

Blogs

While blogs are basically online diaries, in recent times their use has been extended significantly, providing a useful tool for collaboration, self-reflection and peer feedback (Dippold, 2009). Dippold (2009) examined whether blogs could facilitate better peer feedback among a cohort of students enrolled in

Modern Languages. Qualitative findings suggested that students found the blogs useful in receiving feedback from both faculty and peers, though some issues were raised around the asynchronous nature of blogs and an inability to peer-edit work prior to submission. One solution offered by the author was use of combining wikis with the blog, allowing students to use a wiki first so that students could peer-edit.

Microblogging, a relatively new form of blogging (with Twitter as the best-known example), has attracted significant attention from the popular press, and more recently from educators (Honeycutt and Herring, 2009). Twitter lets users create updates or send messages (tweets) of up to 140 characters that are embedded as widgets on blogs or other websites. Given the limitations of the number of characters, large-scale empirical investigations have yet to be undertaken, though smaller-scale studies have examined the use of Twitter for educational benefits surrounding collaboration and conversation. While no studies have specifically examined Twitter and feedback in an education context, Wright (2010) described the use of Twitter during teaching practicums in New Zealand.

Clickers

Clickers, also referred to as personal response systems or audience response systems, are wireless hand-held devices commonly used in many education sectors. Other forms of student response systems are also now available through mobile technologies (Smartphones, etc.). Wireless clicker technology is one of the most effective tools in providing in-class instantaneous feedback (Bruff, 2009). Other pedagogical advantages include the promotion of students' active participation and engagement in learning tasks, the identification of knowledge gaps and misconceptions, and the provision of immediate feedback to the educator about students' knowledge and progress. Clickers, which can now be substituted by mobile phones, allow educators to collect and disseminate information on student learning quickly, and concurrently with teaching and learning activities. They are effective for undertaking peer learning activities (such as debates) with large class sizes (Stav, Nielsen, Hansen and Thorseth, 2010).

While the majority of studies have yet to show evidence that clickers improve learning, their strengths in providing immediate feedback to both learner and teacher are widely acknowledged (Bruff, 2009). This synchronous feedback offers several key advantages. First, it (in a non-threatening manner) exposes any learning or theoretical misconceptions, thus improving study outcomes and study preparation. Second, it allows teachers to adjust their lecture plans *during* class. This type of responsive adjustment is particularly difficult without educational applications such as clickers. Third, if the clickers are used in other types of formative or summative assessments, their responsiveness in collecting student learning data allows much faster marking turnaround times. Finally, they also provide educators with a better sense of student learning over longer timescales, allowing data mining to uncover potential consistent and common patterns.

Bruff (2009) claims these 'patterns can help instructors better understand what students learn, what they have trouble learning, and even how they learn, useful information for designing subsequent learning experiences' (p. 204). Based on our experiences we would echo these views.

Future application to educational practice and recommendations for use

The above section indicates the enormous potential of digital environments for supporting the effective implementation of feedback practices in university and professional education settings, but also the kinds of challenges that may impede effective application to practice.

It is the affordances of Web 2.0 applications that have markedly expanded opportunities for feedback in the digital environment while correspondingly increasing the practical challenges for educators. In Web 2.0 learning contexts where the interactions of the group are fundamental, there is potential for a learning community to be created which can also extend access to public contributions and feedback to enrich knowledge building by the group. For these environments to work effectively, taking advantage of feedback from within the group requires careful learning design, together with the orientation of students, which necessitates the prior professional development or experience of the educator. It also involves a clear vision of the educator's role and responsibilities in guiding the learning process through the provision of appropriate feedback while not undermining the autonomy of the group of students. While these environments can markedly increase the availability of authentic feedback, the practicalities in implementing them may deter many educators.

A further issue to consider in designing digital environments that involve group interaction to complete authentic learning tasks is that feedback becomes an integral component of the learning task as it is completed; if a solution is not 'working' then other alternatives need to be tried until a successful outcome is achieved, and access to feedback via internet-based resources to help in completing the task can be a fundamental component of the design. In these circumstances, the role of the educator is to implement an effective learning design when preparing the environment, and then be available for advice and support while a task is in progress. The concepts of *designed-in* versus *contingent scaffolding* developed by Hammond and Gibbons (2005) are useful in this context, where feedback may provide scaffolding as part of the design of the learning environment as opposed to contingent feedback which occurs in the moment-to-moment interactions between educator and students. Digital environments markedly improve the practical opportunities for *designed-in* feedback but *contingent feedback* from the educator is still required as part of the overall management of learning.

Ultimately, the extent to which the opportunities for timely, relevant feedback in digital environments can be used depends on the characteristics of the providers and users (educator and students) and the context of use. If educators are not familiar and conversant with designing digital environments, do not have access to appropriate applications and continuing professional development support, or are adversely affected by lack of skill, interest, time, workload, confidence and the need to provide orientation and support for students, then the uptake, integration and application to practice may be limited. However, it is always possible to start with small steps and build on these later.

Conclusion

While the principles of effective feedback are the same irrespective of the context in which it is offered and received, digital learning environments are increasing the ways that feedback can be implemented. As we have indicated, this includes the potential to increase peer feedback within learning communities in group-based environments. It also includes extending feedback sources to the public and to the huge range of resources available on the internet, so that giving and receiving feedback becomes more a democratic process than a hierarchical one. This also helps students to prepare for team-based learning in professional contexts. In addition, the potential that digital environments offer for designed-in feedback, through scenarios and ePortfolios where feedback plays an organic role in task completion, provides further simulated experiences for solving real-world problems.

   One of the key issues for educators in designing feedback in these settings is to manage the learning experience while taking advantage of the opportunities that these environments offer for student ownership and opportunities to participate in a learning community of practice. We have suggested that the extent to which the practical application of these opportunities is possible is dependent on the characteristics of educators and students, and the context of learning, including the support and resources available. Nevertheless, developing digital environments, and the feedback opportunities within them, occurs best as an iterative process, with cycles of feedback from users informing the design, so that simple uses of feedback based on first-generation internet technologies can be extended as experience develops. The next generation of digital technology will bring another evolution of approaches and mechanisms whereby feedback may be provided to or generated by students. While the characteristics of Web 3.0 are still emerging, it appears likely to include a fundamental feedback component as 'audit trail' data is created from the activities of users and delivered back to them based on their browsing history.

References

Anderson, T. and Dron, J. (2011) 'Three generations of distance education pedagogy', *International Review of Research in Open and Distance Learning*, 12(3), 80-97.

Archambault, L., Wetzel, K., Foulger, T. and Williams, M. (2010) 'Professional Development 2.0: Transforming Teacher Education Pedagogy with 21st Century Tools', *Journal of Digital Learning in Teacher Education*, 27(1):4-11.

Benson, R. and Brack, C. (2010) *Online learning and assessment in higher education: A planning guide*, Oxford, UK: Chandos Publishing.

Beresford, W. and Cobham, D. (2010) 'The role of eportfolios in higher education: their perceived value and potential to assist undergraduate computing students', paper presented at the International Conference on Education and New Learning Technologies, Barcelona. http://eprints.lincoln.ac.uk/3871/2/Eportfolios.pdf (accessed 20 June 2012).

Biggs, J. and Tang, C. (2007) *Teaching for Quality Learning at University*, 3rd edn, Berkshire: Open University Press.

Boulos, M., Maramba, I. and Wheeler, S. (2006) 'Wikis, blogs and podcasts: a new generation of Web-based tools for virtual collaborative clinical practice and education', *BMC Medical Education*, 6:41 DOI doi:10.1186/1472-6920-6-41.

Bruff, D. (2009) *Teaching with Classroom Response Systems: Creating Active Learning Environments*, San Francisco, CA: Jossey-Bass.

Chang, C., Tseng, K., Chou, P. and Chen, Y. (2011) 'Reliability and validity of Web-based portfolio peer assessment: A case study for a senior high school's students taking computer science', *Computers and Education*, 57:1306-1316.

Charlton, T., Devlin, M. and Drummond, S. (2009) 'Using Facebook to improve communication in undergraduate software development teams', *Computer Science Education*, 19(4), 273-92.

Chen, C. and Chen, M. (2009) 'Mobile formative assessment tool based on data mining techniques for supporting web-based learning', *Computers and Education*, 52:256-73.

Cochrane, T. (2008) 'Mobile Web 2.0: The new frontier', Paper presented at the ASCILITE Conference, Deakin University, Melbourne. http://web.me.com/thom_cochrane/thom/Research_Outputs/ConferenceProceedings/Ascilite2008.pdf (accessed 20 June 2012).

Coulby, C., Hennessey, S., Davies, N. and Fuller, R. (2011) 'The use of mobile technology for work-based assessment: the student experience', *British Journal of Educational Technology*, 42(2):251-65.

Dippold, D. (2009) 'Peer Feedback Through Blogs: Student and teacher perceptions in an advanced German class', *European Association for Computer Assisted Language Learning*, 21(1):18-36.

Dron, J. (2007) *Control and constraint in e-learning: Choosing when to choose*, Hershey, PA: Information Science Publishing.

Duffy, K. and O'Neill, P. (2003) 'Involving medical students in staff development activities', *Medical Teacher*, 25(2):191-4.

Duffy, T. M. and Jonassen, D. H. (eds) (1992) Constructivism: New implications for instructional technology, Hillsdale, NJ: Lawrence Erlbaum.

Gao, T. and Lehman, J. (2003) 'The effects of different levels of interaction on the achievement and motivational perceptions of college students in a web-based learning environment', *Journal of Interactive Learning Research*, 14(4):367-86.

Grabinger, R. S. (1996) 'Rich environments for active learning', in Jonassen, D. H. (ed.), *Handbook of research for educational communications and technology*, New York: Macmillan.

Gray, K., Thompson, C., Sheard, J., Clerehan, R. and Hamilton, M. (2010) 'Students as Web 2.0 authors: Implications for assessment design and conduct', *Australasian Journal of Educational Technology*, 26(1):105-22.

Hammond, J. and Gibbons, P. F. (2005) 'Putting scaffolding to work', *Prospect*, 20(1):6-30.

Holmes, B. and Gardner, J. (2006) *E-Learning: Concepts and practice*, London: Sage.

Honeycutt, C. and Herring, S. C. (2009) 'Beyond microblogging: conversation and collaboration via Twitter'. *Proceedings of the Forty-Second Hawai'i International Conference on System Sciences (HICSS-42)*. Los Alamitos, CA: IEEE Press.

Howe, N. and Strauss, W. (2000) *Millennials rising: the next generation*, New York: Vintage.

Kennedy, G., Dalgarno, B., Gray, K., Judd, T., Waycott, J., Bennett, S., Maton, K., Krause, K-L., Bishop, A., Chang, R. and Churchward, A. (2007) 'The net generation are not big users of Web 2.0 technologies: Preliminary findings from a large cross-institutional study'. In: Atkinson, R., McBeath, C., Soong, A. and Cheers, C. (eds) *Providing Choices for Learners and Learning: Proceedings of the 24th Annual Conference of the Australasian Society for Computers In Learning In Tertiary Education* (pp. 517-525). Singapore, ASCILITE.

Lambert, S. and Corrin, L. (2007) 'Moving towards a university wide implementation of an ePortfolio tool', *Australasian Journal of Educational Technology*, 23(1):1-16.

Li, L. and Pitts, J. (2009) 'Does it really matter? Using virtual office hours to enhance student-faculty interaction', *Journal of Information Systems Education*, 20(2), 175-85.

McCarthy, J. (2010) 'Blended learning environments: Using social networking sites to enhance the first year experience', *Australasian Journal of Educational Technology*, 26(6), 729-40.

McCrindle, M. (2006) *New generations at work: Attracting, recruiting, retraining & training generation Y*, Bella Vista, NSW: McCrindle Research.

Moore, M. G. (2007) 'The theory of transactional distance' in Moore, M. (ed.), *Handbook of distance education*, 2nd edn, Mahwah, NJ: Lawrence Erlbaum Associates.

Neighbours, C., Lewis, M., Atkins, D., Jensen, M., Walter, T., Fossos, N., Lee, C. M. and Larimer, M. E. (2010) 'Efficacy of web-based personalised normative feedback: a two-year randomized controlled trial', *Journal of Consulting and Clinical Psychology*, 78(6):898-911.

O'Reilly, T. (2005) 'What is Web 2.0: Design patterns and business models for the next generation of software'. Online. Available from <http://www.oreillynet.com/pub/a/oreilly/tim/news/2005/09/30/what-is-web-20.html> (accessed 20 April 2012).

Parker, K. and Chao, J. (2007) 'Wiki as a Teaching Tool', *Interdisciplinary Journal of Knowledge and Learning Objects*, 3:52-72.

Richardson, W. (2009) *Blogs, wikis, podcasts, and other powerful web tools for classrooms*, 2nd edn, Thousand Oaks, CA: Corwin Press.

Siegel, M. A. and Kirkley, S. (1997) 'Moving toward the digital learning environment: The future of web-based instruction', in Khan, B. H. (ed.), *Web-based instruction*, Englewood Cliffs, NJ: Educational Technology Publications, Inc.

Siemens, G. (2005) 'A learning theory for the digital age', *Instructional Technology and Distance Education*, 2(1), 3-10.

Smits, M., Boon, J., Sluijsmans, D. and van Gog, T. (2008) 'Content and timing of feedback in a web-based learning environment: effects on learning as a function of prior knowledge', *Interactive Learning Environments*, 16(2):183-93.

Stav, J., Nielsen, K., Hansen, G. and Thorseth, T. (2010) 'Experiences obtained with integration of student response systems for iPod and iPhone into e-Learning environments', *Electronic Journal of e-Learning*, 8(2):179-90.

Su, F. and Beaumont, C. (2010) 'Evaluating the use of a wiki for collaborative learning', *Innovations in Education and Teaching International*, 47(4):417-31.

Tang, C., Lai, P., Arthur, D. and Leung, S. (1999) 'How do students prepare for traditional and portfolio assessment in a problem-based learning curriculum?', *Themes and variation in PBL*, 1, 206-17.

Vickery, A. and Lake, F. (2005) 'Teaching on the run tips 10: giving feedback', *Medical Journal of Australia*, 183(5), 267-8.

Vygotsky, L. (1978) *Mind in society: The development of higher psychological processes*, Cambridge, MA: Harvard University Press.

Waddell, D., Tronsgard, B., Smith, A. and Smith, G. (1999) 'An Evaluation of International Nursing Education Using Interactive Desktop Video Conferencing', *Computers in Nursing*, 17(4):186-92.

Wang, Q., Woo, H., Quek, C., Yang, Y. and Liu, M. (2012) 'Using the Facebook group as a learning management system: An exploratory study', *British Journal of Educational Technology*, 43(3):428-38

Wenger, E., McDermott, R. and Snyder, W. (2002) *Cultivating communities of practice*, Boston, MA: Harvard Business School Press.

Wright, N. (2010) 'Twittering in teacher education: reflecting on practicum experiences', *Open Learning: The Journal of Open, Distance and e-Learning*, 25(3), 259-65.

Xiao, Y. and Lucking, R. (2008) 'The impact of two types of peer assessment on students' performance and satisfaction within a Wiki environment', *Internet and Higher Education*, 11:186-93.

Yonge, O., Myrick, F. and Ferguson, L. (2011) 'Preceptored Students in Rural Settings Want Feedback', *International Journal of Nursing Education Scholarship*, 8(1). DOI: 10.2202/1548-923X.2047.

Zemke, R., Raines, C. and Filipczak, B. (2000) *Generations at work: managing the clash of Veterans, Boomers, Xers, and Nexters in your workplace*, New York, N.Y: American Management Association.

Chapter 9

Feedback in clinical procedural skills simulations

Debra Nestel
Fernando Bello
Roger Kneebone

Health professionals perform procedures on patients. Traditionally, these procedures have been learned on patients in clinical settings with various levels of supervision. The phrase, '*see one, do one, teach one*' reflects some early approaches to skills training in health professional education. Simulation has advanced the practice of teaching and learning procedural skills, enabling learners to practice on simulators before performing the procedure on a real patient in a clinical setting. It is well documented that learners want more feedback on their performance (Holmboe, 2004; Holmboe et al., 2004; Liberman et al., 2005; Ende 1983).

This chapter focuses on the role of feedback in simulation-based procedural skills training. The chapter has two sections. The first section – *Simulation, procedural skills training and feedback* – outlines current approaches to procedural skills training in medical education and identifies associated challenges. Relevant educational theory is cited and we draw on the discipline of education for further insights into feedback to promote self-regulatory learning.

In the second section we introduce *Patient-Focused Simulations* as a means of addressing some of the limitations with current approaches to procedural skills training, then describe *The Integrated Procedural Performance Instrument (IPPI)* as a case study to illustrate the role of feedback in Patient-Focused Simulations. The IPPI provides learners with an opportunity to practice procedural skills in authentic clinical contexts and to receive multi-source feedback on their performance. The feedback is delivered via the *Imperial College Feedback and Assessment System* (ICFAS). We discuss the benefits and limitations of ICFAS drawing on the content of section one.

Finally, we draw some general conclusions on our experiences of feedback, simulation and learning.

We use the term 'learners' to describe health professionals in training and draw mainly on our experiences with procedural skills training for medical students in the United Kingdom, especially those who have participated in our teaching and research programs at Imperial College London.

Simulation, procedural skills training and feedback

Simulation and training in procedural skills

Simulation is well established as a means of learning procedural skills (Nestel et al., 2011; Cook et al., 2011). Learners can be provided with opportunities to practice psychomotor skills necessary for safe performance of procedures. For example, they may learn steps for giving injections, taking blood, inserting an intravenous drip, inserting a urinary catheter, suturing, etc. (Figure 9.1). Bench top simulator models (sometimes known as simply task trainers) enable learners to acquire these skills through repetitive practice. Learners may (or may not) receive feedback during such training. For the simulators shown in Figure 9.1, feedback would most likely be verbal from a clinical teacher or peer. In the United Kingdom, these types of simulators are available in medical schools and clinical sites in *skills labs*. Most clinical skills programs for medical students offer this type of training (Ker and Bradley, 2010).

A key advantage of simulation is that it allows procedural skills to be practised and assessed outside clinical settings, away from the complexities of actual patient care. However, clinical practice needs to be holistic and patient-centred. Learners must be able to integrate clinical knowledge and skills with professionalism, communication and patient safety (Kneebone and Nestel, 2011; Kneebone et al., 2006a). Fundamental to performing procedural skills are specialized psychomotor tasks and specific knowledge and judgment. The procedural skill as

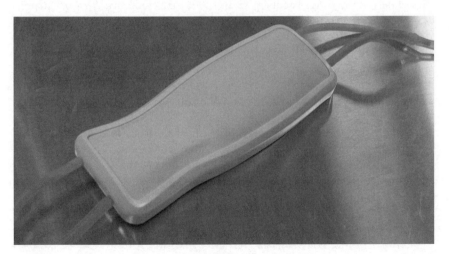

Figure 9.1 Illustrations of procedural skills simulators

performed on real patients is also located in a broader pathway of care, which at minimum commences with the learner explaining the procedure to the patient and obtaining their consent. The task elements of the procedure are conducted, the next steps for care explained to the patient and the procedure documented in the patient's record.

Fragmentation of teaching procedural skills into isolated components can lead to over-emphasis on psychomotor elements of the procedure. Further, feedback to learners on their ability to perform procedural skills is then limited to these psycho-motor elements. Current approaches to assessment in medical education (e.g. the Objective Structured Clinical Examination – OSCE) tend to exacerbate this imbalance (Hodges, 2010; Nestel et al., 2009). Although this approach to reducing complex tasks to components reflects important principles of instructional design (van Merrienboer and Kirschner, 2007), in medical education the interim steps of fitting the components together are often overlooked. That is, the task is rarely incrementally rebuilt into the *whole* as it will be performed in clinical practice.

Simulation and feedback or debriefing

Current literature on feedback in healthcare simulation is growing. A frequently cited review paper by Issenberg et al. (2005) on simulation-based education in healthcare identifies feedback as its most important feature. The paper explores feedback in manikin-based simulations (Figure 9.2). These simulations often focus on supporting learners in recognizing and managing acutely ill patients and support the development of a range of skills – psychomotor, communication, teamwork and clinical decision-making. Issenberg et al. (2005) conclude that *'feedback appears to slow the decay of acquired skills and allows learners to self-assess and monitor their progress toward skill acquisition and maintenance.'* The authors describe different sources of feedback in the papers they reviewed – simulator (built-in) or instructor (verbal or written) generated – and consider the varied timing of feedback from real time to post hoc. Despite the importance attributed to feedback in healthcare simulation, there is surprisingly little published literature (Raemer et al., 2011) on the subject, and even less is empirically based (Arora et al., in press).

In healthcare simulation, a specialist form of feedback is considered – that is, debriefing. Prominent scholars in healthcare simulation, Fanning and Gaba (2007) define debriefing as *'facilitated or guided reflection'* and argue that this *'reflection on an event or activity and subsequent analysis is the cornerstone of the experiential learning experience'* (simulation). The authors write that

> Not everyone is naturally capable of analyzing, making sense, and assimi-lating learning experiences on their own, particularly those included in highly dynamic team-based activities. The attempt to bridge this natural gap between experiencing an event and making sense of it led to the evolution of the concept of post-experience analysis or debriefing.

(Fanning and Gaba, 2007, p. 117)

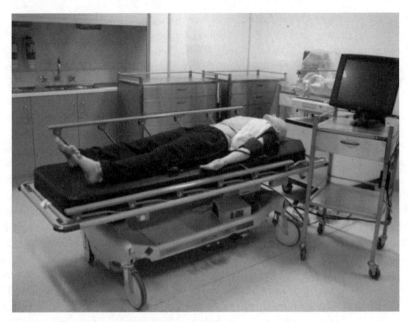

Figure 9.2 Illustration of manikin simulator

Fanning and Gaba (2007) identify structural elements common to debriefing that include considerations for the debriefer/s, learner/s, the experience (simulation), the impact of the simulation, the recollection of what happened, the reporting (sharing reflections on the simulation and learning) and the timing (variable but usually soon after the simulation). The authors describe different models of debriefing, the role of learning objectives in debriefing, the level of involvement of the facilitator, and explore the use of video in debriefing finding mixed evidence for its value. However, they conclude that *'video playback may be useful for adding perspective to a simulation, to allow learners to see how they performed rather than how they thought they performed, and to help reduce hindsight bias in assessment of the scenario'* (p. 122). With advances in technology, audiovisual capture is now highly accessible and, therefore, it expands the repertoire of data teachers have to support feedback processes.

Educational theory underpinning simulation and procedural skills training

There are several accounts of the application of educational theory to clinical education (White and Gruppen, 2010; Mann et al., 2011) and specifically simulation (Kneebone et al., 2004; Kneebone 2009). Elsewhere, Kneebone and Nestel (2010) have described educational theory relevant to procedural skills. It is beyond the scope of this chapter for a detailed review of relevant educational theory. Instead we direct readers to the references above and the original theorists writings. Of particular note are literatures on the development of expertise (Ericsson, 2004, 2005), situated learning and communities of practice (Lave and Wenger, 1991; Wenger, 1998), reflection (Schon, 1983, 1987), experiential learning (Kolb and Fry, 1975), transformative learning (Mezirow, 2000) and instructional design (van Merrienboer and Kirschner, 2007).

In exploring the role of feedback in procedural skills training, the education literature also offers guidance, especially that focusing on the development of self-regulatory learners. Zimmerman refers to self-regulatory learners as those able to self-observe, self-assess and self-react to *performance* outcomes (Zimmerman, 1990). The conceptual analysis of feedback by Hattie and Timperley (2007) provides a model of feedback to enhance learning. Their basic premise is that feedback is intended '*to reduce discrepancies between current understandings and performance and a goal*' (p. 87). They propose that feedback must answer three questions: '*Where am I going? How am I going? Where to next?*' and argue that an important role for teachers is '*to create a learning environment in which students develop self-regulation and error detection skills*' (p. 88). They describe feedback at four levels – task, process, self-regulation and self – with feedback at the *process* and *self-regulation* levels the most powerful. However, their work was located in school-level education and appeared to focus on knowledge acquisition. Often the tasks were assessment-oriented rather than skills that would be practiced in the workplace. We posit that feedback at the task level in procedural skills may have more power than that attributed by these authors.

We also consider the work of Nicol and Macfarlane-Dick (2006) on formative assessment and self-regulated learning. Derived from their synthesis of the literature in higher education, they propose seven principles of feedback practice that support self-regulation (Box 9.1). In medical education, White and Gruppen (2011) have reported the importance of self-regulated learning. However, they describe an overemphasis in curricula on self-assessment with few opportunities for learners to adjust their perceptions, a critical component of Nicol and Macfarlane-Dick's practice (2006). White and Gruppen (2010) propose a four-phased model for self-regulation – *planning, learning, assessment and adjustment*. In the assessment phase they consider the roles of self-assessment and external feedback for learning.

Box 9.1 Feedback principles that support and develop self-regulation (Nicol & Macfarlane-Dick, 2006)

1 Clarify what good performance is
2 Facilitate self-assessment
3 Deliver high quality feedback information
4 Encourage teacher and peer dialogue
5 Encourage positive motivation and self-esteem
6 Provide opportunities to close the gap
7 Use feedback to improve teaching

With these many approaches to feedback (and debriefing) we have distilled features relevant to simulation-based education in healthcare (Box 9.2). Pre-simulation (briefing) is important to prepare learners for feedback by explaining the process. Where possible, learners are encouraged to reflect on their experience with the procedure, to explore their feelings about the procedure and the simulation (acknowledging that simulations are sometimes stressful), to discuss perceptions of likely challenges and strategies for managing them, and to explore the learner's goals for the procedure (and the simulation). Finally, we invite the learner to identify if there is anything they would like observed during their simulation.

Box 9.2 Feedback principles for procedural skills simulations

Pre-simulation
1 Prepare learner/s for feedback by explaining the process
2 Identify learner/s experience with procedure
3 Explore learner/s feelings about the procedure and the simulation
4 Discuss likely challenges and strategies for managing the procedure
5 Explore learner/s goals for the procedure (and the simulation)
6 Explore requests from learners for observers to note

Post-simulation
1 Remind learner/s of the feedback process
2 Invite learner/s reaction (verbal/written) and include expression of feelings
3 Affirm elements of learner/s performance that met/exceeded expectation (be selective)
4 Identify elements of performance that were borderline or did not meet expectations – especially unsafe practices (be selective)
5 Review challenges from pre-simulation discussion
6 Encourage teacher/s (clinicians/SPs) and learner/s dialogue (in present/in future) to:
   • Re-evaluate learner/s goals
   • Maintain learner/s performance
   • Explore learner/s understanding of their performance
   • Develop strategies to improve performance
7 Provide opportunities to practice strategies to improve performance (in simulation and in clinical settings)

While post-simulation, we remind learners of the process for feedback, invite learners' reactions verbally and/or in written formats, and affirm elements of the learner's performance that met or exceeded expectations. It is important that these be articulated clearly so the learner is aware that their performance is effective and should be maintained. Obviously, not everything can be identified because this may simply be too much information. Key items should be noted. Additionally, we identify elements of performance that were borderline or did not meet expectations, especially unsafe practices. We encourage dialogue between teacher (or clinician assessors) and learner to assist in maintaining performance, to explore the learner's understanding of their performance, and to develop strategies to improve performance. Finally, we provide opportunities to practice strategies to improve performance in simulation and in clinical settings.

We now outline our work in attempting to recreate the holistic nature of clinical practice through innovative approaches to simulation.

Patient-focused simulations

Patient-focused simulations are a means of addressing the fragmentary approach to using bench top models for procedural skills training. Patient-focused simulation consists of scenarios in which a simulated patient is *seamlessly* aligned with a bench top model. That is, we combine the bench top models illustrated in Figure 9.1 with a real person (Kneebone et al., 2002, 2006a, 2007) (Figure 9.3 – photos of hybrid simulations). The simulated patient is trained to portray a real patient. This *blended* or *hybrid* approach combines the safety of simulation with the authenticity and unpredictability of a real human encounter. Scenarios are designed to enable learners to explain each procedure to the patient, prepare for the procedure, perform it and then document the activity. Scenarios include a range of patient behaviours, and the level of challenge can be adjusted to reflect the experience of the learner. It is important for learners to practice (and be assessed) in the context in which the procedural skill will be used. This approach to simulation is underpinned by situated or contextualized learning theory (Lave and Wenger, 1991; Wenger, 1998). That is, learners learn in an environment that reflects the physical, psychological and social fidelity of real work settings. Patient-focused simulation provides an interim step between learning on bench top models and before performing procedures on real patients. However, patient-focused simulation can also be used to address more complex procedural skills challenges once the learner has gained experience in real clinical settings.

A feature of patient-focused simulation is the audiovisual capture of the scenario. Clinical assessors and other learners are able to observe the learner in the scenario remotely via a television monitor rather than being in the scenario room. Kneebone and Nestel (2005) describe a model for feedback in patient-focused simulation that invests heavily in preparing the learner for learning before participating in a scenario and receiving feedback from expert observers, simulated patients and peers. The feedback process is augmented by video review. Working in small groups of about six, learners are briefed on the

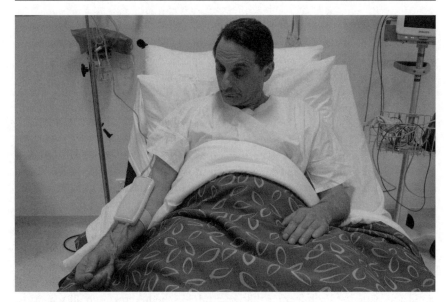

Figure 9.3 Illustration of a hybrid simulation

scenario (task and simulated patient characteristics) according to the principles set out in Box 9.2. The learners are asked about their prior experiences with performing the procedure and with managing the patient's character-istics, exploring learners' anticipated challenges, strengths and goals for the encounter. In addition, learners are asked about their feelings, since simulation can be anxiety-provoking and therefore influence performance. The process for feedback is explained and, where necessary, oriented to the simulator model. Based on this information and the broader curriculum goals, the expert observers and peers identify foci for their observations.

During the feedback process, the learner is first given an opportunity to describe their thoughts and feelings about their performance. The expert observers and peers share their observations based on the preparatory discussion. The simulated patient offers a patient perspective on the encounter. Exchanges of views between all those present are encouraged. Video review provides an oppor-tunity for the learners to see themselves as others did and affirms or prompts further discussion. Key elements of the exchange are summarized and considered with respect to taking the learning into the workplace and ways in which further skills development might occur. The design of the session addresses many of the principles for feedback outlined earlier together with mechanisms for promoting self-regulatory learning. In the example above, the teacher facilitates and engages all learners and the simulated patient in the learning process. In the next section we shift the locus of control for learning from the small group to the individual.

Integrated Procedural Performance Instrument (IPPI)

In this case study we use our experience of a specific application of patient-focused simulation to consider alternative approaches to feedback. The IPPI concept and variations have been reported elsewhere (Kneebone et al., 2006b, 2008b; Nestel et al., 2009; LeBlanc et al., 2009; Moulton et al., 2009; Kneebone and Nestel, 2011). In summary, the IPPI consists of eight ten-minute scenarios built around the clinical procedures expected of new medical graduates and set out in *Tomorrow's Doctors* (General Medical Council 2003) (Box 9.3). In the IPPI, each procedure is performed as part of a clinical scenario, which specifies the patient's role and what the learner (junior doctor) is required to do. Each patient role is played by a simulated patient and designed to reflect situations which junior doctors might be expected to manage in real clinical settings. Alongside the procedural task are specific challenges relating to communication, patient safety and professionalism. These challenges include patients who are distressed, hostile, visually or aurally impaired, have no shared language with the learner or are accompanied by an anxious relative. As in patient-focused simulation, the procedures themselves are performed on models aligned with simulated patients. Each learner follows a timed schedule through all scenarios. Encounters are recorded using webcams and microphones. There is no observer in the scenario room. Instead, the clinician assessor observes the scenario remotely via a computer.

Box 9.3 Examples of clinical procedures in the IPPI scenarios

1 Insert a urinary catheter
2 Take blood from an arm
3 Insert an intravenous cannula and set up infusion
4 Measure peak flow and perform spirometry
5 Administer nebulised drug
6 Administer oxygen at a specified concentration
7 Performa an electrocardiogram and interpret findings
8 Give a subcutaneous injection of insulin and instruct patient in technique

Feedback is a key part of the IPPI, acting as a focus for learner reflection, discussion or remediation. In planning our feedback and assessment system (ICFAS) we had several aims aligned to the principles in Box 9.2. We had a particular focus on wanting our learners to be provided with multiple independent judgments from different perspectives (clinical assessor and simulated patients). We needed to provide learners with a benchmark for safe and competent practice and to promote excellence. We also wanted to shift the locus of control over learning to the learner, allowing the learner (not the teacher) to decide when, what, how often and with whom they review their feedback. The next paragraphs describe elements of the ICFAS, including the feedback data, the rating form, the web pages, training for clinical assessors and simulated patients and, finally, technical elements of the process.

Feedback data

Clinical assessors

Clinician assessors use an on-screen rating form with drop-down pick lists and space for free text comments. Assessors may work in real time using computers within a dedicated assessor station at the same location as the scenarios. Alternatively, assessors can work remotely, from their home or clinical practice, accessing and rating scenario recordings at their convenience via the web (Nestel et al., 2008; Kneebone et al., 2008a; Akhtar et al., in review).

Simulated patients

Simulated patients rate learners' ability to address the patient's needs during each procedure, using a wireless handheld computer with drop-down pick lists to complete a global rating after the scenario. Each simulated patient also provides one minute of structured spoken feedback to the camera, after the learner has left the scenario room. This provides a brief but personal summary of key points from the patient's perspective, together with guidance on areas for development.

Learners

Learners assess their own performance after each encounter, using wireless handheld computers.

Rating form

For each IPPI scenario, assessors, simulated patients and learners complete a rating form similar to that used in the Foundation Programme for junior doctors in the United Kingdom for the Direct Observation of Procedural Skills (DOPS) workplace based assessments (Foundation Programme, 2012). Aligning these rating forms is intended to help learners transfer learning between settings. Ratings of competence are made for eleven categories, each requiring a judgment on a 6-point scale, where '4' represents the standard expected of a safe, competent practitioner (Box 9.4). Drop-down boxes allow each field to be rated on-screen. Assessors are encouraged to enter free text comments using the keyboard, commenting on strengths and areas for development. Simulated patients and learners have access to the form on a wireless handheld computer. Simulated patients have an additional six items to rate that explore their satisfaction with 'patient-centredness' (Box 9.5).

Box 9.4 Items on the rating form rated by clinical assessors, simulated patients and trainees

1 Introduction/establish rappor
2 Explanation of intervention including patient's consent to proceed
3 Assessment of patient's needs before procedure
4 Preparation for procedure
5 Technical performance of procedure
6 Maintenance of asepsis
7 Awareness of patient's needs during procedure
8 Closure of the procedure including explanation of follow-up care
9 Clinical safety
10 Professionalism
11 Overall ability to perform the procedure (including technical and professional skills)

Box 9.5 Items on patient-centredness rated by simulated patients for satisfaction from 1 (not at all satisfied) to 6 (completely satisfied)

1 Facilitates patient's expression of concerns
2 Seeks patient's specific requests
3 Identifies and acknowledges patient's feelings
4 Provides information throughout the interaction
5 Treats patient as an individual and with respect
6 Communicates sensitively throughout

Feedback web pages

Soon after an IPPI session, each learner receives by email a password and a link to the secure website which provides a composite graphical summary from three perspectives (the assessor's, the patient's and the learner's own) (Figure 9.4). Further levels of detail provide numerical scores for each element of each scenario, and written feedback where relevant (Figure 9.5). Crucially, learners can access the video recordings of their own performances, including the spoken feedback by simulated patients. In this way, learners can review and reflect on their procedural skills practice in the light of feedback. The web design allows

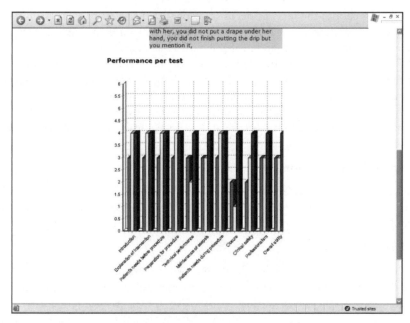

Figure 9.4 Illustration of summarized ICFAS data for one participant with red yellow and blue bars representing self, patient and assessor perspectives for one procedure

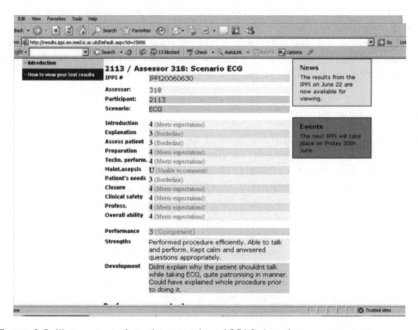

Figure 9.5 Illustration of single procedure ICFAS data for one participant

learners to choose the level of detail of feedback and when they access it. This means that the learner receives feedback from eight different clinical assessors (one per scenario) – a rich and probably rare experience.

The IPPI feedback is detailed and confidential and may be accessed by the learner alone or moderated by a clinical supervisor/teacher. The ICFAS integrates multiple assessments, using a content management program (Librios CMS www.librios.com). Feedback data is provided over the web via password protected login access, so it is secure and accessible from any online computer.

Feedback training for IPPI

The complexity of the feedback process meant that training was essential. We are confident that the attention to this training supported clinical assessors and simulated patients, raising the importance of feedback in the learning process.

Clinical assessors

Training for clinical assessors is online and consists of orientation to the concept of the IPPI and to using ICFAS. Assessors practise logging into the website, identifying their workflow (the scenarios they are asked to assess), navigating scenarios and using the rating form. They are provided with sample scenarios for practice ratings and to assist in calibration of judgments. Assessors are provided with guidance on writing free text comments to learners. They are encouraged to use the free text to justify ratings, to affirm excellent performance, to identify unsafe practice, to prompt learner reflection and to suggest ways to improve. Assessors review examples of free text comments and consider the consequences for the learner of ambiguous statements. Clarity is essential since there is no opportunity for discussion between the assessor and the learner. Assessors are asked to view just one type of procedural skill in each IPPI session, enabling them to calibrate performance across several learners.

Simulated patients

Simulated patients participate in training for role-play and feedback. The initial feedback training session takes approximately three hours and simulated patients are reminded about the feedback process immediately prior to each IPPI session. Simulated patients are oriented to the IPPI concept and handheld computer-based ratings. They are provided with an opportunity to calibrate ratings by observing recorded scenarios and speak directly to the camera for up to 90 seconds after completing their rating form (Box 9.6). These videos are made available to learners as part of their feedback. This spoken feedback complements the free text comments from the clinical assessors. Significant skill is required in articulating critical feedback. Spoken feedback must be precise, balanced (strengths and weaknesses), use carefully chosen language (unambiguous), be honest and focus on the simulated patient's experience of the learner as a professional. Simulated patients are given the opportunity to rehearse verbal feedback they would provide to a learner based on an observed recorded scenario (as they used for ratings). Simulated patients are reminded that clinicians will provide feedback on psychomotor elements of the tasks. However, there are elements of psychomotor techniques that patients can feedback such as the loss of their confidence in response to the learner who appears disorganized, clumsy or unhygienic in handling equipment or the simulated patient.

Box 9.6 Example of spoken feedback from simulated patient to trainee (via camera)

"Thanks for that. I am sorry I don't remember your name even though I know you told me when you came in... I thought you did well overall. The things that you did that were helpful for me are: Firstly, using my name at the beginning of the scenario and then again at the end – it felt like I was a person and not just another patient to you; Second, asking me what I already knew about the procedure – I think it meant we were more efficient together; and Third, shaking my hand when you left – again, it just felt personal. Things I would have liked you to have done are: Firstly, speak a little slower and more clearly at the beginning – your talking seemed rushed and I think I missed important information (like your name); Second, when you were having trouble getting your gloves on you let your frustration show – I was losing confidence fast – I was thinking that if you couldn't get your gloves on, I don't really want you sticking things in me. If you'd just said something like, 'The gloves stick when your hands are wet' or something like that I might have been reassured; and Third, you seemed to just run out of the room when it was over. That was odd since you had given me so much time at the beginning (even though you spoke really quickly), I would only have expected a few seconds but you were off. I hope you take some time to watch the video and think about these points. It might be helpful to think about how you were feeling when you did the things I have given you feedback about."

Technical aspects of Imperial College Feedback and Assessment System (ICFAS)

The ICFAS uses wireless networked cameras, standard computer equipment and database facilities, and a proprietary content management software system (Librios) modified for this purpose. ICFAS offers a unique integrated infrastructure for observing and recording multiple encounters, assessing them in real time from several simultaneous perspectives, integrating disparate data streams, and presenting them in a structured format for secure web access within 24 hours of the session.

Benefits and limitations of the ICFAS in the IPPI

The IPPI is an application of Patient Focused Simulation that offers a detailed, safe and patient-centred means to sample and document learners' practices across multiple procedures. A major strength of the IPPI is that it promotes engagement of all facets of performance – psychomotor, clinical judgment, communication and professionalism – in several procedures and in a timely fashion. Importantly, the IPPI forms part of a spectrum of educational activities to support learners in developing safe and competent practice in procedural skills.

The feedback process, ICFAS, serves as a prompt for learners to self-regulate their learning, shifting the locus of control for learning back to them. It offers multiple, independent judgments from different perspectives (clinician, simulated patient) combined to provide rich and layered feedback in several formats (bar charts, free text, spoken feedback, audiovisual review) that is accessible when the learner chooses to review it rather than at the convenience of the providers.

During our various IPPI trials, learners were provided with a benchmark for safe and competent performance. By using the same rating form, the collated results (clinical assessors, simulated patients and learners) offered deep insights into performance, helping learners to develop self-awareness. Free text from clinical assessors and spoken feedback from simulated patients was intended to help learners make sense of global ratings, to signal key elements of performance (including both excellent and unsafe practice), to identify what and how the learner might improve, and to make links with clinical practice. Feedback was sometimes phrased as a question prompting reflection on process and self.

Numerical performance data was valued by trial participants who requested either an additional layer of feedback, their cohort result or normative assessment. This would permit individual participants to see how they performed in comparison to their peers. Learners also requested an alert system in which unsafe practice was flagged immediately after logging into ICFAS to access their results. Feedback on task was seen as important as feedback on process and self-regulation for all participants. Learners often reported that they had never seen themselves performing a procedural skill, placing great value on the video clips, which goes some way to promoting self-regulation as described by Zimmerman (1990) in relation to self-observation.

The IPPI scenarios were designed to align with their broader curriculum and learners were encouraged to consider their performance in this light. Finally, in real clinical settings, patients are often compromised in their ability to give honest feedback to learners and so patient perspectives are frequently overlooked. The feedback from simulated patients ensured that patient perspectives received the same importance as that of clinical assessors.

There are several limitations to the IPPI and ICFAS approach to feedback. Although in the briefing learners were asked about their goals in each scenario, our design did not permit sharing of this information with the clinical assessors or simulated patients. Consequently, feedback from assessors may not align with learners' perceived needs or expectations. Some learners may have chosen not to access the feedback at all. Additionally, learners may access feedback but not act on it. Unsafe practice may persist. Learners may also misunderstand feedback. Although we encouraged learners to contact us if they had concerns, we cannot be certain that no contact meant no concerns.

So, together the IPPI and ICFAS provide an innovative approach to complement other approaches to learning procedural skills. It offers learners rich ingredients to support the development of self-regulatory learning.

Concluding remarks

In this chapter we have outlined the role of simulation in procedural skills training. We have drawn on the literature from healthcare simulation and the broader discipline of education. We distilled principles for feedback relevant to simulation-based learning of procedural skills. We presented patient-focused simulation and IPPI as a means to address some of the challenges associated with the fragmentary approach to procedural skills training and argued that IPPI is best seen as part of a broader curriculum/spectrum of learning activities, while ICFAS serves as a prompt for learners to self-regulate their learning.

Overall, we believe the IPPI and the ICFAS provide a rich and multifaceted learning experience, which resonates with clinical practice, mirrors the problems of real professional life, yet provides learners with a means to observe themselves as others see them. The IPPI and ICFAS approach is designed to return the locus of control over feedback to the learner so that self-regulatory learning can occur.

References

Akhtar, K., Bello, F., Granados, A., Kneebone, R. and Nestel D (in review) 'Real time and retrospective "remote" assessment of procedural skills: An evaluation of assessor perspectives', *Medical Teacher*.

Arora, S., Ahmed, M., Paige, J., Runnacles, J., Hull, L., Darzi, A. and Sevdalis, N. (in press) 'Objective Structured Assessment of Debriefing (OSAD): Bringing Science to the Art of Debriefing in Surgery', *Annals of Surgery*.

Cook, D. A., Hatala, R., Brydges, R., Zendejas, B., Szostek, J. H., Wang, A. T., Erwin, P. J. and Hamstra, S. J. (2011) 'Technology-enhanced simulation for health professions education: a systematic review and meta-analysis', *JAMA : the journal of the American Medical Association*, 306(9):978-88.

Ende, J. (1983) 'Feedback in clinical medical education', *JAMA*, 250(6):777-81.

Ericsson, K. (2004) 'Deliberate practice and the acquisition and maintenance of expert performance in medicine and related domains', *Academic Medicine*, 79(10):S70.

Ericsson, K. (2005) 'Recent advances in expertise research: A commentary on the contributions to the special issue', *Applied Cognitive Psychology*, 19:233-41.

Fanning, R. M. and Gaba, D. M. (2007) 'The role of debriefing in simulation-based learning', *Simulation in healthcare: journal of the Society for Simulation in Healthcare*, 2(2):115-25.

Foundation Programme (2012) Online. Available at: http://www.foundation programme.nhs.uk/pages/home (viewed June 2012).

General Medical Council (2003) *Tomorrow's Doctors*, London: General Medical Council.

Hattie, J. and Timperley, H. (2007) 'The power of feedback', *Review of Educational Research*, 77(1):81-112.

Hodges, B. (2010) *The Objective Structured Clinical Examination*, Koln: LAP Lambert Academic Publishing.

Holmboe, E. S. (2004) 'Faculty and the observation of trainees' clinical skills: problems and opportunities', *Academic Medicine*, 79(1):16-22.

Holmboe, E. S., Yepes, M., Williams, F. and Huot, S. J. (2004) 'Feedback and the mini clinical evaluation exercise', *Journal of General Internal Medicine*, 19(5 Pt 2):558-61.

Issenberg, S. B., McGaghie, W. C., Petrusa, E. R., Lee Gordon, D. and Scalese, R. J. (2005) 'Features and uses of high-fidelity medical simulations that lead to effective learning: a BEME systematic review', *Medical Teacher*, 27(1):10-28.

Ker, J. and Bradley, P. (2010) 'Simulation in medical education', in Swanwick, T (ed.), *Understanding Medical Education: Evidence, Theory and Practice*, Chichester: Wiley-Blackwell.

Kneebone, R. (2009) 'Perspective: Simulation and transformational change: the paradox of expertise', *Academic Medicine*, 84(7):954-7.

Kneebone, R., Bello, F., Nestel, D., Mooney, N., Codling, A., Yadollahi, F., Tierney, T., Wilcockson, D. and Darzi, A. (2008a) 'Learner-centred feedback using remote assessment of clinical procedures', *Medical Teacher*, 30:795-801.

Kneebone, R., Kidd, J., Nestel, D., Asvall, S., Paraskeva, P. and Darzi, A. (2002) 'An innovative model for teaching and learning clinical procedures', *Medical Education*, 36(7):628-34.

Kneebone, R. and Nestel, D. (2005) 'Learning clinical skills – the place of simulation and feedback', *The Clinical Teacher*, 2(2):86-90.

Kneebone, R. and Nestel D (2011) 'Learning and teaching clinical procedures', in Dornan, T., Mann, K., Scherpbier, A. and Spencer, J. (eds), *Medical Education: Theory and Practice*, Edinburgh: Churchill Livingstone Elsevier.

Kneebone, R., Nestel, D., Bello, F. and Darzi, A. (2008b) 'An Integrated Procedural Performance Instrument (IPPI) for learning and assessing procedural skills', *The Clinical Teacher*, 5:45-8.

Kneebone, R., Nestel, D., Vincent, C. and Darzi, A. (2007) 'Complexity, risk and simulation in learning procedural skills', *Medical Education*, 41(8):808-14.

Kneebone, R., Nestel, D., Wetzel, C., Black, S., Jacklin, R., Aggarwal, R., Yadollahi, F., Wolfe, J., Vincent, C. and Darzi, A. (2006a) 'The human face of simulation: patient-focused simulation training', *Academic Medicine*, 81(10):919-24.

Kneebone, R., Nestel, D., Yadollahi, F., Brown, R., Nolan, C., Durack, J., Brenton, H., Moulton, C., Archer, J. and Darzi, A. (2006b) 'Assessing procedural skills in context: Exploring the feasibility of an Integrated Procedural Performance Instrument (IPPI)', *Medical Education*, 40(11):1105-14.

Kneebone, R., Scott, W., Darzi, A. and Horrocks, M. (2004) 'Simulation and clinical practice: strengthening the relationship', *Medical Education*, 38(10):1095-1102.

Kolb, D. and Fry, R. (1975) 'Toward an applied theory of experiential learning', in Cooper, C. (ed.), *Theories of Group Process*, London: John Wiley.

Lave, J. and Wenger, E. (1991) *Situated Learning: Legitimate Peripheral Participation*, Cambridge: Cambridge University Press.

LeBlanc, V. R., Tabak, D., Kneebone, R., Nestel, D., MacRae, H. and Moulton, C-A. (2009) 'Psychometric properties of an integrated assessment of technical and communication skills', *American Journal of Surgery*, 197(1):96-101.

Liberman, S., Liberman, M., Steinert, Y., McLeod, P. and Meterissian, S. (2005) 'Surgery residents and attending surgeons have different perceptions of feedback', *Medical Teacher*, 27(5):470-2.

Mann, K., Dornan, T. and Teunissen, P. (2011) 'Perspectives on learning', in Dornan, T., Mann, K., Scherpbier, A. and Spencer, J. (eds), *Medical Education: Theory and Practice*, Edinburgh: Churchill Livingstone Elsevier.

Mezirow, J. (2000) *Learning as Transformation: Critical Perspectives on a Theory in Progress*, New York: John Wiley.

Moulton, C-A., Tabak, D., Kneebone, R., Nestel, D., MacRae, H. and LeBlanc, V. R. (2009) 'Teaching communication skills using the integrated procedural performance instrument (IPPI): a randomized controlled trial', *American Journal of Surgery*, 197(1):113-18.

Nestel, D., Bello, F., Kneebone, R. and Darzi, A. (2008) 'Remote assessment and learner-centred feedback using the Imperial College Feedback and Assessment System (ICFAS)', *The Clinical Teacher*, 5:88-92.

Nestel, D., Groom, J., Eikeland-Husebo, S. and O'Donnell, J. M. (2011) 'Simulation for learning and teaching procedural skills: the state of the science', *Simulation in Healthcare*, 6 Suppl:S10-13.

Nestel, D., Kneebone, R., Nolan, C., Akhtar, K., Darzi, A. (2009) 'Formative assessment of procedural skills: Students' responses to the Objective Structured Clinical Examination and the Integrated Performance Procedural Instrument', *Assessment and Evaluation in Higher Education*, 34:1-13.

Nicol, D. and Macfarlane-Dick, D. (2006) 'Formative assessment and self-regulated learning: a model and seven principles of good feedback practice', *Studies in Higher Education*, 31(2):199-218.

Raemer, D., Anderson, M., Cheng, A., Fanning, R., Nadkarni, V. and Savoldelli, G. (2011) 'Research regarding debriefing as part of the learning process', *Simulation in Healthcare*, 6(7):S52-S57.

Schon, D. (1983) *The Reflective Practitioner: How Professionals Think in Action*, London: Temple Smith.

Schon, D. (1987) *Educating the Reflective Practitioner*, San Francisco: Jossey-Bass.

van Merrienboer, J. and Kirschner, P. (2007) *Ten Steps to Complex Learning: A Systematic Approach to Four Component Instructional Design*, New Jersey: Lawrence Erlbaum Associates.

Wenger, E. (1998) *Communities of Practice: Learning, Meaning and Identity*, Cambridge: Cambridge University Press.

White, C. and Gruppen, L. (2010) 'Self-regulated learning in medical education' in Swanwick, T. (ed.), *Understanding Medical Education: Evidence, Theory and Practice*, Chichester: John Wiley & Sons.

Zimmerman, B. (1990) 'Self-regulated learning and academic achievement: An overview', *Educational Psychologist*, 25:3-17.

Chapter 10

Implementing multisource feedback

Jocelyn Lockyer
Joan Sargeant

The general purpose of multisource feedback (MSF) is to collect data about an individual's performance from those working with the person being assessed in order to guide their learning and improvement. Data are compiled and presented to the person in aggregate form, often with comparator data. Individuals can then use the data to direct learning, obtain additional feedback and create a learning plan for improvement. MSF is also known as 360-degree assessment, multi-rater appraisal and full circle appraisal.

MSF has been used in a many different settings. It originated and is still commonly used in business and industry, particularly to assess managers and leaders (Lepsinger and Lucia, 2009). In business applications, questionnaires obtain feedback about an individual from peers, direct reports, supervisors, and occasionally clients. It is increasingly being used in health care, especially to assess physicians in practice and in training (Lockyer and Clyman, 2008). In medical settings, the raters may include medical colleagues, non-medical co-workers (i.e. nurses, pharmacists and psychologists), and patients. The person often completes a self-assessment questionnaire as part of the assessment. It has a place in higher education to assess academics whose respondents might include students, mentors, managers, and peers. In these settings, observable behaviors that tap into skill, knowledge, and style are assessed (Berk, 2009).

Items on surveys query observable behaviors which people can change. Thus skills like written and oral communication skills, teamwork, interpersonal skills, professionalism, and collegial interaction are usually part of survey instruments. These domains are not easily assessed by more traditional approaches yet these are the ones found critical to success in business and the professions. While MSF is more commonly used in North America and the UK, it is being adopted worldwide in industry (Brutus et al., 2006).

The specific goals of MSF may vary but the overall intent is usually developmental. MSF provides feedback about performance to enable people see the gaps in their performance (related to observable and changeable behaviors) and, in response, to learn and change. MSF is consistent with views of quality improvement; participants receive data about themselves that will enable them to improve their workplace performance. Goals may include ensuring that critical behaviors in the individual are developed, evaluated, and reinforced. In cases where an organization is changing, MSF may be designed to help achieve organizational strategies by clarifying the behaviors that individuals must meet (Lepsinger and Lucia, 2009).

However, implementing MSF is complex. Successful implementation requires that attention be paid to the organization, the questionnaires, and the approach taken to delivering feedback and follow-up. The chapter discusses each of these components and presents recommendations for successful implementation, monitoring, and evaluation of MSF programs.

Best practices and key decisions when introducing MSF into workplace

Not all contexts are suitable for the use of MSF. There are four features that characterize the organizational requirements for it to operate successfully. There are parallel features to be considered in predominantly educational contexts. These features are: organizational readiness, the culture and values of the context, the need for leadership, and the importance of MSF adding value.

Organizational readiness

Organizational readiness is key to the successful introduction of MSF. Significant resources, both human and information technology (IT), are required for successful implementation and sustainability.

Culture and values of the organization

There is an optimal environment for implementing an MSF program. The reasons for introducing this type of feedback must be aligned with the organization's needs. MSF must assess behaviors critical to the organization's success (e.g. working collaboratively, communicating essential information). Feedback from colleagues and others must be valued. It is often implemented when the direct supervisor is not able to observe and evaluate critical aspects of performance. People have to trust the system to provide useful data and protect their anonymity before they commit to rate peers and supervisors or be evaluated themselves (Fleenor and Taylor, 2008; Lockyer and Clyman 2008; Lepsinger and Lucia, 2009).

Leadership

Leadership must support an MSF program philosophically and with resources. Funding along with redeployment of people to guide, monitor, and ensure communication with all stakeholders is needed. Tasks include finding or developing questionnaires, implementing the program, creating the feedback system, and ensuring that the educational resources are in place to support individuals as they develop their learning plans.

Value-added

MSF must add value to an organization. Given that most organizations will have appraisal and feedback systems in place, it is important to determine the role that MSF will play. It may replace current systems or supplement them.

Key decisions

Several key decisions are required when considering an MSF system:

Formative or summative

Determining whether MSF is formative or summative needs to be made early and without ambiguity as participants may respond differently based on the program's purpose. In formative systems, the goal is quality improvement and the stakes are low. People are encouraged to use the data for self-reflection and change, often with the assistance of another person. When MSF is summative, progress may be monitored and decisions such as appointments and promotion may result. Using MSF for summative purposes requires more rigor.

Domains, constructs, and competencies

Questionnaires can assess a variety of competencies. It is important to select key areas that will be examined and ensure these are in alignment with organizational goals. For example, in private industry where teamwork is critical to an organization's success, team-based behaviors and communication skills may be emphasized. In medicine, British physicians are likely to receive feedback about their attention to core duties: good clinical care, teaching and training, relationships with patients, working with colleagues, probity, and physician health (Campbell et al., 2008; Archer et al., 2006). In higher education, a professor may be assessed on questioning skills and rapport with students (Berk, 2009).

Source of the instruments

Some organizations develop their own questionnaires. Others will work with other organizations that have created MSF systems. Considerable work is required to develop and psychometrically test instruments to ensure that the scores demonstrate evidence of reliability and validity. When instruments are purchased, they need careful scrutiny to ensure the program is a good fit for the organization and its goals and values. Due diligence requires a careful examination of the instruments (items and rating scales), technical manuals, and feedback reports. Information about the evidence for the instrument's reliability, validity, and use in different geographic and workplace settings should be requested (Fleenor and Taylor, 2008; Lepsinger and Lucia, 2009).

Assessors

Determining the raters is important. In some MSF systems, the feedback recipient determines who will be asked to respond. In others, a combination of assessee and supervisor make the decision, or the supervisor makes the decision (Brutus et al., 2006). In medicine, the person is most likely to select their own raters as early research showed that ratings differed little based on whether the individual selected their assessors or assessors were assigned (Ramsey et al., 1993) – although that has been challenged more recently in work involving physicians who were referred for assessment following complaints about performance (Archer and McAvoy, 2011). Nonetheless, at a practical level, it is often difficult for anyone other than the person being assessed to determine the people most able to answer the questions. The numbers of assessors required needs consideration. Too few assessors may mean that the data inferences are not reliable (stable). Too many assessors may mean respondents are being asked to rate people whom they haven't closely worked with and observed.

Data access

It is important to determine who will have access to the data. Reports may go only to the person being assessed, or to both the person and their supervisor. Sometimes, someone who is not a supervisor (e.g. mentor, or someone in Human Resources) receives the data. This can vary by country. For example, in China, supervisors receive the data (Brutus et al., 2006). But it can also vary by the level of the position. For physicians in training programs, supervisors or program directors will generally receive the data. Physicians in practice may be the only ones to receive the data unless scores fall below a pre-specified threshold.

The feedback

Results are generally provided to individuals as aggregate scores for all raters, by item or for a group of items (e.g. all items related to communication). Data might also include comparator scores based on people within the person's organization, people holding similar positions, or across multiple organizations. Data might be presented as numbers or graphs. Some instruments collect comments. Decisions must be made about whether the comments are screened for possible editing, particularly in cases in which it is believed that anonymity and confidentiality cannot be preserved.

Feedback delivery

Feedback can be delivered in a number of ways. Some organizations provide feedback as a report in the mail or through a computerized system on a password protected site. In other cases, feedback is facilitated in a meeting with a supervisor or other person who can help the person understand and use their data.

Ensuring instrument integrity: Validity and reliability considerations

In this section, we assume that an organization is developing and evaluating its own questionnaires; although the approaches to testing would be similar if an organization was adopting (purchasing) another organization's MSF program. Ensuring the evidence for the validity and reliability of inferences from scores within and across workplaces is a complex and multi-stage process. Attention needs to be paid to a number of aspects using generally accepted standards for survey instruments development and testing (Streiner and Norman, 2008; Berk, 2006). Approaches to undertaking a psychometric assessment of instruments are described by several research teams (Archer et al., 2006; Campbell et al., 2008; Violato et al., 2006).

Constructs and competencies

As noted above, the competencies (e.g. teamwork, communication) on which the MSF is based have to be determined. This is a fundamental decision as it will inform survey length (i.e. large numbers of competencies may lengthen the questionnaires too much or the items may provide a very superficial overview of the construct). Competencies must align with the organization's goals and values. The competencies must be able to be described in behavioral terms that are observable by respondents.

The questionnaires

Decisions need to be made about whether there will be one questionnaire for all sources (e.g. different types of respondents) or whether multiple questionnaires for different sources will be adopted. This is best determined in conjunction with the competencies to be assessed and people's ability to observe the behaviors. When one questionnaire is being used by diverse sources, the types of observable behaviors may be more limited than when different sources assess different competencies. In medical applications, there may be different questionnaires for medical colleagues, health care professionals (e.g. nurses, pharmacists), and patients (Sargeant et al., 2005; Violato et al.,2006; Violato et al., 2008). Whereas medical colleagues can provide information about clinical competence and communication with other physicians, nurses can provide data about professional respect and responsiveness to patients. Patients can provide information about instructions, explanations, and wait times.

The items

The items or individual questions need to be determined. Organizations often begin with existing literature to determine the items that might be applicable in their setting. Through a guided process of discussion, review, and more discussion, a list of possible items will emerge. Attention needs to be paid to ensuring that all the items are behavioral and observable. Once preliminary lists are determined, focus groups with both assessors and raters are required to ensure that these are observable items, the items can be answered, and the information to the questions will guide learning.

The scales

There are many options for scales. Likert-type scales may be most common, providing one sentence (e.g. "Is accessible for communication") followed by scales that require the respondent to answer based on agreement (strongly disagree – strongly agree); frequency (never – always); expectations (does not meet expectations – exceeds expectations); or quality (unacceptable – acceptable). In some cases there are additional words along the continuum. Behavioral anchored scales can also be used (this employee does not listen to co-workers – this employee listens to co-workers); these are more difficult to write so that both ends are equal. The choice of scale type depends on what is customarily used in that particular work environment and ensuring that the match between the item and the scale makes sense. Surveys should also include an option for "unable to assess".

Pilot test

Once a preliminary questionnaire is developed and approved, the instrument should be tested within the organization. If possible at least 20-30 people should be included with an appropriate number of assessors (e.g. 6-8 per person). Those selected should be as representative as possible of the group(s) who will be assessed using the instruments. This evaluation should include an assessment of scores on the items (are they all high for each respondent and thus unlikely to provide much guidance to the person being assessed), response rates, and percentages of unable to assess for each item. It should also involve feedback about the items, how well people were able to answer the questions, and people's perceptions about the process and its potential utility to respondents and the organization. This may be done by questionnaire, face to face or group interviews, but should involve as many participants in the process as possible. Information from this evaluation must be used to inform revisions to the questionnaires.

Testing for evidence of reliability and validity

Once an instrument is approved for use, more testing is required to assess the evidence for reliability and validity on a large sample (i.e. >100). It is important to remember that reliability and validity are temporal concepts and must be established empirically (through testing) in different groups at different times.

While a detailed description of these analyses is beyond the scope of this chapter, a brief description follows.

Reliability assessment addresses the question of whether the data are dependable, stable, and consistent. It often involves examining the overall instrument's internal consistency reliability (e.g. through Cronbach's alpha assessment) and an assessment of whether the numbers of items and the numbers of raters are sufficient to provide stable data to the individual (e.g. through Generalizability/G and Decision/D studies) (Lockyer and Clyman, 2008). Clearly parsimony in both the numbers of items and numbers of respondents is warranted. Too many items may result in respondent fatigue and carelessness. Too many raters may draw on people who are not in a position to observe and thus fairly assess the individual.

Assessing the evidence for validity asks whether the instrument assesses what it is intended to address. This can take many forms. Feedback may be obtained from expert panels who review the items to ensure they are in alignment with the constructs. Feedback from end-users will provide information about their perceptions of MSF and its utility. It may involve examining whether scores demonstrate a bias for men or women or younger or older people or whether there are interaction effects whereby younger respondents provide lower/higher scores for younger/older individuals. Factor analyses may be conducted to determine whether the items that are intended to measure a specific construct (e.g. communication) are inter-correlated with that construct and not another construct. (Lockyer and Clyman, 2008). Studies have also been done to see what happens over time when assessments are repeated as scores should increase if those assessed use the data (Violato et al., 2008; Smither et al., 2005). Other studies have examined how recipients of feedback use the data to inform change (Fidler et al., 1999).

MSF as a feedback approach for promoting development and change

MSF can be both a powerful and sensitive process. It can increase individuals' awareness of how their performance is viewed by their colleagues and, importantly, how it compares with their own views of their performance. It can serve as a strong stimulus for development and behaviour change. Yet, to achieve these ends the feedback process needs to be managed sensitively (Gray et al., 2007).

Ideally feedback should increase the recipient's awareness of their performance, provide insight into areas for improvement, and stimulate practice change. Human resources research indicates that MSF can achieve changes in attitudes and behavior, albeit these are usually modest (Atwater et al., 2007; Smither et al., 2005). Domains in which change most commonly occurs are in interpersonal communication, team, management, and leadership skills. Similarly in medicine, participants have reported increased awareness arising from feedback in domains such as communication with patients, colleagues and co-workers; professionalism and management of stress, and office management. About two-thirds of participants reported either intending to or actually making changes in their practice in communication with patients and office management, as a result of MSF (Fidler et al.,1999).

However, other studies report that acceptance of feedback and subsequent learning and improvement don't always result (Smither et al., 2005). Two important studies in the business and human resources fields illustrate this. The first (Kluger and DeNisi, 1996) was a meta-analysis of 600 performance appraisal and feedback studies. Results were surprising: only in one-third of studies did participants improve; in one-third they stayed the same and in one-third they actually decreased their performance. The second study was of Masters in Business Administration (MBA) students receiving MSF (Brett and Atwater, 2001) and contributes to understanding these results. MBA students who received negative or disconfirming scores did not see the ratings as accurate or useful, rejected the scores and hence did not accept or use the ratings to make changes. Negative scores actually led to discouragement, anger and demotivation. Such findings demonstrate that scores perceived as negative can evoke strong emotional responses which can interfere with accepting and using the feedback for improvement.

Factors influencing MSF acceptance and use

Multiple factors affect acceptance and use of feedback. In particular, knowing why people may resist and not act upon negative feedback is particularly important. Here it is important to recognize that MSF provides personal information. It is often hard to treat it objectively and it tends to be emotionally charged (Ashford et al., 2003; Goodstone and Diamante, 1998).

DeNisi and Kluger (2000) provide a useful model of performance feedback based on internal organization of individuals' performance goals. They propose that performance goals are arranged hierarchically in three levels: the highest is a meta or "self" level where goals relate to self-concept, the middle is a "task" level where goals relate to task performance, and the lowest is a "task learning" level where goals relate to task details and specifics of performing it. They suggest that negative emotional responses most commonly occur when feedback intended for the "task" or middle level is interpreted at the "self" or meta level. This diverts attention from the task and instead focuses it upon the "self" where it is perceived as a generalized criticism and leads to negative feelings like self-doubt, anger, or frustration. They suggest this has particular implications for MSF, as using comparator data which encourages participants to compare their individual scores with aggregate scores may focus interpretation at the "self" level and away from the "task" level.

In business settings, eight factors have been identified that influence people's abilities to make changes in practice, engage in follow-up meetings, and accept and use feedback (Smither et al., 2005):

- characteristics of the feedback – whether the feedback is perceived as positive or negative.
- initial reactions to feedback – as noted above, negative or disconfirming feedback can elicit emotional reactions such as disappointment, anger, frustration, sadness, which can interfere with its acceptance.
- personality – some personality characteristics, such as being generally self-directed, are related to development and improvement.
- feedback orientation – individuals differ in their predisposition to seeking out and using feedback; i.e. some seek it out and tend to be more accepting, while others do not.
- perceived need for change – perceiving the need for a change as indicated by feedback can enhance the likelihood of setting goals for change and making that change.
- beliefs about change – self-efficacy is the belief that one can actually develop and make a specific change. High self-efficacy is linked to positive use of feedback.
- goal setting – once one accepts the feedback, perceives that it indicates a need for change, and believes that one can make that change, setting goals for that change facilitates the implementation of the change.
- taking action – performance improvement is only possible for those who actually implement their goals for change by taking appropriate action.

Smither et al. (2005) suggest a model for understanding how these factors interact to influence the use of MSF. They propose that reactions to feedback, goal setting and taking action are influenced by personality and feedback orientation. Initial reactions and goal setting are influenced by beliefs about change. Goal setting and taking action are influenced by perceived need for change. Hence, changing and improving in response to MSF is an intricate and complex process. Supervisors or others facilitating the feedback need to consider all the influential factors and their interactions; failure in any one of the eight areas can prevent feedback acceptance and use. Moreover, the authors remind us that MSF assessment and feedback always takes place within an organizational culture and context which influences both appraisal and feedback.

Within medicine, qualitative studies demonstrate the influence of similar factors upon acceptance and use of MSF (Sargeant et al., 2005, 2007). In addition to those described above, perceived credibility of the data and fairness of the MSF process influenced acceptance of the feedback. If the process were perceived as being biased or unfairly judgmental, feedback was less frequently accepted. The degree of specificity of the feedback was also influential upon acceptance and use – i.e. general statements were found to be less helpful than specific items or examples. In many cases, narrative feedback which provided specific instances or examples was valued over numerical scores.

Feedback strategies in an MSF program to enhance its acceptance and use

The feedback process occurs in three phases: preparation for providing the feedback, providing or facilitating the feedback, and follow-up after the feedback (Atwater et al., 2007; Bruce and Sargeant, 2008). As the ultimate goal of MSF is improvement, then the focus of providing the feedback is to enhance feedback acceptance and subsequent use for improvement. Even when the MSF is generally positive, it can give clues to the learner about how they might further change to become even better at what they do.

Moreover, active involvement of both teacher/facilitator and feedback recipient/learner in the feedback process can enhance acceptance and use of the feedback. A description of the activities of each of the three phases and implications for both teachers/facilitators and learners is included below in Table 10.1:

Table 10.1 Feedback phases and implications for feedback delivery and acceptance

Feedback phase and activity	Implications for teachers/ feedback facilitators	Implications for learners/feedback recipients
Before providing the feedback		
1. Consider the environment, culture and context of MSF To be effective feedback, MSF needs to be well integrated and valued.	- Ensure integration of MSF and a culture of improvement into the learning/work environment.	- Observe others, inquire about opportunities for self-direction and share beliefs about using feedback for improvement.
2. Ensure that the MSF process is credible and that the feedback will be specific and relevant.	- Be active on committees overseeing and implementing MSF to ensure its rigor for both assessment and feedback.	- Seek representation on committees overseeing and implementing MSF.
3. Prepare for the individual feedback session; support opportunities for facilitated discussion of the confidential feedback with a supervisor or teacher.	- Review the individual's report; consider facilitation approaches for enhancing acceptance and use of data and improvement (e.g. the ECO model below).	- Remember that receiving feedback from co-workers and peers can feel sensitive. Prepare emotionally for feedback that might be surprising, and cognitively, for using feedback to improve. - Review and reflect on your report before meeting with your teacher/facilitator if possible.

During the feedback discussion

1 Consider the impact of the nature of the feedback (i.e. positive or negative) upon the recipient and his/her reaction to it.

- Remember that feedback, especially disconfirming feedback, can be surprising and create a negative emotional response.
- Teachers/facilitators must help the learner move beyond the emotional response to looking at the data.

- Consider your emotional response to the feedback and how that might influence your ability to attend to and use it.

2 Ideally allow for a conversation with the recipient about the feedback, what it means to him/her, and how they might use if for improvement, after they have had time to review and reflect on it.

- Consider using an organized feedback format for facilitating the conversation; e.g. see below.
  See yourself as a facilitator and coach.

- Think honestly about your performance and how this feedback might provide a different perspective. View it as an opportunity for improvement.

After the feedback

1 Consider providing support for individual development and coaching.

- Help the learner in identifying their learning goals and implementing a plan for change as indicated by the feedback.

- Ask your teachers to assist with developing and implementing learning plans.

2 Consider assistance in bringing about change in attitudes and/or behavior and offering resources for supporting identified changes.

- Become aware of resources within your institution.

- Remember that sometimes other resources may be needed to help with change.

An example of a model for feedback facilitation in MSF

As the intent of MSF is individual development and improvement, the goal of providing the feedback information is to enhance its acceptance and subsequent use for improvement. Guidance in meeting this goal comes from the therapeutic counseling field which suggests, rather than just "delivering" or "providing" the feedback, that the supervisor or teacher engage the learner in a conversation about their feedback. The purpose of the conversation is to explore learners' views on their progress and performance, perceptions of the feedback, and plans for improvement. The role of the teacher or supervisor is central, especially if feedback is perceived to be negative. It is one of facilitator and coach rather than the more traditional teacher and assessor roles. In fact, the relationship between the teacher and learner may be more influential than the feedback itself (Goodstone and Diamante, 1998; Atwater et al., 2007). Where there are differences between the learners' self-perceptions of their progress and performance and the views offered by their reviewers via the MSF scores, the challenge is to resolve the differences in a positive manner which will lead to acceptance and subsequent change.

Drawing on this earlier work, a practical, evidence-based model for facilitating feedback from MSF has been proposed in medical education (Bruce and Sargeant, 2008). Ideally the learner receives their feedback report prior to the interview and has had a short period of time to reflect on it before the feedback interview or conversation. The interview model is comprised of three steps, each one exploring a particular facet of the feedback: Emotional reactions, Content of feedback, and feedback Outcomes, and hence is referred to as the ECO model (Bruce and Sargeant, 2008). Each step is particularly important when the feedback is perceived as negative. In the first phase the facilitator asks about their emotional reaction to the feedback and explores the reasons for these reactions. Negative emotional reactions generally occur when the feedback is in some way disappointing and disconfirms their own views of how they thought they were doing. Because such reactions can get in the way of using the feedback, it's helpful to understand and acknowledge them as a normal part of the process. Once emotions have been addressed, the facilitator can then move to the second phase addressing feedback content, by querying and clarifying the learner's understanding of the feedback and its implications. When this is clear and mutually agreed to, the final phase involves coaching the learner in the development of outcomes in response to the feedback. The facilitator explores how the learner sees the feedback as an opportunity for improvement, their goals and plan for that improvement, and resources required to help them achieve it.

Practical implications for implementing MSF in teaching, higher education and professional development

In summary, MSF is relatively new and its advantages, disadvantages and limitations are continuing to be determined in various settings in which it is being implemented. Attention needs to be paid throughout all phases of the program to communication about the program and the goal of MSF to enhance learning and continuous improvement. Table 10.2 summarizes the key requirements for a successful MSF program.

Table 10.2 Implementation of a successful MSF program: practical implications

Ensure organizational and program support and buy-in	Ensure full support from all people in the organization that are involved. There must be leadership commitment to creating and sustaining program and participant commitment to thoughtful completion of questionnaires, and review and use of data.
	Develop an effective communication plan to build awareness and support at all levels within the organization.
	Involve representatives from all levels of the organization including those who will be assessed and be assessors.
Determine whether MSF is for formative (quality improvement) for summative purposes.	Formative MSF will guide individual improvement and learning. There will be few penalties.
	Summative MSF can result in promotions, salary increments and other organizational advantages. Summative use is less common and caution is needed as raters may respond differently. Increased attention will need to be paid to the defensibility of MSF development, implementation and feedback.
Ensure psychometric quality of the data provided.	Ensure that the content domains (i.e. major themes) and items (individual questions) are relevant to the recipient and can be answered by the respondents.
	Conduct the appropriate statistical analyses to assess and develop the evidence for the validity and reliability of the MSF questionnaires for both the overall surveys and for the data provided to individuals.
Implement the MSF program.	Orient those being assessed and those doing the assessments about the purpose, rationale, questions, scales and use of the data.
	Test with a small (or typical) group if possible before expanding to the larger population.
	Use the results of the pilot to improve the MSF program.
	Share the results, improvements and subsequent implementation plan with the organization.
	Prepare to modify the communication plan, questionnaires, and feedback plan as needed.

Provide the feedback and enhance its acceptance and use.	Ensure MSF processes and practices that protect confidentiality for recipient and anonymity for assessor.
	Provide MSF data (results) that are summarized in a clear, concise and confidential report.
	Enhance acceptance and use of the feedback, through a processes of facilitated feedback with a trained facilitator to guide learners in considering their results and developing an improvement plan.
	Develop a culture to support using MSF for improvement.
Evaluate the MSF Program.	Create an oversight committee with appropriate stakeholder representation to oversee program implementation, monitor the program and evaluate the program.
	Develop an evaluation of the program to obtain feedback from those assessing and being assessed.
	Use the feedback to continuously improve the program.

Conclusions

MSF is a powerful tool that can be used for professional and personal development. As the data are provided by those who work closely with the individual, care and attention is needed to address the sensitive nature of the data. Unlike data that is provided by people in "authority" (i.e. a supervisor), these data come from peers and people who work closely together. Further, the expectation is that those who provide and receive feedback will continue to work closely together. Feedback can have unintended consequences. For some recipients, negative feedback may be demotivating. New dynamics within the learning or workplace environments may result.

MSF appears to be most useful at assessing interpersonal skills including communication. teamwork, leadership, management, and collaboration. While MSF can be used to assess technical skills, there are likely more objective approaches for their assessment such as observation check-lists, record reviews, and examination of longer-term outcomes.

Establishing an MSF program requires attention be paid to assessing organizational readiness, obtaining a buy-in at all levels of the organization, carefully selecting and assessing the questionnaires that will be used, determining the type and processes for providing feedback and developing improvement plans, implementing the program initially in a limited way and gaining feedback about the pilot, and finally implementing and evaluating the program. When such processes are carefully put in place, MSF can be a strong and helpful process for providing performance feedback and enhancing learners' acceptance and use of that feedback.

References

Archer, J., Norcini, J., Southgate, L., Heard, S. and Davies, H. (2006) 'mini-PAT (Peer Assessment Tool): A valid component of a national assessment program in the UK?' *Advancement in Health Science Education*, DOI 10.1007/s10459-9033-3.

Archer, J. and McAvoy, P. (2011) 'Factors that undermine the validity of patient and multi-source feedback', *Medical Education*, 45:886-93.

Ashford, S. J., Blatt, R. and VandeWalle, D. (2003) 'Reflections on the looking glass: a review of research on feedback- seeking behaviour in organizations', *Journal of Management*, 29(6):773-99.

Atwater, L. E., Brett, J. F. and Charles, A. C. (2007) 'Multisource Feedback: Lessons learned and implications for practice', *Human Resource Management*, 46(5):285-307.

Berk, R. A. (2006) *Thirteen Strategies to Measure College Teaching*. Sterling VA: Stylus.

Berk, R. A. (2009) 'Using the 360° multisource feedback model to evaluate teaching and professionalism', *Medical Teacher*, 31:1073-80.

Brett, J. F. and Atwater, L. (2001) '360 Feedback: accuracy, reactions, and perceptions of usefulness'. *Journal of Applied Psychology*, 86(5):930-42.

Bruce, D. and Sargeant, J. (2008) 'Multi-Source Feedback', in Mohanna, K., Tavabie, A. (eds), *General Practice Specialty Training: make it happen a practical guide for trainers, clinical and educational supervisors*, London: Royal College of General Practitioners.

Brutus, S., Derayeh, M., Fletcher, C., Bailey, C., Velazquez, P., Shi, K., Simon, C. and Labath, V. (2006) 'Internationalization of Multi-Source Feedback Systems: a six-country exploratory analysis of 360-degree feedback', *The International Journal of Human Resource Management*, 17(11):1888-1906.

Campbell, J. L., Richards, S. H., Dickens, A., Greco, M., Narayanan, A. and Brearley, S. (2008) 'Assessing the professional performance of UK doctors: an evaluation of the utility of the General Medical Council patient and colleague questionnaires', *Quality and Safety in Health Care*, 17:187-93.

DeNisi, A. S. and Kluger, A. N. (2000) 'Feedback effectiveness: Can 360-degree appraisals be improved?', *The Academy of Management Executive*, 14:129-39.

Fidler, H., Lockyer, J., Toews, J. and Violato, C. (1999) 'Changing Physicians' Practices: The effect of individual feedback', *Academic Medicine*, 74:702-14.

Fleenor, J. W. and Taylor, S. (2008) *Leveraging the impact of 360-degree feedback*, San Francisco: Pfeiffer: a Wiley Imprint.

Goodstone, M. S. and Diamante, T. (1998) 'Organizational Use of Therapeutic Change Strengthening Multisource Feedback Systems through Interdisciplinary Coaching', *Journal of Consulting and Clinical Psychology: Practice and Research*, 50(3):152-63.

Gray, A., Lewis, A., Fletcher, C., Burke, E., Mackay, J., Kubelius, E. and Lindley, P. (2007) '360 degree feedback: Best practice guidelines,' Online. Available from <http://www.psychtesting.org.uk/> (accessed 8 April 2012).

Kluger, A. N. and DeNisi, A. (1996) 'Effects of Feedback Intervention on Performance: A historical review, a meta-analysis, and a preliminary feedback intervention theory', *Psychology Bulletin*, 119(2):254-84.

Lepsinger, R. and Lucia, A. D. (2009) *The Art and Science of 360° Feedback*, 2nd edn, San Francisco: Jossey-Bass.

Lockyer, J. and Clyman, S. (2008) 'Multi Source Feedback', in Holmboe, E. and Hawkins, R. (eds), *A Practical Guide to the Assessment of Clinical Competence*, Philadelphia, PA:Mosby/Elsevier.

Ramsey, P. G., Wenrich, M. D., Carline, J. D., Inui, T. S., Larson, E. B. and LoGerfo, J. P. (1993) 'Use of Peer Ratings to Evaluate Physician Performance', *Journal of American Medical Association*, 269:1655-60.

Sargeant, J., Mann, K. and Ferrier, S. (2005) 'Exploring Family Physicians' Reaction to MSF Performance Assessment: Perceptions of credibility and usefulness', *Medical Education*, 39:497-504.

Sargeant, J., Mann, K., Sinclair, D., van der Vleuten, C. and Metsemakers, J. (2007) 'Challenges in Multi-Source Feedback: Intended and unintended outcomes', *Medical Education*, 41:583-91.

Smither, J. W., London, M. and Reilly, R. R. (2005) 'Does Performance Improve Following Multisource Feedback? A theoretical model, meta-analysis and review of empirical findings', *Personnel Psychology*, 58:33-66.

Streiner, D. L. and Norman, G. R. (2008) *Health Measurement Scales: A practical guide to their development and use*, 3rd edn, Oxford, UK: Oxford Medical Publications.

Violato, C., Lockyer, J. and Fidler, H. (2006) 'The assessment of pediatricians by a regulatory authority', *Pediatrics*, 117:796-802.

Violato, C., Lockyer, J. and Fidler, H. (2008) 'Changes in Performance: a 5-year longitudinal study of participants in a multi-source feedback programme', *Medical Education*, 42:1007-13.

Chapter 11

The role of peers in feedback processes

Richard K. Ladyshewsky

It is of no surprise to those who work in higher education that students often provide each other with feedback in informal ways through discussions of examination and assignment results, questions about classroom content, and in project groups. The extent to which this 'peer feedback' is effective in changing the knowledge and performance of students is difficult to measure. However, systems can be put in to place to improve its efficacy.

Peer feedback is a process where learners of equal status and training, without any formal authority over each other (Finn and Garner, 2011), provide information to one another about their performance. It can be reciprocal or unilateral and be evaluative or non-evaluative in nature. It can occur within the higher education setting between students, or in work settings between colleagues. In the higher education system, this process of peers giving feedback to one another about their learning and performance, which occurs outside of the formal educational system, is called the 'hidden curriculum'. The term 'hidden curriculum' was first used by sociologist Philip Jackson, who argued that what is taught in schools is more than just the sum total of the curriculum (Jackson, 1968).

Peer feedback, however, doesn't have to exist outside the formal education system or be left to its own devices. It can, and should, be formalised in well-designed curricula and work integrated learning experiences. Work integrated learning experiences refer to the learning and teaching components of curricula that occur in real world contexts – for example, medical students working in a hospital, law students doing work within a legal practice.

Academics and staff developers can build peer feedback systems that increase the scope, frequency and depth of learner feedback. To do this, staff need to constructively align (Biggs, 2003) learning outcomes related to peer feedback, with evaluation and assessment (Nofziger, Naumburg et al., 2010). This occurs by linking peer feedback to professional behaviour and ensuring that this is assessed when making an overall decision about the learners' performance. If this doesn't occur, learners may lack engagement with the peer feedback system (Ladyshewsky, 2010a) and instead, turn to the educator solely for feedback. Teachers and workplace supervisors are in higher status positions and have evaluative power; hence, learners are more inclined to want feedback from these individuals.

However, insisting that learners rely on their peers for some of their feedback indicates to them that the educator puts great value and weight on this peer feedback. An astute educator will encourage learners to work together by providing mutual feedback in regards to their learning and development needs. They will then ask the students to explain what they have learned from one another, and only then will the educator provide their additional input if necessary. They can then tie this back to the evaluation of the learner's professional behaviour and reflective practice. This signals to the students that they must assign value to the peer feedback process. This constructive alignment process links desired activity to rewards and encourages the cooperative behaviour necessary for the peer feedback system to work (Deutsch, 1949).

Of course, this is only one part of the equation for a successful peer feedback program. Students also need opportunities in the curriculum to practice peer feedback along with appropriate background theory so they understand its relevance in the context of professional development (Nofziger, Naumburg et al., 2010) and reflective practice (Schon, 1991).

Evidence in support of peer feedback

There is substantial research in a range of disciplines and associated curricula that demonstrate educational gains through peer feedback systems (Fantuzzo et al., Riggio et al., 1989; Riggio, Whatley et al., 1994; Ladyshewsky, 2002; Ladyshewsky, 2004; Topping, 2005). Peers are often the most accessible and most involved parties in the learning experience. Hence, they offer great potential to provide feedback to each other in addition to the formative and summative feedback provided by supervisory staff. Unfortunately, supervisors have limits on the amount and frequency of feedback they can provide to learners. Learners often can learn more themselves, from the act of giving feedback to others, as a result of the peer interaction. Earlier research in peer tutoring substantiated that this process positively benefits both parties, but it is usually the peer tutor who receives greater cognitive gains from the process (Fantuzzo, 1989; Topping, 1996). This occurs because the peer tutor must reorganise and explain the material in simple terms to the peer tutee. In doing so, this leads to a better understanding of the material by the peer tutor.

To gain positive benefits from peer feedback, it is important that all staff understand the theory and principles of how to give and receive appropriate feedback, and model this behaviour to learners. Otherwise peers will be less effective in implementing this development strategy. A 'one size fits all' approach to feedback is inadequate for understanding the complexities of having peers provide feedback to one another. Academics and supervisors who throw learners together and expect them to automatically know how to give each other feedback are setting up the process to fail.

Traditional views of giving positive and negative feedback have fallen under criticism (Wysocki and Kepner, 2002) and telling a person how they performed may not necessarily reinforce the behaviour or lead to further improvement. Negative feedback may be rejected by the individual, may not lead to any change, and may even lead to disengagement from the person giving this feedback and the work/study environment. The purpose of giving feedback should be to engage the receiver of this feedback with their thinking that led to their action in the first place, whether the action was positive or negative. This type of engaged feedback involves the learner in a thinking process that increases opportunities for social constructivist learning (Vygotsky, 1986; Wertsch, 1997). It also reinforces reflective practice (Schon, 1991) and enhances meta-cognition (Flavell, 1979), both of which are important components of building knowledge and performance through feedback.

Social constructivist learning is an opportunity for peers to share what they know, and what they know they don't know, about their learning activities. Often things learners don't know that they didn't know, become discoveries in themselves. By engaging in dialogue about their knowledge and performance with peers, opportunities emerge for conversations about what they are learning and how this links in to their performance or knowledge base. Where discrepancies and disagreement about knowledge or practice occur between peers, a state of constructive cognitive conflict emerges, which, when handled appropriately, creates opportunities for dialogue and reflective practice between peers to resolve this disequilibrium (Johnson, 1981; Johnson, Johnson et al., 1998).

The advantage of peer feedback and engagement in this process is that it is a safe way to resolves discrepancies and to further increase knowledge. This is due to the feedback being peer-based, as it does not come from a supervisor or instructor who often possesses evaluative power over the learner. This power difference can impact learning because learners want good grades, and don't necessarily want to reveal lack of knowledge and performance gaps to those parties responsible for evaluation. This is called the 'hidden area' in the Johari Window and is a place where individuals withhold information from others (Luft and Ingham, 1955).

The feedback between peers is often more timely and immediate, important factors for effective feedback, which can be very helpful to a learner when they need to learn things quickly, in context, and when they are currently engaged with the task, without waiting for a response from their instructor or supervisor. The peer nature of the relationship also encourages 'open area' discussions (Luft and Ingham, 1955) as the lack of status difference promotes self-disclosure.

Before engaging students in a formative or summative feedback process, one of the first determinants to consider is the underlying objective for this process. Depending on the objective, a range of peer feedback processes and systems may then have to be set up, as this will influence the degree of mutuality and equality in the relationship (Damon, 1984; Damon and Phelps, 1989) and the outcome. Mutuality refers to the level of peer engagement and interactivity the peers embrace, which is important for learning. Equality refers to how equal each peer feels in the relationship. Equality moderates mutuality, and equality can be influenced by factors such as age differences, differences in knowledge, or referential power.

Design and implementation of peer feedback systems

There is a range of methods for designing peer feedback arrangements between students and the terminology behind these can be quite overlapping (Ladyshewsky, 2000; D'Abate, Eddy et al., 2003) so it is necessary to clarify distinctions between peer coaching, peer tutoring and cooperative learning, the three peer feedback systems that are commonly referred to in the literature. Five important considerations that educators need to consider in designing their peer feedback system are whether:

- the feedback processes will flow in one direction or be reciprocal;
- the peer network will be a paired relationship or a group;
- students select their peers themselves or whether they are assigned by staff (randomly or using learning styles or another matching dimension);
- the feedback system, and how it is embedded in the curriculum, is formative and/or summative in nature; and
- the feedback provided by students comprises part of the student's final grade or formal summative evaluation.

Topping (2005) provides some other important considerations, such as how frequent and for what duration is the contact between the peers, what resources training and guidelines will be provided to the peers, how will educators monitor the quality of the process, and how will the overall system be evaluated to ensure it is working. While it is not possible to cover every one of these points in this chapter, some key principles will be covered to ensure those who set up a peer feedback system get off to a good start.

Paired student feedback systems

Paired peer feedback processes can be structured as a peer coaching (Ladyshewsky, 2010b) or peer tutoring (Topping and Ehly, 1998; Topping, 2005) relationship. The former has more equality and, as a result, has more potential for mutuality. The latter, because of the implied status or ability difference between peer tutor and peer tutee, can impact on mutuality due to the difference in equality (while students may still be in the same year and class, equality differs because the peer tutor is being put in the higher status position of instructor). Pairings can be left to the students, be organised by educators to meet specific objectives, or use other strategies such as learning styles to match students (Sandmire and Boyce, 2004). Again, depending on the objectives of the program, educators need to consider what arrangements will best lead to an achievement of desired outcomes.

The objective behind a peer coaching relationship is to provide peers with ongoing formative feedback opportunities as they are learning new skills or knowledge. Under this feedback system, peers liaise with each other to discuss questions, explore practice dilemmas, observe practice or review knowledge. The peer coachee drives the process, seeking specific non-evaluative feedback which is linked to a set of specific goals or objectives. The peer coaching can be reciprocal. One example, described more fully in the literature, discusses paired nursing students in a clinical placement providing formative feedback on sterile dressing change procedures (Waddell and Dunn, 2005). Another example described in the literature involves pairs of postgraduate business students (acting as peer coaches) providing reciprocal formative feedback to one another as they work through their leadership development plans (Ladyshewsky, 2001; Ladyshewsky, 2007).

Peer coaching, as a term, can often be used interchangeably with peer feedback. However, one has to be cognisant of how information is exchanged between peers and whether summative evaluation occurs, as this can change the dynamics of the relationship. Peer coaching relies on non-evaluative feedback and does this through the use of open-ended questioning that requires peers to self-reflect. Peer feedback is more evaluative and while it may involve open-ended questioning, peers offer direct positive and developmental feedback to their peer. Peer coaching is a good starting point in a newly structured peer learning relationship. Once the relationship builds trust and confidence, it is easier to then shift into more direct peer feedback.

Peer tutoring, in contrast, emulates at least in part the traditional teacher-student relationship, although the peer tutor does not have the same authority or expertise as a professional teacher (Falchikov, 2002). This narrower difference in authority and expertise ('near-peer') positively influences the instructional discourse because the peer tutee feels more able to express opinions and ask questions (Damon and Phelps, 1989). Hence, while peer tutoring is lower on the equality scale, it has less impact on the mutuality scale. Mutuality and the feedback that flows from the peer tutor to peer tutee depends to a large degree on the peer tutor's interpersonal and feedback skills, and the peer tutee's responsiveness to these (Damon and Phelps, 1989). Training and preparation of the peer tutor is essential (Topping, 1996). An example of a peer tutoring relationship is one where medical residents tutor medical clerks in an ortho-paedic clinic, and provide formative verbal feedback on the more junior medical student's performance around a set of established tasks or objectives.

Group peer feedback systems

When peer feedback moves in to a group situation, it becomes a cooperative or collaborative learning group. A cooperative learning group is more structured with clearly defined objectives and outcomes whereas a collaborative learning group is more informal and loosely structured. Again, whether a cooperative or collaborative group is established depends on the objectives of the curriculum. The objective of a cooperative learning group is usually to complete a set task, which, when structured appropriately, provides each student with a specific role and set of responsibilities to complete (Slavin, 1995). Failure to do so usually results in varying degrees of group conflict and loafing because participants have to decide what role to take, how to parcel out the tasks, and personalities and power dimensions take hold during this process (Tuckman, 1965). As a result, equality differences may develop which influence the mutuality of the group.

In a well-structured cooperative group, as each person works through their specific role and tasks, opportunities for more focused and directed feedback can occur at individual and group levels. In any group situation, equality issues become more of an issue and clear objectives, roles and tasks help to reduce these issues and help facilitate clearer feedback processes. For example, a group of marketing interns may be given the responsibility to develop a marketing plan for an agency. Each intern is given a specific role and set of tasks to complete. Each task is integrated in a way that is central to the overall end result, and failure of one component leads to the failure of the entire project. This ensures that each intern's role and task set is unique (individual accountability) which minimises boundary overlap. Feedback process can then be focused on each individual's particular area more readily and with more clarity.

The same approach could be applied to a group of three medical clerks working through a complex referral. One individual would be given responsibilities for the medical interview, the second for the physical examination, and the third for ordering and interpreting test results. Whilst they would do this together during the assessment of the client, the peer feedback would come together when they share their results and work together to understand the diagnosis and required therapeutic intervention of the overall case. In a discussion of the client with their supervisor, each student would be held accountable for understanding the complete needs of the client, regardless of what sub-role they took.

Using peer feedback in assessment

Peer assessment involves peers giving formative or summative feedback to another peer, with the assignment of an actual grade or formal written feedback in the form of an evaluation. The important determinant here is that evaluation is being introduced into the relationship, which influences equality, and if not managed properly may lead to group conflict or student collusion, which influences the validity of the formative or summative feedback. The impact of evaluation on peer feedback, if not managed properly, may also result in students migrating away from the intended cooperative learning system intended by this experience towards more individualistic or competitive learning approaches (Johnson, Maruyama et al., 1981; Ladyshewsky, 2006). For example, a group of four students is given a project by an academic staff member with each student having responsibility for allocating a portion of the final grade to each of the other three peers. Without clear project roles and tasks, a student who is after a high grade may take over the leadership of the group and start controlling the activities. Another student, who sees this occurring, may see this as an opportunity to loaf and reduce effort, but still reap the benefits of the controlling student's efforts.

In this situation the students are engaging in competitive and individualistic learning behaviours, which will make the provision of feedback from students in this group difficult. A more structured project brief, with clear roles and tasks for each participant and clear marking guidelines, would encourage more cooperative behaviour for achieving the overall group reward (Johnson and Johnson, 1991; Johnson, Johnson et al., 1998), thus creating more equality and making the provision of formative and summative feedback more mutual. It is also important to consider how much weight is being given to peer assessment. A weighting of up to 25 per cent of a final grade may be acceptable to peers. However, weightings greater than 25 per cent may make peers uncomfortable. Peers may collude on grades or inflate grades to mitigate fears about failing or adversely affecting the overall academic progress of their peers.

More junior students may need more direction in establishing these peer assessment practices because of their younger age, less developed meta-cognitive skills, and inclination to be more influenced by affiliation needs than more mature age students who are more established adult learners (Knowles, Holton et al., 1998).

Peer assessment can provide great value to students and a study by Nofziger and colleagues confirms this fact (Nofziger, Naumburg et al., 2010). In their research, they found that approximately two-thirds of second year and fourth year medical students found peer assessment created transformations in attitude, awareness and behaviour. This success was predicated on appropriate training, clear guidelines, and rewards that aligned expected behaviour to performance. Peer assessment programs require a significant amount of thought and planning and a range of structures and processes needs to be put in to place to ensure effectiveness. Finn and Garner (2011), for example, outline twelve specific requirements for peer assessment, some of which are noted here: developing appropriate criteria; deciding on the format of the peer assessment framework; timing; staffing requirements; and providing support to students.

The psychodynamics of non-evaluative peer feedback

Up to this point in this chapter the term peer feedback has been used in a general sense, interchangeably with peer coaching, and distinct from peer assessment. As noted earlier, students are very powerful sources of feedback for one another and it makes sense to have them work collaboratively. Peers are learning the same information and skills, hence they often have similar challenges and questions. They also reason quite differently from experts or individuals who have mastered the material or practice. In research on chess players and in the health sciences, for example, it is well established that novices employ a different reasoning framework than experts (Chi, Feltovich et al., 1981; Higgs and Titchen, 2000; Boshuizen and Schmidt, 2008). Novice reasoning is often fraught with errors as they try to transfer newly acquired knowledge to practical situations (Ladyshewsky, 2004). Hence, the deductive or backward reasoning process used by novices can be facilitated through peer feedback and coaching and reduce many of the errors associated with knowledge transference (Boud, 1988; Ladyshewsky, 2004).

Experts may not be the best source of feedback in these situations because of their use of inductive or forward reasoning, which is different to the reasoning of novices. By creating peer feedback systems, peers gain valuable insights that further support their learning and performance that they would not have been able to achieve individualistically (Ladyshewsky, 2002; Ladyshewsky, 2004; Waddell and Dunn, 2005).

Peers are equals – as a result there is generally no evaluation pressure, and peer feedback, when provided in a non-evaluative manner, is more readily acceptable as it is less threatening to one's self esteem. However, further exploration of the construct of peer feedback is needed here to position it in the form of 'non-evaluative' feedback which is central to the success of peer feedback and coaching systems in educational settings.

In their work on peer feedback between teachers, Joyce and Showers found that traditional forms of feedback (e.g. making positive or negative statements about another person's performance) are difficult to administer in a peer feedback system as the process often becomes evaluative and influences the peer learning experience (Joyce and Showers, 1995). Hence, they omitted traditional forms of feedback from their peer feedback model. The omission of this notion of feedback is an interesting yet confusing point. How does a peer guide his or her peer or group without providing feedback? The key is to keep feedback non-evaluative. In other words, by providing assistive comments through key questions (coaching) that are not judgmental, the integrity of the peer feedback experience is maintained. This integrity is important as the feedback process is highly influenced by the social and psychological aspects of the relationship.

Evidence from students participating in peer coaching and feedback processes suggests that a formal structure is needed to gain the most from the experience (Ladyshewsky and Varey, 2005). Participants found that they need to be clear about what they want from the peer coaching experience, and communicate in such a way as to maintain their peer status. Social relationships have different psychological contracts to pedagogic ones, and often students cannot be objective in their feedback in these instances because the social contract interferes with the need to be objective. As a result, formality and structure will make the peer feedback experience more productive.

To illustrate this point, the following example is provided. Two of three learners have just given a presentation on their project. After the presentation they meet to give feedback to each other. The observer then summarises all the things they did well, and not so well, to the other two in the form of a list. The positive feedback is largely ignored and the two learners move into a defensive dialogue with the observer who provided the negative feedback. Most likely the learners will move into an individualistic or competitive learning space as a result of this peer feedback situation for the remainder of the project because the feedback was evaluative and altered the equality dimensions of the relationship. To avoid this occurring, the observer should have asked participants open-ended questions (coaching) about what they felt they did well, and where they felt they could have improved in their presentation. Where the presenters do not see their weaknesses, the peer could ask more probing questions to help them discover the weaker aspects of their presentation. For example, the peer observer might have asked 'how did you feel you answered the questions?', 'during the facilitation phase of the presentation what could you have done to manage the collection of ideas more effectively?'. In this example, the peers are getting feedback about their presentation, in a non-evaluative way, by making them reflect on their performance. The peer observer is moving them through an experiential learning (Kolb, 1984) reflection which will have a greater impact on further development (Boud, 1999). If a grade or formal written feedback is required, it is developed through consensus and more likely to be accepted.

Peers, therefore, need to be prepared to provide non-evaluative feedback (in both written and verbal form) by asking their peers for explanations using 'who', 'what', 'where', 'when' and 'how' questions, which focus the peer(s) who is/are receiving this feedback to reflect on their performance (Zeus and Skiffington, 2002). Peers should use 'why' questions sparingly as these often make the receivers of feedback defensive as it forces justification. Evidence from neuropsy-chology suggests that providing non-evaluative feedback in this manner, which forces the receiver to reflect on their knowledge and performance, leads to more transformative restructuring of knowledge networks in long-term memory (Rock and Schwartz, 2006), in comparison to just telling individuals what they did wrong or right, which is what more traditional feedback has done. Clearly, peers require training and practice so they understand how to give non-evaluative feedback to their peers.

The final section of this chapter provides examples of some peer feedback systems that have been successfully employed in academic and work integrated learning settings.

Example 1: Peer feedback in a hospital based work integrated learning placement

Peer feedback has been used successfully in placements as a strategy to provide ongoing formative feedback support to learners in both educational and real work settings (Ladyshewsky, Barrie et al., 1998; Ladyshewsky, 2007). For example, in hospital-based placements involving physical therapy students, learners worked cooperatively on shared work tasks as well as provided coaching support to their peers on individual work. The supervisor set the framework for the learners by assigning individual and shared tasks, and indicated expectations for peer feedback which comprised part of the formal evaluation in the category of professional behaviour. This encouraged students to work cooperatively, rather than individualistically or competitively, because they knew they were also being evaluated on their ability to provide peer feedback and coaching. Students in this peer feedback system also significantly outperformed their peers who worked independently on the same task when tested in a quasi-experimental setting (Ladyshewsky, 2002).

Supervisors, because of their expert status, however, have to be somewhat cautious about how much they will delegate to learners, particularly around more complex skill-based tasks that learners are doing for the first time. There is some evidence to suggest that expert assisted learning is superior to peer assisted learning in complex psychomotor tasks, particularly when it comes to transfer of the learning to future tasks (Walsh, Rose et al., 2011). This outcome is not surprising given that experts would have completed the complex task numerous times beforehand and have well-established patterns for execution. Hence, they would be able to provide deeper support to learners undertaking this task for the first time. Peers would not have this background experience and therefore would not be able to provide the same level of support. What this indicates is that appropriate planning has to go into structuring peer learning and feedback, so that the appropriate level of support is given in the right situations. At times peer feedback may be an appropriate learning strategy. At other times, expert input may be needed.

Example 2: Peer feedback in a business leadership course

Peer feedback has been used successfully in helping leadership and management executives learn more about their leadership performance through formative feedback strategies (Ladyshewsky, 2007). Learners in this executive management course undertook a 360-degree assessment of their managerial leadership skill by collecting data from their work colleagues and supervisors on a survey tool (Quinn, Faerman et al., 2011). The results of this survey were analysed and collated by their peer coach, whom the learner self-selected. The peer coach provided the 360 survey results to their peer coachee, and they in turn prepared a managerial leadership development plan. Once the development plan was completed, the two learners engaged in three peer coaching sessions where they provided formative feedback, through open-ended non-evaluative questioning (coaching), to help their peer move forward with their development plan. Peers maintained reflective learning journals about their development plan progress, and brought these reflections and questions to the peer feedback/coaching sessions. The learning that evolved helped to transform leadership and management behaviours in a non-evaluative and supportive manner. Learners were prepared for these sessions by receiving tuition and practice on coaching practices and non-evaluative feedback respectively. They used the framework for peer learning in Table 11.1 to structure their peer coaching and feedback sessions.

Table 11.1 A Peer Learning (Coaching) Framework

Stage	Description	Objective	Effect if Missing
1	Assessment	Peers assess each other for compatibility, stage of development and needs.	Trust and understanding are not built and relationship fails.
2	Planning	The timing and place for formal coaching sessions are agreed.	If sessions cancelled, or inappropriately timed, sessions seen as unproductive.
3	Scoping	Learner's needs and scope of session determined based on balance of priority and time.	If coach drives the process, actions will not be relevant to learner and motivation will lapse.
4	Purpose	Coach explores with learner real purpose, asking them to re-define the central question or goal	Only symptomatic and surface level solutions discovered. Main goals not uncovered or achieved
5	Assumptions	Coach asks learner to separate assumptions from facts. May provide alternative objective and non-evaluative perspective.	Concerns may be misconceived and easily resolved by third party. Self-awareness of unknown areas for improvement not discovered.
6	Possibilities	Conversations move from the problem to creative solutions. Learner finds own path out of maze assisted by coach.	If range of solutions not developed by learner and owned by them, process leaves learner feeling unempowered and dependent on coach.
7	Actions	Conversation moves to verbal commitment and identified actions with clear outcomes.	If unrealistic constraints not explored, actions will be frustrated. Trust in process declines as does follow-up of accountability of learner.
8	Support	Follow-up accountability structured to assist in motivation, recognition and trust building and assessment.	Without support, follow-up is resented as accountability only. Process stops with once cycle, trust declines, and learner less confident.

(Ladyshewsky and Varey, 2005)

Example 3: Peer Feedback to Assess Client Interviewing Skills

In this example, peers gave a formal grade and written feedback to another peer who completed a twenty-minute interview. The interview was a simulation, using an actor, and was captured on videotape. The student received feedback and evaluation from their peer who evaluated the interview on videotape. Initially, the peer feedback and assessment process involved two students, who exchanged their videotape with one another. The end result was unsatisfactory with nearly all students receiving a high grade and minimal written feedback (collusion). Several students expressed dissatisfaction with this process as they knew there was room for improvement and wanted useful feedback to develop their interviewing skills.

The peer feedback system was restructured and a group of four students were given the videotapes of another four peers in the class. As a group they were required to review each videotape and collectively provide a grade and written feedback. This group feedback strategy worked very well, with the mean student-assigned grade and standard deviation closely matching the mean instructor-assigned grade and standard deviation for a matched sample (Ladyshewsky and Gotjamanos, 1997). Students were also more satisfied with this approach. Using peer feedback to provide summative evaluation requires that well-established guidelines be in place to guide students. Similarly the academic weighting of the peer feedback is an important determinant. As the value or significance of the grade provided through peer feedback increases, peers become more reluctant to provide lower grades and developmental feedback. This can be minimised by having the grade decided on a group basis, as done in this example, as this seems to enable students to make more difficult decisions with more confidence as a result of the support of the group.

Example 4: Using Peers to Benchmark Performance in Academic Writing Assignments

Another well-established way of providing peer feedback is to identify the top five student assignments and invite these students to share their excellent assignments with students who want to see why those assignments received high grades. This benchmarking system provides a useful way of giving best practice exemplars to students, in addition to the individual feedback provided by the instructor. It is important, though, to explain to students that this is a method to increase peer feedback to them on their assignments and not an honour list, which is why only a few assignments were selected. Competitive students who receive a good grade for their assignment but do not get identified may get upset if they don't understand this. As a summative feedback process, it increases the use of peer feedback in a non-threatening manner and may yield transfer of training effects to future assignment preparation, which is a formative process in itself.

Example 5: Using group peer feedback to promote reflective practice in work integrated learning

In this example, final year physiotherapy students spend their year rotating through a range of placements. To promote reflective practice, students were allocated to peer groups and used blogs to maintain contact with their peers as they transferred across different placements. While each blog had an academic monitor, they only had a monitoring and evaluation role. The blog was largely peer driven with training and guidelines relating to involvement, confidentiality and focus provided to the group. Students provided peer feedback to one another throughout the year on issues of professional practice and found the process very valuable (Ladyshewsky and Gardner, 2008; Tan, 2009), particularly since the group remained the same throughout the year and could build a trusting learning community. The experience supported the development of clinical reasoning throughout the year and was driven by the students, who provided written peer feedback to another.

Conclusions

This chapter has attempted to illustrate some of the key theoretical and practical principles of establishing peer feedback systems in educational settings along with providing some examples. To make peer feedback work effectively, the design of these systems must consider the overall scope of the process and consider a range of factors identified in this chapter. Whether a paired or group experience, peer feedback and coaching should be driven by objectives and have established guidelines so learners understand the scope of their responsibilities in the process. Training is critical, and learners must learn how to provide non-evaluative feedback to one another so as to ensure the ongoing viability of the peer feedback system, particularly where assessment is also a responsibility of the peer. The opportunities for building effective peer feedback systems are limitless, provided those setting up the systems understand some of the key principles outlined in this chapter.

References

Biggs, J. (2003) *Teaching for quality learning at university*, Buckingham: Open University/Society for Research into Higher Education.

Boshuizen, H. and Schmidt, H. (2008) 'The development of clinical reasoning expertise', in Higgs, J., Jones, M., Loftus, S. and Christensen, N. (eds) *Clinical Reasoning in the Health Professions*, London: Butterworth Heinemann Elsevier.

Boud, D. (1988) 'How to help students learn from experience', in Cox, K. and Ewan, C. (eds), *The Medical Teacher*, London: Churchill Livingstone.

Boud, D. (1999) ' Situating academic development in professional work: using peer learning', *International Journal for Academic Development*, 4(1):3-10.

Chi, M., Feltovich, P. and Glaser, R. (1981) 'Categorisation and representation of physics knowledge by experts and novices', *Cognitive* Science, 5:121-52.

D'Abate, C. P., Eddy, E. R. and Tannenbaum, S. I. (2003) 'What's in a name? A Literature-Based Approach to Understanding Mentoring, Coaching, and Other Constructs That Describe Developmental Interactions', *Human Resource Development Review*, 2(4):360-84.

Damon, W. (1984) 'Peer education: the untapped potential', *Journal of Applied Developmental Psychology*, 5:331-43.

Damon, W. and Phelps, E. (1989) 'Critical distinctions among three approaches to peer education', *International Journal of Educational Research*, 13:9-19.

Deutsch, M. (1949) 'A theory of co-operation and competition', *Human Relations*, 2(2):129-52.

Falchikov, N. (2002) *Learning Together: Peer Tutoring in Higher Education*, London: Routledge.

Fantuzzo, J. W., Riggio, R. E., Connelly, S. and Dimeff, L. A. (1989) 'Effects of reciprocal peer tutoring on academic achievement and psychological adjustment: a component analysis', *Journal of Educational Psychology*, 81(2):173-7.

Finn, G. and Garner, J. (2011) 'Twelve tips for implementing a successful peer assessment', *Medical Teacher*, 33:443-6.

Flavell, J. (1979) 'Metacognition and Cognitive Monitoring', *American Psychology*, 34(10): 906-11.

Higgs, J. and Titchen, A. (2000) 'Knowledge and Reasoning', in Higgs, J. and Jones, M. (eds), *Clinical Reasoning in the Health Professions*, Oxford, UK: Butterworth-Heinemann Ltd.

Jackson, P. (1968) *Life in Classrooms*, New York: Holt, Reinhart & Winston.

Johnson, D. (1981) 'Student-student interaction: the neglected variable in education', *Educational Researcher*, 1:5-10.

Johnson, D. and Johnson, R. (1991) *Learning Together and Alone: Cooperative, Competitive and Individualistic Learning*, Boston: Allyn and Bacon.

Johnson, D., Johnson, R. and Smith, K. (1998) 'Cooperative learning returns to college: what evidence is there that it works?', *Change*, 30(4):27-35.

Johnson, D., Maruyama, G., Johnson, R., Nelson, D. and Skon, L. (1981) 'Effects of Cooperative, Competitive, and Individualistic Goal Structures on Achievement: A Meta-Analysis', *Psychological Bulletin*, 89(1):47-62.

Joyce, B. and Showers, B. (1995) *Student Achievement Through Staff Development: Fundamentals of School Renewal*, White Plains, N.Y.: Longman Publishers.

Knowles, M., Holton, E. and Swanson, R. A. (1998) *The Adult Learner*, Woburn, MA: Butterworth Heinemann.

Kolb, D. (1984) *Experiential Learning*. Englewood Cliffs: Prentice-Hall.

Ladyshewsky, R. (2000) 'Peer Assisted Learning in Clinical Education: A Review of Terms and Learning Principles', *Journal of Physical Therapy Education*, 14(2):15-22.

Ladyshewsky, R. (2001) *Reciprocal Peer Coaching: A strategy for training and development in professional disciplines*, Jamison, ACT, Australia: Higher Education Research and Development Society of Australasia Inc.

Ladyshewsky, R. (2002) 'A Quasi-experimental study of the differences in performance and clinical reasoning using individual learning versus reciprocal peer coaching', *Physiotherapy Theory and Practice*, 18(1):17-31.

Ladyshewsky, R. (2004) 'The impact of peer coaching on the clinical reasoning of the novice practitioner', *Physiotherapy Canada*, 56(1):15-25.

Ladyshewsky, R. (2006) 'Building cooperation in peer coaching relationships: understanding the relationships between reward structure, learner preparedness, coaching skill and learner engagement', *Physiotherapy*, 92(1): 4-10.

Ladyshewsky, R. (2007) 'A Strategic Approach for Integrating Theory to Practice in Leadership Development', *Leadership & Organization Development Journal*, 28: 426-43.

Ladyshewsky, R. (2010a) 'Building Competency in the Novice Allied Health Professional through Peer Coaching', *Journal of Allied Health*, 39(2):e75-e80.

Ladyshewsky, R. (2010b) 'Peer Coaching', in Cox, H., Bachkirova, T. and Clutterbuck, D. (eds), *Handbook of Coaching*, London: Sage Publications.

Ladyshewsky, R., Barrie, S. and Drake, V. (1998) 'A comparison of productivity and learning outcome in individual and cooperative physical therapy clinical education models', *Physical Therapy*, 78(12): 1288-1301.

Ladyshewsky, R. and Gardner, P. (2008) 'Peer assisted learning and blogging: A strategy to promote reflective practice during clinical fieldwork', *Australasian Journal of Educational Technology*, 24(3):241-57.

Ladyshewsky, R. and Gotjamanos, E. (1997) 'Communication Skill Development In Health Professional Education: The use of standardised patients in combination with a peer assessment strategy', *Journal of Allied Health*, 26(4):177-86.

Ladyshewsky, R. and Varey, W. (2005) 'Peer Coaching: A practical model to support constructivist learning methods in the development of managerial competency', in Cavanagh, M., Grant, A. and Kemp, T. (eds) *Evidence-Based Coaching: Volume 1; Theory, research and practice in the behavioural sciences*, Bowen Hills, Qld:Australian Academic Press.

Luft, J. and Ingham, H. (1955). *The Johari Window: a graphic model for interpersonal relations*, California:University California Western Training Laboratory.

Nofziger, A., Naumburg, E., Davis, B. J., Mooney, C. J. and Epstein, R. M. (2010) 'Impact of Peer Assessment on the Professional Development of Medical Students: A Qualitative Study', *Academic Medicine*, 85(1): 140-7.

Quinn, R., Faerman, S., Thompson, M., McGrath, M. and St Clair, L. (2011) *Becoming a Master Manager: A Competing Values Approach*, New Jersey: Wiley.

Riggio, R., Whatley, M. and Neale, P. (1994) 'Effects of Student Academic Ability on Cognitive Gains Using Reciprocal Peer Tutoring', *Journal of Social Behaviour and Psychology*, 9(3): 529-42.

Rock, D. and Schwartz, J. (2006) 'The Neuroscience of Leadership' *Strategy and Business*, Online. Available from <http://www.strategy-business.com/article /06207 > (retrieved May 2006).

Sandmire, D. and Boyce, P. (2004) 'Pairing of Opposite Learning Styles Among Allied Health Students', *Journal of Allied Health*, 33(2): 156-63.

Schon, D. (1991) *The Reflective Practitioner: How Professionals Think in Action*, London: Ashgate Publishing Ltd.

Slavin, R. (1995) *Cooperative Learning: Theory, Research and Practice*, Boston: Allyn and Bacon.

Tan, M. (2009) *The Influence of Blogging on Physiotherapy Students' Clinical Reasoning Skills*, Bachelor of Science (Honours) Thesis, School of Physiotherapy. Perth WA: Curtin University of Technology.

Topping, K. (1996) 'The effectiveness of peer tutoring in further and higher education: a typology and review of the literature', *Higher Education*, 32: 321-45.

Topping, K. (2005) 'Trends in Peer Learning', *Educational Psychology*, 25(6): 631-45.

Topping, K. and Ehly, S. (eds) (1998) *Peer Assisted Learning*. London: Lawrence Erlbaum and Associates.

Tuckman, B. (1965) 'Developmental Sequences in Small Groups', *Psychological Bulletin*, 63(6): 384-99.

Vygotsky, L. (1986) *Thought and Language*. Cambridge, MA: M.I.T. Press.

Waddell, D. and Dunn, N. (2005) 'Peer coaching: the next step in staff development', *Journal of Continuing Education in Nursing*, 36(2): 84-91.

Walsh, C., Rose, D., Dubrowski, A., Ling, S. C., Grierson, L. E., Backstein, D. and Carnahan, H. (2011) 'Learning in the Simulated Setting: A Comparison of Expert-, Peer- and Computer-Assisted Learning', *Academic Medicine*, 86(10 Suppl):S12-6.

Wertsch, J. (1997) *Vygotsky and the social formation of the mind*. Cambridge: Harvard University Press.

Wysocki, A. and Kepner, K. (2002) 'Managerial Feedback, Associate Performance, and Eleven Positive Feedback Rules'. Online. Available from: <http://edis.ifas.ufl.edu/pdffiles/HR/HR02600.pdf>. (accessed June 2012).

Zeus, P. and Skiffington, S. (2002) *The Coaching at Work Tool Kit*, Roseville, Australia: McGraw Hill Australia.

Chapter 12

Utilising the voice of others

The example of consumer-delivered feedback

Lisa McKenna
Fiona Kent

Feedback in the work-based setting is complex and multifaceted, comprising both direct and indirect feedback. Useful information can be gained by a wide variety of other people who would not conventionally be seen as contributors to education and training. This chapter explores how consumers (clients, customers, patients, etc.) give feedback that can enhance professional practice. Traditionally, in most workplaces, learners have received feedback formally from a supervisor but they also receive it informally from whoever they are providing a service to. While formal educator-led feedback is important, if used constructively to assist the learner, formal and informal consumer-delivered feedback may play a powerful role in assisting professional development.

The clients of professionals have the capacity to meaningfully comment on trainees' performance in relation to communication skills and they are willing to provide this feedback directly to learners. The authors offer strategies to help formalise consumers' capacities to support learners' practice in the workplace setting. The aim of this chapter is to review the role of consumers as teachers and providers of feedback. It does this through the medium of patients in healthcare settings. It presents key findings from research conducted by the second author describing how patients' appraisals of students can be used to further professional learning. The sensitivities and vulnerabilities around patients are such that what works for them may be applicable in many different professional contexts where recipients of services have an important voice to contribute to the formation of the professional.

Roles and sources of feedback in clinical settings

Feedback is a fundamental component of practice-focused education in the professions. Clynes and Rafferty (2008) report that feedback is 'an interactive process which aims to provide learners with insight into their performance' (pp. 405-6). It is provided to guide development of the learner and may be formative or summative in nature, and build across a range of areas, including motivation and confidence. For health professional students in clinical settings, there can be multiple sources of formal and informal feedback including from clinicians, clinical educators (however titled), other students, families, patients and others, further adding to the complexity of the learning environment.

Despite being fundamental to students' learning, often such feedback is unstructured, and may be indirect (Sargeant et al., 2007). For feedback to be sensitive and of optimal benefit, it should be presented in a structured way. Van de Ridder et al. (2008) suggest that there are four procedures involved in the feedback process, that is, 'information gathering, content, direction of the provided information and intention of providing information' (p. 194). *Information gathering* entails observing the learner's performance, *content* requires evaluating the learner's performance against required standards, *direction* refers to from whom the feedback is provided, and finally, *intention* should be on performance improvement.

Patients as teachers

Learning from patients has always been part of clinical or fieldwork education in the health professions. Patients provide first-hand information about clinical conditions and managing care priorities having actually experienced them, and offer opportunities for applying, and developing competence in, psychomotor and other skills. Yet, despite its continual presence, such contribution to learning has often been understated, passive and unstructured. More recently, educational researchers in the health professions have begun to examine how patients can play more formal roles in enhancing student learning in practice. Wykurz and Kelly (2002) undertook a literature review to explore roles and settings in which patients contributed to teaching in medical education. They found that trained patients were commonly engaged in teaching examination skills, and also participated in students' assessments and direct teaching. Other researchers have explored the role of patients in the teaching of communication skills (Lown, Sasson and Hinrichs, 2008; Reinders et al., 2008) and chronic conditions (McKinlay, McBain and Gray, 2009; Phillpotts, Creamer and Andrews, 2010).

Patients can provide additional benefits and a different dimension to teaching and learning for students in the health professions. Kelly and Wykurz (1998) purport that patients have the benefit of offering students opportunities to 'understand the experience of a condition ... rather than observing a discrete incident in a clinical setting'(p370). In describing their 'Patients as Partners Programme', Kelly and Wykurz (1998) report that through their partnerships with patients, medical students developed respect for the patients and their rights, appreciation of lifestyles and personal situations and how these impacted on health, as well as improved students' communication and listening skills. In another study, Jha et al. (2009b) explored tutors' and medical students' experiences of patient involvement in learning. Patients were reported to provide a type of knowledge that was not accessed through traditional educational approaches. A patient's own words were found to be more 'evocative and powerful than any reinterpretation of a patient's views' (p. 453). Hence, patient involvement in teaching and learning offers an additional dimension of feedback to students.

Employing patients as teachers has not only been used in clinical areas. Many studies also report the use of patient teachers as 'standardised' or 'simulated' patients within classroom environments. Standardised patients are individuals who are prepared to simulate patients with 'illnesses in a standardized, unvarying way' (Barrows, 1993, p. 444), incorporating spiritual and psychosocial dimensions of the person.

What are potential benefits of patient feedback in learning and teaching?

Working in educational contexts with patients clearly has potential to provide benefits for student learning outcomes. A number of studies have directly examined the development and impact of real and standardised patients in providing student feedback. Turan, Üner and Elçin (2009) evaluated the use of standardised patients in developing first year medical students' communication skills in Turkey using a control group post-design approach. They found that students who had received patient feedback were less anxious and had higher self-efficacy, impacting on overall motivational level. Furthermore, Sargeant, Mann et al. (2007) investigated the potential of multi-source feedback to induce a change in performance. They concluded 'the feedback most consistently used was specific, received from patients, and addressed communication skills' (p. 584). This reported learner receptivity to patient comment further adds to the evidence supporting patient feedback in clinical education.

There has also been a call in recent years to increase the 'voice' of the patient in medical education (Towle, 2006; Howe, 2007; Jha et al., 2009a). The empowerment of patients as active participants in the education process has been advocated in order to develop patient-centred care, better utilise patients as a source of learning, reduce the hierarchy between health professionals and patients and reduce the reported problems of patients feeling misunderstood (Howe, 2007). The invitation to contribute to learner feedback offers an opportunity to increase patients' involvement and 'voice' in their own care.

However, the use of patient feedback requires careful planning if it is to optimise learning outcomes. Reinders et al. (2008) evaluated a patient feedback programme for trainees in general practice around acquisition of consultation skills using a questionnaire. They found that patients' responses regarding the trainees' skills were positively biased. They also found that where patient conditions were relatively simple, feedback was not useful.

Benefits of employing patients in student learning

- Facilitate patient centred learning and care
- Offer first-hand knowledge of a particular condition
- Add social, cultural, spiritual dimensions to understanding particular situations
- Allow the opportunity to increase the 'voice' of the patient in education
- Have experience of living with a condition
- Provide information about effectiveness of management in particular conditions
- Offer opportunities for the application of communication, psychomotor and other skills
- Allow the opportunity for development of mutual respect and understanding

How can consumer feedback be gathered?

The means by which consumer feedback should be sought depends upon the context of the learner and consumer, and the stakes of the evaluation. Standardised or purpose-written questionnaires may be utilised and delivered either in paper format or electronically, with electronic tools offering the benefit of simplified collation. Quantitative or qualitative data may be obtained by questionnaire. Alternately, verbal feedback may be gathered either directly by the learner, with the consumer adopting a role as teacher, or indirectly by a third party (for example, the clinical supervisor). The options for gathering verbal consumer feedback include both face-to-face or by telephone conversations. Furthermore, the sampling strategy and number of opinions sought, which will in turn affect the reliability and validity of the consumer feedback, also requires careful consideration.

Researching patient feedback in professional learning

This section presents key findings of one mixed methodology study that investigated patient feedback in physiotherapy clinical education (Kent, 2009). This research sought to investigate the role that untrained patients would like, and were able, to play in the delivery of feedback to undergraduate students. Feedback was sought from eighty-one patients who had received physiotherapy care from an undergraduate student in a metropolitan teaching hospital. A purposeful sampling strategy was utilised to minimise selection bias. Patients who had been treated by a student were approached by a Research Assistant after their student consultation and invited to provide anonymous student feedback.

The patient feedback questionnaire asked for both a rating of the students' competency on a five-point Likert scale and allowed open responses to a series of questions about their student consultation. Quantitatively, the four areas of competence rated by the patients were communication, assessment, treatment and education. The five-point patient scale was chosen in order to replicate the five levels of competence described in the formal physiotherapy assessment tool (Dalton et al., 2009). This enabled student scores to be sensibly compared with the formal clinician marking. In the open-ended qualitative section of the questionnaire, patients' views on, and experiences of, providing feedback to students were collected.

There were three key findings from this feedback research:

1   Patients wanted to deliver feedback to students
2   Patients may be reluctant to deliver 'negative' feedback to students
3   Patient feedback should focus on communication skills

Patients want to deliver feedback

When asked how comfortable patients were to deliver feedback to students, the response was clearly positive as 93% reported feeling comfortable or extremely comfortable in providing this information to students. See Table 12.1.

Table 12.1 Patient Feedback

	Frequency	Per cent
Not at all comfortable	6	7.5
Comfortable	46	57.5
Extremely Comfortable	28	35
Total	**80**	**100.0**

Two sub-themes emerged when analyzing patient responses about their reasons for wanting to deliver feedback to students: patient-centred and student-centred benefits. Firstly, patients reported the need to inform the students of the effectiveness of their intervention as a means of maximising the quality of their care. Comments about therapeutic outcomes and adverse events were included in this group.

'if I don't tell someone [about the student's intervention], it only hurts myself'

Some patients expressed their willingness to give feedback as an expression of their rights, rather than necessarily serving an educative function for the student's benefit.

'would I ever? [give feedback] Yes I would say something. I speak my mind wherever I go'

Second, patients described the importance of feedback to assist student learning.

'[Feedback is] the only way they know and learn'

'good for them to be there and she hears what the physio says and what I say!'

These comments suggest that some participants saw themselves beyond 'the patient role' (requiring help from the student), and rather positioned themselves as co-teachers with the clinical educator (helping the student). Patients in hospital are dependent on practitioner attention and skill and therefore may perceive themselves as disempowered in the hospital setting. They are typically the recipients of diagnoses, treatments and information. It could be argued that participation in feedback events allows patients the opportunity of contributing to something that they see as tangible and useful for students in the hospital setting. Despite lack of formal implementation of patient feedback, many patients in this study reported already delivering student feedback. Students embarking on clinical education placements may need to be prepared for patients delivering feedback, without being prompted.

When assessing student performance, many patients made reference to their expectations of physiotherapy competence. As expected, there was a tendency for patients to compare their student experience to previous physiotherapy encounters. Of the fourth year encounters, 31% were described as being as good as a physiotherapist, one even exceeding previous experiences,

'he was very good, better than some older staff'

Other patients, such as this example on the cardiothoracic ward, commented that they were unaware of the benchmark,

'hard to compare – only had sports physio in the past'

It is reassuring in this study to find that the patients appeared to critique students with reference to a previously determined benchmark. However, for some patients the student-led care may be their first experience of physiotherapy. Without an awareness of the performance target, useful feedback is unlikely. At the other end of the spectrum, there may be some patients with a health or education background, well positioned and skilled to deliver feedback. As one patient commented,

'I was a nurse and dealt with students all the time'

Reluctance to deliver negative feedback

Some patients, although happy to deliver feedback, reported their reluctance to deliver feedback based on students' deficits.

'more likely if something nice to say, otherwise harder to upset anybody'

Such reluctance to raise criticism has also been reported in the literature. Ende (1983) describes the concept of 'vanishing feedback', where negative feedback may be avoided for fear of upsetting a student. Other patients in this study indicated that they would be comfortable delivering feedback, but preferred to deliver it to the clinician (as a form of mediator) than to the student.

'would probably tell supervisor first – depends on what the problem is. Would tell him if he was doing well though'

The study by Feletti and Carney (1984) of medical students in Australia also found that patients were reluctant to be critical. The reasons were cited as not wanting to discredit and discourage the student and that the students were young and would improve. The incentives and disincentives for patients providing honest negative appraisal warrant further investigation. Politeness theory, as proposed by Brown and Levinson (1987), suggests that all competent adult members of society cooperate to maintain each others' 'face'. The authors propose that individuals estimate the risk to themselves, before choosing to threaten the 'face' of the student.

Validity of patient feedback

To establish the validity of patient feedback, patient scores were compared to the educator scores for each student. For each of the four domains, communication, assessment, treatment and educating ability, the degree of agreement between the patient rating and clinician rating was calculated using Pearson's r. In the domain of communication there was a weak, but statistically significant correlation between the patient and educators ratings ($r=0.23$, $n=81$, $p=0.04$). See Figure 12.1. In the other three domains, the correlation was very poor.

   Despite patients' intentions to participate in student feedback, the validity of their feedback warrants comment. Within the quantitative data, patients appeared to be poor discriminators of student performance in the domains of assessment, treatment and educating ability, with a global tendency to rate students positively. Feletti and Carney (1984) also reported a tendency of patients to rate students favourably. An example of discrepancy in the rating of treatment choices was found on the neurological ward, where one patient noted,

'he doesn't seem to know what is wrong with me – making me stand up!'

This treatment intervention, essentially encouraging the mobilisation out of bed, was quite likely to be the correct intervention for this patient, despite the patient critique. Burford et al. (2011) also reported that both doctors and patients felt that patients did not have sufficient expertise or knowledge to give meaningful feedback on clinical skills.

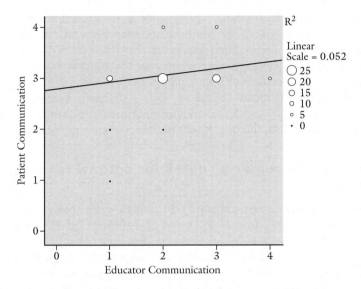

Figure 12.1 Correlation between patient and educator rating of student communication

The results of the current study and the previous literature suggest that the utilisation of patient feedback should therefore be focused on students' demonstrated communication ability. Patient feedback should also be focused on formative assessment to aid learning rather than higher stakes summative assessment.

Patients in hospital prefer to give verbal feedback

The study design allowed a Research Assistant the time to approach each selected patient individually. After gaining consent, patients were offered the option of either completing the paper questionnaire independently or responding verbally and having the Research Assistant transcribe their responses verbatim. Although no patients declined involvement in the research, all except two patients chose to respond verbally rather than fill in the questionnaire. Implementing written patient questionnaires in the hospital setting in the UK (Burford, Bedi et al., 2009) also uncovered a reluctance or inability of hospital patients to complete a paper form. The implementation of patient feedback must be considerate of the potential burden on the patient.

Limitations

The health education literature describes the use of 'simulated' (Kneebone, R., Scott, W. et al., 2004), 'standardised' and 'trained' patients (Jha et al., 2009a)

in clinical education. By contrast, 'real' patients, as investigated in this study, are recipients of routine clinical care and have not undergone any training prior to their clinical education encounter. The distinction between 'real' and 'trained' patients requires consideration when interpreting the education literature.

Finally, the extrapolation of these findings beyond the system and idiosyncrasies of hospital-based care should be made with careful consideration. For example, the demographics, clinical caseload and patient expectations in a private health setting may yield differing patient responses to student-led care.

Harnessing consumer feedback for optimal teaching and learning

To deliver feedback on performance, the clinical performance needs to be observed (Ende, 1983; van de Ridder et al., 2008). Clinical educators are not necessarily present throughout a novice clinician's consultation. The ever-present audience is the patient. Bleakley and Bligh (2008) argue for a shift in medical education to a 'patient-centred model', where the relationship between the student and patient is of priority and the educator is utilised as an expert resource. They propose that the patient play an active role as educator, rather than a passive role to the educational activities initiated by the doctor.

Patients are well positioned to determine the effectiveness of their clinical care and their progress toward their desired outcomes. They also report that they are equipped to deliver feedback to novice practitioners, and some report already doing so. Some patients believe it is in fact their 'right' to provide feedback to students and the vast majority report feeling comfortable with the concept. In addition, the patient's experience provides an important perspective to triangulate student assessment. Multiple data points (from multiple stakeholders) on student performance can help to shape a clearer view of the student's demonstrated behaviours. Triangulation of assessment data has been deemed important in the literature due to the nature of assessment, which is inherently subjective (Ende et al., 1995). However, although there is a reasonable argument for the involvement in patients in student feedback, implementation requires the consideration of boundaries to both maximise validity and minimise potential harm to students and consumers.

The authors propose several recommendations.

Recommendation 1: Prepare consumers to deliver student feedback

Alongside the patient 'consent to education' that occurs prior to any clinical teaching episode, patients should be invited to contribute to student learning by providing feedback to assist learning. The importance of honest appraisal and value of their perspective should be communicated. The invitation to deliver feedback, particularly on the students' communication skills, either during or at the completion of the consultation should be made clear. In addition, the option for patients to provide any anonymous feedback should be provided, without student presence, if preferred. To reduce the burden on the patient, this feedback should be verbal and informal.

The delivery of feedback needs to be introduced and supported, to ensure that students are not exposed to damaging critique on their performance. As one option, patients could be asked to contribute to teaching by indicating one thing that the student did well, and one thing they could do better next time at the completion of the consultation.

Recommendation 2: Encourage students to use consumers as a source of feedback

Students should also be made aware, prior to their clinical education, of the potential to use patients as a source of feedback. They should also be prepared for the fact that patients do deliver feedback, without being prompted. Most patients in this study reported feeling comfortable with the idea of delivering feedback, so students should be encouraged to ask for it, informally and regularly. Eva, K. W., and Regehr (2008) describe the need for 'self-directed assessment seeking' (p. 15), a process whereby students take responsibility for looking outward and seeking information about their performance. Soliciting feedback from patients is a viable alternative allowing triangulation from multiple data sources.

Informal feedback on both student performance and patient reactions are of use to assist student learning. Student performance may include feedback about handling skills such as 'let me know if I am pressing too hard' or communication skills – 'have I explained this treatment clearly?' Patient reactions or outcomes may also be elicited by targeted questions such as 'how did you feel after the last session?'.

Key aspects for effective consumer feedback

- Consumers should be invited and prepared to provide balanced, honest, constructive feedback
- Feedback should be timely and related to observed behaviour
- Use of consumer feedback should be carefully planned
- Educators should undertake careful selection of consumers to ensure appropriateness
- The role of feedback should be understood by all parties involved
- Feedback should focus on communication skills
- Consumers should be provided with the opportunity to provide anonymous feedback
- Verbal feedback should be prioritised
- Awareness that there may be the tendency for consumers to avoid the delivery of negative feedback

Conclusion

Workplace settings can be complex and unpredictable learning environments, yet they also offer learning opportunities that classroom settings may not. Students have opportunities to apply their learning to the workplace setting and aim to develop their performance in line with standards of practice. Feedback is a vital part of learning in these settings to assist students to develop expertise. Consumer feedback has the potential to be a powerful source that complements formal feedback from educators through adding different dimensions to learning. Consumers are willing and able to make such a contribution and educators should consider ways to include this element. This chapter has contextualised the use of patient feedback in the health setting and has offered strategies to enhance students' learning experiences.

References

Barrows, H. S. (1993) 'An overview of the uses of standardized patients for teaching and evaluating clinical skills', *Academic Medicine*, 68:443-51.

Bleakley, A. and Bligh, J. (2008) 'Students learning from patients: let's get real in medical education', *Advances in Health Sciences Education*, 13(1):89-107.

Brown, P. and Levinson, S. (1987) *Politeness. Some universals in language usage*, Cambridge: Cambridge University Press.

Burford, B., Bedi, A., Morrow, G., Kergon, C., Illing, J., Livingston, M. and Greco, M. (2009) 'Collecting patient feedback in different clinical settings: problems and solutions', *The Clinical Teacher*, 6:259-64.

Burford, B., Greco, M., Bedi, A., Kergon, C., Morrow, G., Livingstone, M. and Illing, J. (2011) 'Does questionnaire-based patient feedback reflect the important qualities of clinical consultations? Context, benefits and risks', *Patient education and Counseling*, 84(2): e28-e36.

Clynes, M. P. and Rafferty, S. E. C. (2008) 'Feedback: An essential element of student learning in clinical practice', *Nurse Education in Practice*, 8, 405-11.

Daelmans, H. E. M., Overmeer, R. M., van der Hem-Stokroos, H. H., Scherpbier, A. J., Stehouwer, C. D. and van der Vleuten, C. P. (2006) 'In-training assessment: qualitative study of effects on supervision and feedback in an undergraduate clinical rotation', *Medical Education*, 40(1):51-8.

Dalton, M., Keating, J. and Davidson, M. (2009) 'Development of the Assessment of Physiotherapy Practice (APP): A standardized and valid approach to assessment of clinical competence in physiotherapy', *Australian Learning and Teaching Council (ALTC) Final report*, Brisbane: Griffith University, 6-28.

Ende, J. (1983) 'Feedback in clinical medical education', *Journal of General Internal Medicine*, 13: 155-8.

Ende, J., Pomerantz, A. and Erickson, F. (1995) 'Preceptors' strategies for correcting residents in an ambulatory care medicine setting: a qualitative analysis', *Academic Medicine*, 70(3): 224-9.

Eva, K. and Regehr, G. (2008) '"I'll never play professional football" and other fallacies', *Journal of Continuing Education in the Health Professions*, 28(1):14-19.

Feletti, G. I. and Carney, S. L. (1984) 'Evaluating patients' satisfaction with medical students' interviewing skills', *Medical Education*, 18(1): 15-20.

Henderson, P., Ferguson-Smith, A. C. and Johnson, M. H. (2005) 'Developing essential professional skills: a framework for teaching and learning about feedback', *BMC Medical Education*, 5(1):11.

Howe, A. (2007) 'Ally, advocate, authority: strengthening the patient voice in medical education', *The Clinical Teacher*, 4: 170-4.

Jha, V., Quinton, N. D., Bekker, H. L. and Roberts, T. E. (2009a) 'Strategies and interventions for the involvement of real patients in medical education: a systematic review', *Medical Education*, 43: 10-20.

Jha, V., Quinton, N. D., Bekker, H. L. and Roberts, T. E. (2009b) 'What educators and students really think about using patients as teachers in medical education: A qualitative study', *Medical Education*, 43: 449-56.

Kelly, D. and Wykurz, G. (1998) 'Patients as teachers: A new perspective in medical education', *Education for Health*, 11:369-77.

Kent, F. (2009) *Physiotherapy clinical education – the patients' perspective*, Master's Thesis, Monash University: Melbourne, Australia.

Kneebone, R. L., Scott, W., Darzi, A. and Horrocks, M. (2004) 'Simulation and clinical practice: strengthening the relationship', *Medical Education*, 38:1095-1102.

Lown, B. A., Sasson, J. P. and Hinrichs, P. (2008) 'Patients as partners in radiology education: An innovative approach to teaching and assessing patient-centred communication', *Academic Radiology*, 15:425-32.

McKinlay, E., McBain, L. and Gray, B. (2009) 'Teaching and learning about chronic conditions management for undergraduate medical students: Utilizing the patient-as-teacher approach', *Chronic Illness*, 5:209-18.

Phillpotts, C., Creamer, P. and Andrews, T. (2010) 'Teaching medical students about chronic disease: Patient-led teaching in rheumatoid arthritis', *Musculoskeletal Care*, 8:55-60.

Reinders, M. E., Blankenstein, A. H., Marwijk, H. W .J., Schleypen, H., Schoonheim, P. L. and Stalman, W. A. B. (2008) 'Development and feasibility of a patient feedback programme to improve consultation skills in general practice training', *Patient Education and Counseling*, 72:12-19.

Sargeant, J., Mann, K., Sinclair, D., van der Vleuten, C. and Metsemakers, J. (2007) 'Challenges in multisource feedback: Intended and unintended outcomes', *Medical Education*, 41, 583-91.

Towle, A. (2006) 'Where's the patient's voice in health professional education?', *Nurse Education in Practice*, 6: 300-2.

Turan, S., Üner, S. and Elçin, M. (2009) 'The impact of standardized patients' feedback on the students' motivational levels'. *Procedia-Social and Behavioral Sciences*, 1(1):9-11.

van de Ridder, J. M., Stokking, K. M., McGaghie, W. C. and ten Cate, O. T. (2008) 'What is feedback in clinical education?', *Medical Education*, 42:189-97.

Wykurz, G. and Kelly, D. (2002) 'Developing the role of patients as teachers: Literature review', *British Medical Journal*, 325:818-21.

Chapter 13

Decision-making for feedback

David Boud
Elizabeth Molloy

As the earlier chapters have shown, there is now considerable research-based knowledge about feedback for learning in a wide variety of modes and contexts. There are also a vast number of different ways of undertaking feedback that have been used. Many of these authors challenge common taken-for-granted assumptions about what feedback is and how it should be conducted. However, even if the challenge is accepted and our notion of feedback reframed, there is the problem of choice of particular strategies and approaches. On what basis should feedback strategies be selected for any given purpose in any given situation? At what stage is it appropriate that such decisions are made? Who should be involved in them? And, should these decisions change as learners advance along the novice to expert spectrum in their field of study?

This chapter brings together the themes of the book to focus on the design and choice of feedback approaches. It seeks to provide a summary resource to aid decision-making. It starts by reviewing some of the main messages that have arisen so far and moves to what needs to be done to establish a program climate conducive to healthy feedback practices and produce a particular feedback episode. Rather than provide a reference-rich account, we have used our own judgement about what has been presented earlier to generate key decision points in planning for learning and the issues that need to be considered at each point. We do not seek to be prescriptive but to raise questions about what might be considered at each stage of thinking about a program. The chapter ends by reflecting on how organisational and dispositional changes might be made to move from a conventional view of feedback to one that has a serious influence on learning.

An important emphasis here is that consideration of the role of feedback, like that of assessment more generally, is something that needs to be dealt with at an early stage in the sequence of the planning and conduct of programs. It is not something determined once courses have been settled and assessment tasks designed. It is a fundamental part of curriculum decision-making. This is not to say that there are not particular local or real-time choices to be made by those giving and receiving feedback at the time of its occurrence, but these micro-decisions need to be framed within a context set by some macro ones at the time of course planning. Effective feedback is not something that can be slotted into a program as an afterthought.

Feeding back the main messages

The many and diverse contributions to this book have canvassed a great deal of research about feedback and assembled much useful advice about feedback in a variety of circumstances. In closing the book, we review what we take the main messages about feedback to be.

Feedback is undeniably seen as problematic, both for the learner, and from the educator's perspective. This 'problem' has been reported across disciplines, across learning contexts and across countries. However, other than the adoption of a few standard, and different, recipes, there is little agreement on what should be done about it. This is mainly because there is little consensus on what is the nature of the problem of feedback and, remarkably, little engagement with the research evidence that does exist.

Feedback is often perceived not to work well because it is not being implemented at all. Key elements of the feedback process are ignored or omitted from consideration. The most important omission is that feedback information needs to be organised to influence the learner to usefully act. Knowledge of effects of feedback information is needed, and students must have an active role in producing these effects. Without these features it does the notion of feedback a disservice to have lesser processes labelled with this name. As commonly used in practice, 'feedback' is really a surrogate for 'hopefully useful information'.

Feedback must necessarily lead to noticeable positive differences in what students can do. This is the principal justification for it. Feedback therefore needs to be judged primarily in terms of its impact on learning. Discerning what is this impact is an important role for teachers and all others involved in feedback processes. Without this knowledge, they cannot provide effective inputs to learners and they cannot learn from feedback on their own interventions to attune their interventions effectively.

Learners must have an active role in feedback. If they are passive recipients of inputs from others, feedback for learning is not occurring. It is only the learner who can ultimately act to change what they do. Students must therefore develop the skills of engagement, including seeking feedback, self-evaluating, and making sense of internal and external judgements, at the earliest stage. This is a priority not only to prepare students for 'feedback interactions' but to be self-regulating in all aspects of their work in the course and beyond. Feedback processes must be specifically designed to mobilise student activity. This involves dialogue to appreciate and clarify standards of performance and criteria for judgement, to identify ways of noticing qualities of work, and to show how improved work can be generated. Feedback necessitates learners becoming aware of the standards that need to apply to their work and being able to discern how these standards can be manifest in the work they produce. These standards can rarely be simply transmitted to students through explanation or text. The appreciation of standards and how they are applied is a central part of study. While the degree and intensity of dialogue may vary from task to task, the default assumption can never be that feedback is unilateral and unsolicited.

Feedback must build learners' capacity to make their own judgements about their work. Learners will only change what they do once they have made their own judgements that this is necessary. The judgements of other parties always inform this self-judgement by the student. It is in the influencing of these decisions to which the energy of the teacher or peer or other person needs to be directed. The sharing of their own opinion, in itself, is not feedback and is not sufficient.

Feedback should not be seen as an exclusively teacher-student interaction. Other parties – peers, practitioners, clients and others – have important and varied roles to play on different occasions and for different tasks. Learners must look to other parties for the particular kinds of knowledge they can contribute, not just because this provides an additional data source to complement their learning in the institutional setting, but because seeking and making sense of feedback from multiple sources is a key practice for lifelong learning in the workplace. Peers and consumers are an under-utilised source of information and support for learning.

Feedback must be viewed as a part of overall course and program design and planned and organised accordingly. Left solely to individual teachers, its potential will not be realised. Considerations of feedback and where it will fit must be undertaken before the timing and nature of assessment tasks are resolved. Thinking about feedback needs to occur not as an adjunct to existing fixed tasks, but as a teaching and learning feature of the curriculum as a whole. Conditions therefore need to be created for feedback at the level of decisions about the curriculum, the forms of pedagogy to be used and everyday interactions between teachers and students and among students.

Feedback information needs to be thoughtfully directed at the appropriate level if it is to be expected that it will be acted upon. The nature of the information provided needs to be framed more in terms of its effects on the learner and what they can do with it, than in terms of decontextualised or essential qualities of the work. No one form, mode or strategy for feedback is appropriate. Feedback needs to take on different forms for different purposes in different contexts.

Expectations of feedback change throughout a program, especially across major transitions: from school to higher education, from higher education to the workplace and from workplace to workplace. Feedback practices need to be staged and designed to anticipate and accommodate such transitions. As learners become more experienced, their reliance on 'external feedback from the teacher' should be reduced as they increasingly seek feedback from other useful sources including peers and consumers. Their self-monitoring and self-regulatory practices should be more finely tuned (and utilised) compared to their entry point into a program or discipline of study.

Discrepancies in judgements between learners and others almost always have emotional import and commonly touches on the emerging professional and personal identity of the learner. Feedback, like assessment, is an emotional business. This impact must be considered in the design and utilisation of feedback. Providers of feedback must therefore be seen to have the best interests of the learner at heart and should be mindful of the way they construct the language they use to comment to learners – both in written and verbal forms. This sensitivity in language choice and prioritisation of message content should ensure that the currency in feedback is behaviours or outputs (that can be changed), not the person (that for the present purposes cannot, and is resistant to change). Orientating learners to the explicit purpose of feedback, that it is a tool for the learner to help the learner, may help the process enormously. The more that students are given opportunities to practise giving, receiving and utilising feedback, the more likely they are to build their capacity to benefit from it. Building their self-regulatory system should help learners to make increasingly sound judgements about their own work and that of others so as to improve their work practices.

Making choices about feedback

Before considering the many decision points involved in creating and implementing feedback strategies, it is useful to return to the definition of feedback we introduced at the beginning of the book. This provides the overall frame and focus for planning. There we identified feedback as:

> *a process whereby learners obtain information about their work in order to appreciate the similarities and differences between the appropriate standards for any given work, and the qualities of the work itself, in order to generate improved work.*

When making decisions about what to build into a program this definition directs our attention to the following:

1   The learner is central to the process and the learner is the person who benefits from it. This implies an active role for the learner throughout. Other parties may be important, but what they do is subordinate to what is of benefit to the learner. Of course, all learners are different, so that implies the need to have processes which adapt to this variation.
2   The standards applicable to the work produced is the second most important consideration. Learners need to understand what are the appropriate standards and how they can be applied to their own work. Being told what they are is seldom an effective strategy on its own, as it would not be worth the effort of introducing a feedback activity at all if all that was required was simple instruction. The investment of feedback in a course is only needed when learning is not straightforward. Also, standards need to be appreciated and utilised effectively before they can be deployed well in the production of new

work. Any occasion of feedback requires that standards be made explicit and this may need exemplification of them through the use of examples of good work.

3   Feedback events are not isolated 'reception of information' episodes supplemental to learning activities or assessment tasks. They can only be effective if they are an integrated part of the course. They are needed to achieve the desired learning outcomes at the level required. In areas of learning that are hard won, multiple occasions of feedback are likely to be necessary. For example, students do not learn to become adept at academic writing through one or two writing tasks that involve feedback. Likewise, a physiotherapy student is unlikely to develop effective joint mobilisation skills after working on a few patients, even with feedback from supervisors and the patients themselves. Refinement, or learning, comes with multiple practice opportunities with continual uptake of feedback from multiple sources.

4   If the focus of learning is on an appreciation of variation between the standards of work and the work itself, then active and sustained engagement by the learner is needed. If a learner could readily see the differences between their own work and the relevant standards, then feedback processes would be redundant. Such engagement involves a working with the information provided, the standards involved and what the implications are for their own work. Learning is not a case of clear input that determines a predictable output; a process of making sense is involved. This may involve some form of discomfort or disruption or ambiguity in what to do next. Such engagement is a normal part of the feedback process.

5   Finally, such a view of feedback means that action leading to the production of new work is a necessary part of the process. The generation of information for learners through most feedback mechanisms is too time-consuming or resource-intensive for it to just hang in anticipation that learners might, at some stage, do something with it. The generation of information to students about their work is one of the most time-consuming activities teachers and supervisors engage in. It cannot be justified if there is no explicit expectation that it will be specifically used. In any situation where it is apparent that information to learners about their work is not being used, there is a need for a intervention to stop the wasting of valuable time that could be used more productively elsewhere.

Decision points for feedback

While proposals for improving feedback throughout the book may appear to be quite complex, decisions can be simplified to some extent by considering the stage at which each is taken. Some are made only when a new course is being designed (macro-decisions), and some when particular students are enrolled in a course unit (micro-decisions). The first of these relate to what kinds of information are required from whom at what stage in order to reach the course outcomes. They are part of the basic structure of the course and events such as the timing of assignments and their relationship to each other are determined well in advance. The second set of decisions relate to the particularities of the cohort, the nature of student needs and real-time decision-making. These can be varied readily to respond to local circumstances. They adapt to the students and the challenges they specifically face. Once some of the earlier decisions are taken, they won't need to be revisited until the whole program is revised. Also, some decision-making is simplified as soon as it is known what kind of work is being produced by learners at which stage of the program.

At what stage of planning and execution of a program should different feedback decisions be made? This will depend a great deal on the type of course, what it is seeking to do and the experience of the learners in managing their own learning. For example, first year students will need to be carefully inducted into understanding what counts as good work and taking responsibility for their own learning, postgraduate courses may contain more experienced, self-regulating learners. In either case, the assumptions made need to be tested against the actual response of learners and modified accordingly. Macro and micro levels are not either/or distinctions, and some issues reoccur at each level. However, general features of what needs to occur at each stage can be identified.

These decision points are formulated for the principal decision-makers at each stage: program, course, unit and practice coordinators. In many cases, other parties – teachers and tutors, workplace supervisors, students – have important roles in the decision process. Coordinators therefore need to involve others as appropriate in making decisions. An important tension should be identified however: it is easy to inhibit full student engagement by locking in too many decisions at an early stage. A locked-down agenda leaves little opportunity for learners to identify and enact what they see as meaningful or useful in their learning. Scope is needed for meaningful participation by the actual group of students who will be involved in the specific feedback processes to be designed.

Macro-decisions about feedback (curriculum decisions)

Macro-decisions apply to long-term planning. They are major curricular decisions decided ahead of students commencing a course. They form part of overall design of courses. They relate to learning outcomes and structural features of the course. They are made once program-level learning outcomes have been identified and the final kinds of work to be produced by students are determined. Here are some questions that educators may ask themselves in program design.

What is the **place** of feedback in the program? What work does feedback do in the curriculum vis a vis other elements?

What **purpose** does it seek to fulfil? Is it a principal driver of learning? A confirmation? A correction? A supplement? To develop judgement? To give practice in using feedback?

How is it **allocated** across a course, what kinds of feedback are needed for which aspect? When is it most needed? When is 'hopefully useful information' sufficient? What kinds of learning outcome might most benefit from feedback, e.g. threshold concepts, key skills and practices, high risk outcomes, academic literacies?

What is the **relationship** between different occasions of feedback? How do they complement each other? How can they be made more effective together than being seen as separate events? What feedback activity is allocated to each task, how are tasks timed with respect to each other, what is the relationship between them?

What **conditions** are required for feedback to be successful? Is feedback tied or not tied to formal assessment tasks? How much is enough?

What **medium** of feedback is needed for each purpose, e.g. written, verbal? With an accessible record/without a record (of performance or information on performance)? If it is recorded, which **form** of record is needed: in text, in learning management system, audio, video?

What kind of **expertise** is needed to generate information? When can non-experts (e.g. peers, consumers, patients) be used, and for what purposes?

Who provides information? If there is more than one person involved, how do the different parties link together? That is, self, teacher, peers, practitioners, workplace supervisors, recipients of service (clients/customers/patients).

What are the distinct **feedback loops** that need to occur within the course? How many are needed, what form should they take? Is sufficient time allowed between occasions of feedback, provision of information and subsequent tasks to allow information to be fully used? What turnaround times in the provision of information are needed for each occasion of feedback be effective?

What **preparation of students** is needed for them to understand the role of feedback in the program and their role in it? How will student activity and responsibility for **learning be mobilised**? What initiatives by students are required at each stage? What strategies are to be used for this? What will be the signs that they are being successful?

What are the **standards** to be applied to the work? How can students learn to identify and utilise such standards from the resources at their disposal? How can students come to a sufficient and progressive understanding of appropriate standards to enable them to apply them? How will they be able to check that they are applying them appropriately?

How are feedback practices designed to **develop** over the course of study and over time? Are different forms and approaches to be used at different stages? How will students be scaffolded across course units to take increasing responsibility?

How will the notion of **feedback processes be presented** (sold) to students? How will it be ensured that students embrace the notion of feedback and take its practices seriously?

What **preparation of staff** is needed in order for them to understand the role of feedback in the program and the centrality of the learner in this process? What kinds of work are required to 'undo' previous conceptions or practices of feedback that may have been based on the teacher as teller?

Micro-decisions about feedback (local pedagogical decisions)

Micro, or local level, decisions are those within course units, or within workplace learning settings, applicable when the characteristics of the particular learners involved and specific tasks are known. They take into account the macro decisions already made and operationalise feedback in the day-to-day activities of teaching, learning and assessment.

What is the specific **nature of the content** of the information to be provided on any given task? To what features of the work is it directed?

To what **end** is feedback directed? In Hattie's sense, is it primarily to be task focused, process focused or self-regulation focused? How will it avoid being self-focused?

How much information should be shared? Do aspects of work need to be prioritised to ensure that there is not cognitive overload for the learner?

What **mode** of operation is needed? Does it need to be uniquely tailored for each learner? Can collective responses be used? Will individual feedback in front of a group lead to good outcomes for the others, or will this lead to public humiliation? Where are electronic systems that respond to students' correct and incorrect answers appropriate?

What **invitations or opportunities** are provided for students to **seek feedback?** Are they encouraged to cue educators or any other external source to the type of feedback they are looking for? That is, particular areas of work or practice that they feel need attention.

How is information to learners to be **formulated?** What characteristics should it have? How will the use of inappropriate formulations of information be avoided? That is, picking up use of final vocabulary, comments on persons rather than features of work, positioning the student as capable or incapable of achieving the desired change through selection of language, etc.

What **expectations** need to be set up for learners' actions after receiving information? What kinds of **student responses** are anticipated, e.g. replying to comments, contesting comments, deflecting comments, action on the basis of comments, etc.?

When is information most needed? To secure understanding of key material/ practices before moving on? To provide for immediate skill development? To assure key learning outcomes?

What is the specific **role of the learner** on each occasion of feedback? Are they expected to generate their own responses first, compare their judgements with those of others, articulate this comparative judgement or keep it to themselves, produce further work, etc.?

What emotional or identity **issues** need to be considered in the form and type of feedback used? What resistances might reasonably be expected? How might they be addressed, and at what stage will it be necessary to do so?

How is the feedback **loop completed** for learners? What tangible products and outcomes manifest the effects of the feedback intervention? Who notices this and how do they do so? Who is this fed back to, other than the learner, for what purpose?

How will information about learners' work **influence teaching**, learning and feedback practice with this group of students? That is, how will the feedback loop be completed to help the educator improve their teaching?

Application of feedback decision-making

How might this framework for decisions be applied? The following two examples illustrate how decisions might be prompted by questions such as these. On the left hand side of the table is the 'story' and this is marked by annotations on the right hand side of the table to highlight the underpinning rationale for the feedback design.

Table 13.1 Scenario 1. A lecture-based undergraduate course with a common first year

Practices in a first-year university setting	Feedback design rationale
In this course students enter with a wide range of experience and capability. One of the main aims is to bring the students up to a common standard of academic literacy to enable them to benefit from the rest of the program.	Macro decision: The purpose of feedback is to drive particular kinds of learning which focus students on the particular kinds of academic skills (writing, use of references, etc.) they will need in other parts of the course and practice them.
In each lecture, questions are posed to enable students to check their own understanding, responses from students are collected through a student response system and immediately portrayed to the group. Sometimes discussion with other students is prompted before an answer is sought. The lecturer then discusses the results with the class and devotes additional time to misconceptions or poorly understood points.	Macro decision: As the first year is a vital base for all that follows, feedback activities are distributed across all the courses and all parts of the courses, focusing on the production of work that meets the standards required. Macro decision: Feedback is regarded as so important that it is not just used for set tasks and tutorial activities but in lectures as well.
The first tutorial exercise in the second week of the semester uses the well-known exercise (commonly attributed to Graham Gibbs) of distributing three short completed assignments from a previous year to small groups of students for discussion. This is a prelude to them completing a similar assignment for themselves. The groups are asked to differentiate between the three: why is one better than another, what can be noticed in the work that leads to this conclusion, what can then be inferred about the qualities being sought in this assignment? They draw up a list of features to look for in this kind of assignment. This acts as a task on appreciating standards, not through being told what they are, but through appreciating what they are through interaction with others.	Macro decision: Find ways of making competencies or standards of work explicit to students so that they know what they are trying to achieve. Feedback activities are staged so they start with exercises that all students can complete and the level of challenge raised subsequently.

For the first assignment students are asked to complete an assignment, but before submission to check it against the list their group has generated and include a statement on the cover sheet saying what they think their assignment does well and what not so well. After marking, it is handed back without a grade, but with comments that refer directly to their own judgements and suggestions for actions they might take for the upcoming second assignment. Grades are given, but need to be accessed by logging in to the learning management system.

Macro decision: Provide student practice in identifying and using standards to apply to their work. Have them reveal their judgements about their work so they can be commented on to help them calibrate their judgements.

Micro decision: The distraction of grades is removed to focus attention on the information provided.

The second assignment covers new subject matter, but it also focuses on some of the academic writing features emphasised in the first task. In a tutorial, students undertake an exercise on identifying what would constitute a really good submission for this assignment. The list generated by students is transcribed and made available to the whole group. The week before the submission deadline, students are asked to exchange their assignment with a colleague and offer comments to each other using the list of points of a good submission previously generated. When they hand in the assignment they are also asked to comment on the changes they made in response to peer comments.

Macro decision: Further practice in use of standards and application of them to their own work. Structured peer discussions to ensure all students actively contribute.

Macro decision: Learning outcomes are included that overlap with those from the first assignment to ensure that the feedback loop is completed.

The returned assignment from the tutor focuses once again on the process of writing and uses the ideas and vocabulary from the checklist generated in the tutorial.

Macro decision: Learning outcomes are included that overlap with those from the first assignment to ensure that the feedback loop is completed.

The third assignment again includes new subject matter, but the academic skills required overlap with the second assignment. This time students are asked to specifically identify what they want to receive comments about and are given a simple form to prompt their request.

Macro decision: Completion of a second feedback loop is included by overlap of desired learning outcomes in the subsequent assignment.

It is emphasised throughout that students need to be very active in their learning if they are to succeed and this challenge is given great prominence in the lectures and guidance given on how to present their requests.

Further active involvement of students is prompted through the expectation that they will identify the kinds of feedback they need. Hattie's idea of four levels of feedback is provided to them and they are asked to frame their request within this.

Table 13.2 Scenario 2. A fourth year medical student on a surgical ward placement

Practices on the ward placement	Feedback design rationale
The fourth year medical student is placed on a surgical ward with the aim of applying theory to practice. He meets his supervisor on the first day of the four-week placement for orientation. The student had filled out a 'Learning Needs Form" (a requirement sent out prior to the placement) outlining strengths in his own performance to date, and aspects of practice he needs to improve on. The student and supervisor work through this form – it frames the conversation as to the learner's goals and potential needs re support and supervision. The conversation finishes with the supervisor asking 'so in summary, what would be the three key things that you want to improve on in this placement?' He agrees with the student that these goals are achievable and asks that they be written down and emailed to him.	Macro decision: The educator privileges an orientation discussion as a way to empower the learner to analyse and express his past learning experiences, along with articulating goals for the placement. This increases the transparency of learning expectations. The learner comes prepared and is not confronted with this important reflective task on the spot. Micro decision: As the discussion was approximately one hour long, and plenty of ground was covered, the educator asked for a summary of what had been discussed (from the learner's perspective), and also asked for a written account of the summary. The need for the written record is two-fold – an acknowledgement that memory/cognitive load has limits, and that the written account would form an anchor that the pair can revisit throughout performance discussions during the placement.
Over the period of the placement (including in the orientation meeting) the supervisor encourages the learner to cue him in to aspects of his practice that may need improvement, e.g. 'as I watch your physical examination of the patient, is there something that you would particularly like me to focus on?'	Macro decision: This 'cueing activity' is a way for the learner to solicit feedback that is meaningful to them. It puts them into the centre of the feedback process. They often have a good understanding of what they anticipate will be difficult for them, or has proven difficult for them in practice. This helps the educator to

focus on certain activities, and of course does not prohibit them from commenting on performance outside the prompted aspects.

The supervisor draws up a provisional timetable for the placement duration, and provides this to the student. It includes the likely activities to be performed each week, and these activities are repeated and also staggered so that they become increasingly complex throughout the placement based on the learner's likely development. For example, the first day the student is shadowing members of the ward team as a way to warm up and observe expert practices. The second day, the learner will complete a physical examination with a peer and a supervisor observing, and by the second week the student is likely to complete a physical bedside examination independently, and report back on their experience.

Macro decision: The learner is provided with repeat opportunities to perform a task, so as to put into practice the feedback. There are 'overlapping' tasks throughout, but generally these are increasing in complexity to accommodate the student's developing expertise.

Micro decision: Peers are used to observe student performance (so they) can learn through observation without the pressure 'of doing', and so they can provide a different perspective on the task performance, in line with the benefits of multi-source feedback described in the research.

As part of generating the placement timetable, the student and the supervisor together agree on how and when feedback will be provided. They decide on verbal feedback throughout the placement, immediately after the patient encounter (and preferably not in front of the patient, unless there is risk to patient safety, or practitioner safety and the supervisor needs to intervene). The pair also agree to formal verbal feedback sessions at the end of each week, and a final verbal feedback session (placement summary), where summative marks will also be given.

Macro decision: Informal and formal verbal feedback sessions are scheduled into the placement timetable.

Macro decision: The supervisor agrees that feedback should occur as close to the learning episode as possible, and preferably away from the bedside to create a 'safe learning environment' and to avoid the potential for public loss of face. The supervisor also includes the caveat that in some high-stakes circumstances, didactic, unsolicited feedback needs to be given in situ to prevent or minimise error.

When the supervisor observes the student working with a patient post-surgery, he writes his impressions in a notebook. He also prompts the patient to report on

Micro decision: The supervisor records his observations in written form so that he can capture specific behaviours to recount to the student during feedback. Specific examples relating how they felt during the physical examination (i.e. were they comfortable, could they comment on how the student provided information relating to their surgery and recovery?) At the end of the session, the student and the supervisor spend 15 minutes 'debriefing' in the ward tutorial room.

to demonstrable behaviours are more meaningful to students than global statements of 'that was good', or 'that needs more work'.

The supervisor invites the patient to comment on the physical examination (multi-source feedback) to provide another performance-related data point to the student. Hopefully, the student will start to elicit this patient feedback independently throughout the placement. The feedback or debriefing occurs in a private space to maximise the learning potential for the student, and to minimise emotional impact if the conversation brings up challenges for either party.

In the feedback session, the supervisor opens with 'So, tell me about your impressions of your patient examination first'. The student is a little global in his response: 'I think that went OK, but of course there is room for improvement', and waits for what he hopes will be the supervisor's appraisal of this performance. The supervisor replies 'OK, tell me more. Let's focus on the particular aspects that you think you would change next time round ...' The student and supervisor work together to form a list of strategies to improve the task when it is next tackled.

Micro decision: The supervisor provides an invitation for the learner to self-evaluate first. Initially, this invitation is deflected by the student, first because he's not practised at 'doing feedback in this way' and second because he thinks he will learn more from hearing from the expert. He soon learns that this need for expressing his own self-judgement is an implicit part of the feedback process here at this placement and that dodging hard questions does not work.

Both deficits and strengths in performance are raised, and there is a clear action plan for how to improve the approach to the task.

The following day, the student performs another physical examination on a patient (a different patient, but similar in terms of complexity of condition).

Macro decision: In line with Feedback Mark 2, the student is provided with a subsequent opportunity to perform a physical examination on a patient. Both student and supervisor are watchful for the appearance of change in the performance, i.e. that the action plan is actioned. If targets are met, this is acknowledged in the next feedback session, and new goals are set.

Changing feedback practices

The view of feedback presented here is more comprehensive than that found in many contexts. It problematises common taken-for-granted practices and raises questions that may not be normally considered. In such circumstances it is not surprising that resistance to such changes might be generated.

Of course, any of these ideas can be picked up and applied by individuals within the areas of teaching for which they are responsible. If enough people did this then there would be some impact. However, noticeable improvement across the system will only be possible if, across a program, a collective view of the need to address the issue of feedback is taken. The biggest barrier to this is the notion that feedback should be regarded only as a transaction between a learner and a particular person with respect to a given activity, for example, as part of commenting on assignments. This positions feedback normally as a private teacher-student interaction. We take the view here that seeing feedback merely as an extension of local teaching or assessment activity, as an adjunct to marking perhaps, fails to realise the potential it has to offer. It needs to be treated primarily as a key focus of curriculum thinking and the implications worked through until it becomes manifest in specific teaching and learning interactions on particular tasks.

We suggest that the following are some of the issues to be addressed in confronting change about feedback:

An outcomes-centred and standard-based view of learning

The concept of feedback assumes that work can be improved and that the use of relevant information applied by the learner will result in better work. This is essentially an outcomes-centred view. Effectiveness is judged by results demonstrated in learning outcomes in relation to relevant standards. Standards are not some abstraction of worth, but tangible representations which provide yardsticks against which work can be judged. Any view that learning is norm-referenced, that is, learners are to be judged against the performance of others, is antithetical to the views of feedback described here. There must be a notion that anyone can improve against the required standards irrespective of what other learners do.

Common understanding of what feedback is and how it can operate

We believe that the lack of resolution of the public debate about feedback is due to an absence of agreement about what feedback is, built on a poorly articulated conceptual base. While the book goes some way to providing the conceptual base, there is still a need for this to be taken up and widely adopted. In particular there is a need for congruence between learners and teachers about what feedback is. This can only occur when there are sober discussions of the basic ideas and assumptions, followed by agreement on what is to be done.

This agreement in principle is needed before it will be possible to get effective alignment of student and teacher expectations about feedback.

Willingness to take an evidence-influenced view of teaching and learning

So much day-to-day activity in higher and professional education is based upon the cultural practices of the discipline or profession. Things are done because that is the way things get done around here. This is not a sufficient basis to run a system of education or even a particular course. Willingness to base educational practice on evidence of effects is necessary. While this needs to draw on publications based on systematic research, on a local level it depends just as much on the willingness to seek and use evidence about the effects of specific teaching and learning interventions – that is, a commitment to use data about student performance as a driver of change. Feedback is the most obvious arena for this because it provides data about what is and is not working. We just need to set up our own practices so they take notice of it. Data about what students can do following a task needs to necessarily drive what students do, but it also needs to drive teaching interventions. Such actions involve much greater reflexivity on the part of students and of teaching staff than is often apparent.

Many of the arguments presented in the book, particularly the claims around the notion of feedback as Feedback Mark 2, require systematic testing over time. Without this research, the arguments remain plausible suggestions guided by some evidence. In terms of research directions, we need to invest more energy in looking at the role of the learner as seeker and user of feedback. In situ observational studies are also required to examine the micro-skills of both learner and educator in feedback episodes, and in particular, the degree to which these skills can be influenced by explicit orientation and 'feedback training'. Characteristics that need to be captured and analysed include language, content, structure, conditions and, most importantly, the impact of these intersecting factors on the learner.

Leadership to name the problem and mobilise sustained action to address it

Probably the single greatest initiative needed to reform feedback practices is that of working across courses or programs, rather than solely working within them. Feedback is too important to be the concern only of the individual teacher. Exhortations about changing practices are ineffective; action in course design and planning is needed and this requires leadership beyond the immediate context to be exercised. The support of teachers and students in change and sustaining change needs to be enlisted. Even if educators do 'come around' to considering new notions of feedback, many will need to engage in their own reflective practice to avoid operating within old 'feedback as telling' paradigms, or within a limited 'micro' view of feedback that concerns the in situ encounter, rather than the design of the program, enabling feedback to do its work on subsequent learning tasks. Educators may also challenge themselves to consider the transparency of standards of work/learning outcomes that they want learners to achieve. Without a shared understanding of these targets, any feedback practice, in any form, is compromised. For program designers and teachers, this book challenges them to observe their own behaviours and default mechanisms in feedback encounters and in wider design practices – to see how these behaviours and strategies fit into the Feedback Mark 2 framework presented in this book. There is a call to educators to observe, more thoughtfully and with more commitment, the impact of their intervention on student outcomes. There is a need for all those with coordination roles to exert leadership to promote this practice as collective and systematic. We all need to be better at seeking out the effects of our interventions on learners.

In conclusion

Various ideas about feedback and the improvement of feedback practices have been discussed here. Unlike other ideas in teaching and learning which are a challenge to implement, feedback has a unique characteristic: once implemented in its full sense, it can become self-sustaining. It has a two-way benefit: it benefits the learner through information they use to improve their work, and it benefits the teacher and the course through information used to improve what they do. The two features engage students and teachers in a virtuous loop. It is the completion of the loop that is the vital feature of feedback. Without that the cycle is broken and both parties are operating with inadequate information for them to do either of their jobs well. The notion of feedback as presented in this book equips the learner beyond the immediate task and in fact should do more than help students cope, or cope well, within a course. The macro and micro design elements considered within the chapters should help learners develop the capacity to judge their own work. This is the most important work of feedback.

Index

Tables and figures are indicated by page numbers in **bold** type.

action plans 37, **215**
active learning *see* learner-centred
  feedback
Adcroft, A. 4
agency 12, 21–24
Akhtar, K. et al. 149
Anderson, T. 126
anxiety 54, 73, 82; distress and 60, 61
Apter, M. 53, **54**
Archambault, L. et al. 130
Archer, J. 161
Archer, J. C. 115
Archer, J. et al. 160, 162
architecture 132
Arluke, A. 113
Arora, S. et al. 142
arts 28; group work 27–8; nesting tasks
  28; self-evaluation 27–8
Ashford, S. J. et al. 165
assessment 24, 179, **184**, 185; age
  factors 180; on bedside tutorials
  81–5; benchmarking 185, 195; on
  biology 118; on business studies 95,
  95, 96; challenges 179; complexity
  180; constraint 16, 120–1, 179–80;
  digital environments *see* digital
  environments; disparities 96, 118,
  196; group work **212**; on hospital
  placements 131–2; limitations 120,
  154–5, 185, 196; on medicine
  and healthcare 22, 142, 180; on
  patient-centred feedback 148–50,
  151, 152–3, 154–5, 193–4, **194**,
  196, 197, **197**; on peer coaching
  184; on physiotherapy 85–7; on
professional skills and workplaces
  119–21; questionnaires 37, 160,
  162–3, **170**, 192, 193–4, 197; on
  rephrasing feedback 37; scope 13,
  16, 22, 95, 120, 152, 154, 155,
  174, 180, 185; self-regulation
  155; on simulations in interview
  skills 185; success and failure
  180; tailoring from 19–20; time
  factors 119; trust and 93, 96; video
  recordings 185; written feedback
  119–20; *see also* marking; MSF;
  self-evaluation
Atwater, L. 165
Atwater, L. E. et al. 164, 167, 169
audio recordings 107

Balmer, D. F. et al. 113
Barnett, R. 92, 93, 98
Barrow, H. S. 192
Beaumont, C. 133
Beaumont, C. et al. 90, 93, 118
bedside tutorials: anxiety 82;
  assessment 81–5; constraint 82,
  83–4; disengagement 81–2, 83–4;
  metadiscourse 83; scope 82–3, 84–5;
  time factors 82
bench top model simulations 141, **141**,
  146, **147**
benchmarking 185; prior experience
  and 195
Benson, R. 125
Beresford, W. 130
Berg, I. van den et al. 42–3
Berk, R. A. 158, 160
Berners-Lee, T. 127
Biggs, J. 15, 131, 174
Billet, S. 77

biology 17, 18; assessment 118; effects
    6
Bleakley, A. 198
Bligh, J. 198
blogging 131; microblogging 134;
    scope 133–4, 186; self-evaluation 186
Bloxham, S. 118–19
body language **66**; complexity 79; poor
    84
Borrell-Carrió, F. **54**, 63
Boshuizen, H. 180
Boud, D. 1–10, 11–33, 34, 41, 51, 52,
    55, 63, 72, 93, 104–24, 180–1, 182,
    202–18
Boud, D. et al. 23
Boulos, M. et al. 133
Boyce, P. 177
Brack, C. 125
Bradley, P. 141
Brett, J. F. 165
Brewer, W. F. 56
Brown, P. 196
Bruce, D. 167, 169
Bruff, D. 134–5
Brutus, S. et al. 158, 161
Bryson, C. 91
Burch, V. 73
Burford, B., Bedi, A. et al. 197
Burford, B., Greco, M. et al. 196
business studies 94; assessment 95,
    95, 96; classroom atmosphere
    97–8, 100; digital environments
    95; leadership 183; MSF 165; oral
    presentations 98–100; peer coaching
    178; practice and *see* professional
    skills and workplaces; scope 95, 96;
    self-evaluation 95–6
Butler, D. L. 14, 22, 34, 55–6, 57
Butler, R. 109, 111

Campbell, J. L. et al. 160, 162
Campbell, L. 118–19
Carless, D. 62–3, 67, 68, 90–103
Carless, D. et al. 14, 94, 106, 119
Carney, S. L. 196
Chandler, P. 108
Chang, C. et al. 130
Chanock, K. 53
Chao, J. 133
Charlton, T. et al. 132
Chen, C. 131
Chen, M. 131

Chi, M. 35, 43–4
Chi, M. et al. 180
Chi, M. T. H. 39
Chi, M. T. H. et al. 39
Chinn, C. A. 56
Cho, K. 43
CIF (Communication in Interaction
    Framework) 78–87, **79**
Clarke, D. 52, 62–3, 73
classroom atmosphere: dialogic feedback
    97–8; scope 98, 100
clickers: scope 134–5; speed factors 134
clinical practice *see* medicine and
    healthcare
Clyman, S. 158, 159, 164
Clynes, M. P. 190
Cobham, D. 130
Cochrane, T. 131
comments boxes 117
communal constructivism 126
communication 72; challenges 73, 78;
    constraint 74; contextual factors 80;
    frameworks 78–87, **79**; intellectual
    styles 80; managing conversations 80;
    non-verbal cues 79, 87; scope 78,
    79, 80, 81, 92; *see also individual
    terms*
Communication in Interaction
    Framework (CIF) 78–87, **79**
confidence: disparities 58–9, 112; excess
    85–6, 87
connectivism 126
constructivism 14; communal 126;
    scope 126; social 126, 176
consumer-centred feedback 208;
    informality 190–1; questionnaires
    193; scope 190, 193, 200, 204; *see
    also* patient-centred feedback
Cook, D. A. et al. 141
cooperative learning groups: challenges
    178–9; collaborative groups and
    178; equality and 179; formative
    and summative feedback 182–3;
    fragmentation 179–80; leadership
    179–80; marketing plans 179; scope
    179, 180
Corrin, L. 130, 131
Costa, A. L. 92
Coulby, C. et al. 131–2
cover sheets 118–19
Cowan, J. 34
Crossley, J. 120–1

Crossman, J. 93
Curran, J. 107
curricula 25, **26**; constraint 31; cross-curricula 40–1, 175, 217; frameworks **211–13**; group work **211–12**; hidden curricula 174; scope 204, 206–9, 218; time factors 206–7, 209; written feedback 208; *see also individual subjects*
Curzon-Hobson, A. 91
cybernetics 17

D'Abate, C. P. et al. 177
Dalley, K. et al. 31
Dalton, M., Davidson, M. and Keating, J. 119
Dalton, M., Keating, J. and Davidson, M. 193–4
Damasio, A. 50, 51
Damon, W. 176, 178
dangling data 15–16
Davis, A. 12, 51–2
debriefing: scope 142–3; video recordings 143
deference 63
DeNisi, A. 4, 12, 110, 115, 165
Deutsch, M. 175
Dewey, J. 52
dialogic feedback 105, 176, 203–4, **213**; challenges 118; disparities 93; drafts 116–17; expectations 98; limitations 116; portfolios 119; readiness 98; risk-taking 97; scope 90, 93, 97–8, 100, 117, 119, 147; trust 90–1, 92–3, 94, 97, 100, **101**; undervalued 111; *see also* learner-centred feedback
Diamante, T. 165, 169
digital environments: blogging 131, 133–4, 186; challenges 129, 135; clickers 134–5; comments boxes 117; complexity 127–8; connectivism 126; constraint 126, 135–6; dialogic feedback 119; disparities 130; distance and 126; e-business **95**; ePortfolios 130–1; generational factors 127–8; mobile devices 131, 134–5; origins 127, **128**; ratings programs 149–50, 154; scope 45, 125, 126, **128**, 129, 130, 135, 136, 152, 153; social networking 132–3; speed factors 129–30; time factors

127, 130; typed feedback 117; video and 99, 107, 132, 143, 146, 150, 152–3, 185; web pages 150, 152; webcams 148, 149; wikis 133
Dippold, D. 133–4
Direct Observation of Procedural Skills (DOPS) 149
distress 60; effort and 67; scope 67–8; vanishing feedback 61, 113, 195–6
DOPS (Direct Observation of Procedural Skills) 149
Dron, J. 126
Duffy, K. 129
Duffy, T. M. 126
Dunn, D. 181
Dunn, N. 178
Dunning, D. et al. 55
Dweck, S. 58

e-business **95**
e-learning *see* digital environments
ECO model 169
education studies 132
Ehly, S. 177
emotion 59–60, 68, **168**, 169, 204–5, 210; challenges 60; constraint 64, 68; delay and 54; disparities 52–3; frameworks 64, **64–7**, 67; immutability 58; motivation and 52–3; negative 165, **168**, 169; scope 50, 51–2, 54; *see also individual terms*
empathy 97; scope 92
Ende, J. 13, 17, **27**, 54, 60, 61, 62–3, 73, 113, 140, 196, 198
Ende, J. et al. 30, 51–2, 54, 58, 73, 198
engineering 17, 18; digital environments 132; effects 6
episodic feedback 25, 27, **27**; judgementalism 52
ePortfolios 131; challenges 131; scope 130–1; tailoring 131
Epstein, R. **54**, 58, 63
Epstein, R. et al. 63
Ericsson, K. 144
Eva, K. et al. 58, 59, 62, 67
Eva, K. W. 22, 55, 199
evaluative judgement 9, 22–4, 31, 34–5, 37
exams and tests *see* assessment
external and internal feedback 55, 68; challenges 56–7, **56–7**, 59; countering 57–8; disparities 55, 56,

58–9; scope 59, 63–4; self-regulation
55–6; *see also individual terms*
external standards 6

Facebook 132–3
Falchikov, N. 23, 43, 51, 52, 178
Fanning, R. M. 142–3
Fantuzzo, J. W. et al. 175
feedback 1; challenges 1, 3, 11, 18, 54–5,
    202, 203, 216, 218; complexity 25;
    constraint 5, 7, 50–1, 90, 105, 110,
    115, 216; contextual factors 8, 13;
    continuity 16; culture and values 217;
    disparities 17, 106, 108, 109, 144,
    203; effort and 112; evidence based
    217; fragmentation 15, 16; limitations
    17–18, 31, 50; location factors **65**;
    meaning 1, 5–7, 55, 73, 205, 216–17;
    origins 6, 11, 17; person focused
    113–14, 118; personal disparagement
    110; primacy 1, 202; process focused
    111, 120; scope 2, 5–6, 8, 11, 24, 62,
    73, 110, 144, 190, 191, 202, 203,
    204, 206, 209–10, 218; self-regulation
    111–13, 114, 120, 144; sequences 24,
    31; simplistic 16; success and failure
    112–13; systemic 25; tailoring **19**,
    19–20; task focused 110–11, 118,
    120; time factors 6, 31, **66**, 202,
    206, 210; ubiquity 1; uncertainty 11;
    undervalued 203; *see also individual
    terms*
feedback loop 8, 16, 18–20, **19**, 208,
    210, **212**, 218; *see also individual
    terms*
feedback sandwich: constraint 60, 68;
    disparities 61; judgementalism 5;
    limitations 61, 62; praise 60–1; scope
    62
Feletti, G. I. 196
Ferguson, P. 109, 118
Fernando, N. et al. 15, 30
Fidler, H. et al. 164, 165
financial factors 3
Finn, G. 174, 180
Fiorella, L. et al. 108
First Year Experience 30
Flavell, J. 176
Fleenor, J. W. 159, 160
Foundation Programme 149
frameworks 210; on communication
    78–87, **79**; on curricula **211–13**;

on emotion 64, **64–7**, 67; honesty
    in 67; limitations 75; on medicine
    and healthcare **76**, 76–8, 81–7,
    213–15; on MSF **170–1**; on peer
    coaching **184**; on professional skills
    and workplaces 75–87, **79**; scope 75;
    on self-evaluation 64, **64–7**, 67; on
    trust **91–4**
Fry, R. 144

Gaba, D. M. 142–3
Gan, M. 114
Gao, T. 130
Gardner, J. 126
Gardner, P. 186
Garner, J. 174, 180
General Medical Council 148
Generation X 127
Generation Y 127–8
Generation Z 127–8
generic feedback 8
Gibbons, P. F. 135
Gibbs, G. 93, **211**
Gigerenzer, G. 51
Gilbert, D. T. 56, 59, 68
goals 15, 166, 168, **213**; emotion 165;
    honesty 24; limitations 15; scope 41,
    110; self and task levels 165; tailoring
    22; uncertainty 60
Goffman, E. 51, 58
Goodstone, M. S. 165, 169
Gotjamanos, E. 185
Grabinger, R. S. 126
Graduate Careers Australia 106
Gray, A. et al. 164
Gray, K. et al. 129
groupwork 27–8, 185; assessment
    212; communal constructivism
    126; cooperative learning groups
    178–80, 182–3; digital environments
    45, 135, 186; nesting tasks **212**;
    oral presentations 98–100; patient-
    centred feedback 146–7; peer feedback
    and **212**; scope 45, **211–12**; time
    factors 108; written feedback 37, 45,
    212
Gruppen, L. 143, 144

Haber, R. J. 73, 74
Hammond, J. 135
Hampden-Turner, C. 79
Hand, L. 91

handwritten feedback 117
Hargie, O. et al. 108
Harré, R. 51, 52, 58
Hattie, J. 4, 12, 41, 51, 52, 54, 67,
    107–8, 109, 110–14, 115, 118, 120,
    144, 209, **213**
healthcare *see* medicine and healthcare
help-seeking 113
Henderson, P. et al. 54, 68
Herring, S. C. 134
hidden curricula 174
Higgs, J. 180
Higgs, J. et al. 60
Hodges, B. 142
Hofstede, G. 78
Holmboe, E. S. 140
Holmboe, E. S. et al. 140
Holmes, B. 126
homeostasis 17
honesty 63, 67; constraint 24;
    disparities 93; distress and 195–6;
    scope 67
Honeycutt, C. 134
hospital placements 28; assessment
    131–2; bedside tutorials 81–5;
    dialogic feedback **213**; disparities 29;
    goals **213**; limitations 29; nesting
    tasks 29, **214**; physiotherapy 182–3,
    193–8; scope 28, **213–14**; tailoring
    28–9; time factors **214**; written
    feedback **213**, **214–15**; *see also*
    patient-centred feedback
Hounsell, D. 14, 61
Howe, A. 192
Howe, N. 127
human circulatory system 39
Huxham, M. 118
Hyland, F. 52
Hyland, K. 76

ICFAS (Imperial College Feedback and
    Assessment System) 148–50, **151**,
    152–3, 154–5
Iedema, R. et al. 114
Ilgen, D. 12, 51–2
Imperial College Feedback and
    Assessment System (ICFAS) 148–50,
    151, 152–3, 154–5
Ingham, H. 176
Integrated Procedural Performance
    Instrument (IPPI) 148–50, **151**,
    152–5

internal and external feedback
    55, 68; challenges 56–7, **56–7**,
    59; countering 57–8; disparities
    55, 56, 58–9; scope 59, 63–4;
    self-regulation 55–6; *see also*
    individual terms
internet *see* digital environments
interview skills simulations 185
IPPI (Integrated Procedural
    Performance Instrument) 148–50,
    151, 152–5
Isen, A. M. 59
Issenberg, S. B. et al. 142

Jackson, P. 174
Jha, V. et al. 191, 192, 197–8
Johari Window 176
Johnson, D. 176, 180
Johnson, D., Johnson, R. and Smith, K.
    176, 180
Johnson, D., Maruyama, G. et al. 179
Johnson, R. 180
Jolly, B. 104–24
Jonassen, D. H. 126
Joyce, B. 181
judgementalism 5, 52; anxiety 60;
    learned helplessness 12; linguistic
    factors 62–3; tempering 5

Kallick, B. 92
Kaufman, J. H. 42
Keating, J. 31
Keating, J. et al. 119
Kelly, D. 191
Kennedy, G. et al. 127
Kent, F. 190–201, **194**, **197**
Kepner, K. 175
Ker, J. 141
Kift, S. et al. 30
Kirk, P. 119
Kirkley, S. 125
Kirschner, P. 142, 144
Kluger, A. N. 4, 12, 110, 115, 165
Kneebone, R. 141, 143, 146, 148
Kneebone, R., Bello, F. et al. 107, 149
Kneebone, R., Kidd, J. et al. 146
Kneebone, R., Nestel, D., Bello, F. and
    Darzi, A. 148
Kneebone, R., Nestel, D., Vincent, C.
    and Darzi, A. 146
Kneebone, R., Nestel, D., Wetzel, C. et
    al. 141, 146

Kneebone, R., Nestel, D., Yadollahi, F. et al. 148
Kneebone, R., Scott, W. et al. 143, 197–8
knowledge building 35; digital environments 133; primacy 35; scope 111; *see also* reflective knowledge building
Knowles, M. et al. 180
Kohn, A. 61
Kolb, D. 144, 182

labelling 2, 3–4, 19, 60–1, 203
Ladyshewsky, R. 68, **184**
Ladyshewsky, R. et al. 182
Ladyshewsky, R. K. 174–89
Lake, F. 129
Lambert, S. 130, 131
Land, R. 20–1
landscape design 131
Larson, M. 92
Latting, J. 52
Lave, J. 74, 118, 144, 146
leadership: disparities 179–80; peer coaching and 183; scope 159, 183, 217–18
learned helplessness 12, 52
learner-centred feedback 6, 7, 14, 15, 21, 22, 23, **26**, 29–30, 52, 203, 205, 210, **213**; challenges 25; complexity 25, 34; constraint 4, 21–2, 52; disparities 2, 6, 14; limitations 17; scope 22, 30, 31, 203, 204, 206; *see also individual terms*
learners 1, 21, **26**, **211**; constraint 207; scope 3, 30, 32, 207, 208–9; self-regulation **26**; *see also individual terms*
learning impacts 216; disparities 12; limitations 4; *see also individual terms*
LeBlanc, V. R. et al. 148
Lee, I. 116
Lehman, J. 130
Lempp, H. 115
Lepsinger, R. 158–9, 160
Levinson, S. 196
Li, L. 132–3
Liberman, S. et al. 140
Likert scales 163
Lilly, J. et al. 116–17
Lingard, L. A. 73, 74

linguistic factors 62, **66**, 72, 77, 177, 210; constraint 62–3, 115; digital environments 133–4; disparities 115; labelling and 2, 3–4, 19, 60–1, 203; scope 115–16, 205; SIK 74
listening: empathy 92; scope 86–7
Liu, N. F. 93
Lockyer, J. 158–73
Lown, B. A. et al. 191
Lucia, A. D. 158–9, 160
Lucking, R. 133
Luft, J. 176
Lunt, T. 107

McAllister. S. M. et al. 119
MacArthur, C. 43
McAvoy, P. 161
McCarthy, J. 132
McCrindle, M. 127
Macfarlane-Dick, D. 31, 34, 55, 67, 73, 144
McKenna, L. 190–201
McKinlay, E. et al. 191
McManus, I. C. 73
manikin-based simulations 142, **143**
Mann, K. et al. 143
marketing studies 179
marking 42; burdensomeness 4–5; disparities 111; fragmentation 21; limitations 39–40; scope 47; *see also* written feedback
medicine and healthcare 105, 140; anxiety 73; assessment 22, 142, 180; challenges **57**, 57–8, 73, 77–8; complexity 12; constraint 74; cooperative learning groups 179; digital environments 131–2; disparities 73; fragmentation 142; frameworks **76**, 76–8, 81–7, **213–15**; human circulatory system 39; informality 190–1; knowledge building and 111; limitations 15; linguistic factors 77; midwifery 59; MSF 158, 160, 161, 162, 164–5, 166, 69; nursing 31–2; participants 76–7; peer coaching 178; peer tutoring 178; personal disparagement 110; prior experience 77; scope 73, 77, 141–2; self-evaluation 118; self-regulation 144; time factors 107; written feedback 115–16; *see also*

hospital placements; physiotherapy; simulations in medicine and healthcare
Merriënboer, J. J. G. van 13–14, 108
Merriënboer, J. van 142, 144
Merry, S. 39
metadiscourse 76; scope 83
Meyer, J. H. F. 20–1
Mezirow, J. 144
microblogging 134
midwifery 59
Minkov, M. 78
mirroring 15
mobile devices: clickers 134–5; PDAs 131–2; scope 131; Smartphones 131; time factors 131
modern languages 133–4
Molloy, E. 1–10, 11–33, 72, 73, 108, 202–18
Molloy, E. et al. 50–71
Moore, M. G. 126
Moss, F. 73
Moulton, C. 58, 63
Moulton, C. A. et al. 148
MSF (multisource feedback, also known as 360 degree feedback): access to data 161; age factors 164; challenges 169; committees 167, 171; complexity 159, 161, 162, 166; constraint 165; culture and values 159; digital environments see digital environments; disparities 161, 162; emotion 165, 168, 169; fairness and 166; formative and summative 160, 170; frameworks 170–1; goals 166, 168; leadership 159; pilot tests 170; questionnaires 160, 162–3, 170; readiness 159; scope 158–9, 160–1, 162, 164–5, 166–7, 167–8, 168–9, 170–1, 171, 192; sensitivity 171; tests 163, 164; time factors 163; value-added 160
music 131

National Student Survey (NSS) 36
Neighbours, C. et al. 129–30
Nestel, D. 141, 143, 146, 148
Nestel, D., Bello, F. and Kneebone, R. 140–57
Nestel, D., Bello, F., Kneebone, R. and Darzi, A. 149
Nestel, D., Groom, J. et al. 141

Nestel, D., Kneebone, R. et al. 142, 148
nesting tasks 20, 20, 26, 28, 37, 44, 212, 214; limitations 29; scope 20–1, 31; time factors 20
net generation 127–8
Newton, J. M. et al. 119
Nicol, D. 31, 34–49, 55, 67, 73, 90, 104, 105, 117, 144
Nofziger, A. et al. 174, 175, 180
Nooteboom, B. 92
Norcini, J. 73
novice-authority relationships 52, 72, 180–1, 183; episodic feedback 52; linguistic factors 62–3
NSS (National Student Survey) 36
nursing 31–2

Objective Structured Clinical Examination (OSCE) 142
O'Neill, P. 129
oral feedback 80, 208; questionnaires and 197; time factors 14, 108; written feedback and 107; see also individual terms
oral presentations: disparities 99; scope 98–9, 100; self-evaluation 100; video recordings 99
O'Reilly, T. 127
Orsmond, P. 39
Orsmond, P. et al. 93
OSCE (Objective Structured Clinical Examination) 142
over-confidence 85, 86; informality 85, 86; prior experience 85; safety and 85–6, 87
overlapping 20, 20, 26, 28, 37, 44, 212, 214; limitations 29; scope 20–1, 31; time factors 20

Parker, K. 133
patchwork text 37; recorded feedback 37–8
patient-centred feedback: action plans 215; anonymity 198–9; assessment 148–50, 151, 152–3, 154–5, 193–4, 194, 196, 197, 197; bench top models 146, 147; benchmarking 195; challenges 148; complexity 198; dependency and 195; dialogic feedback 147; digital environments 148, 149–50, 152,

153, 154; disparities 196, 197–8;
honesty and 195–6; informality 199;
limitations 154–5, 192, 196–7; MSF
192; primacy 195; privacy **215**;
questionnaires 192, 193–4, 197;
rights and 194; safety 154, **214**;
scope 146–8, 152–3, 154, 155, 190,
191–2, 193, 194, 195, 198, 199,
214–15; self-evaluation 154, **215**;
self-regulation 155; video recordings
146, 150, 152–3
Paul, A. et al. 72–89
PDAs (personal digital assistants) 131–2
peer coaching 177; assessment **184**;
constraints **184**; formative and
summative feedback 177–8, 183;
fragmentation 181–2; frameworks
184; leadership and 183; scope 177,
181, 182, **184**; time factors **184**;
trust and **184**
peer feedback 119, 174; benchmarking
185; constraint 175–6, 181, 183;
disparities 93; equality and 176;
formative and summative 178, 179,
182–3, 185; group work and **212**;
limitations 175; linguistic factors 177;
profusion 45; safety 176; scope 42–7,
174–5, 176, 177, 180–1, 182, 186,
214; speed factors 176; value-added
175; *see also individual terms*
peer tutoring: equality and 177; scope
177, 178
Pendleton, D. et al. 108, 115
Peräkylä, A. 74
perception of feedback: countering
36; disparities 12, 31–2, 93, 96,
106, 116, 118; external and internal
feedback 55–9, **56–7**, 68; limitations
8; linguistic factors 63; poor 2, 3,
11, 12, 13, 30, 36, 107–8, 165;
profusion and 13; scope 93, 96,
97–8, 132, 133; shared meaning 4;
short-termism 2, 3–4; unawareness
and 2, 4, 13
personal digital assistants (PDAs) 131–2
Phelps, E. 176, 178
Phillpotts, C. et al. 191
physics 39
physiotherapy 14–15, 206; assessment
85–7; cooperative learning groups
182–3; disparities 86; group work
185; listening 86–7; non-verbal

cues 87; over-confidence 85–6, 87;
patient-centred feedback 193–8;
profusion 13–14; respect and 86;
risk-taking 86; scope 86
Pitts, J. 132–3
policy documents 38
politeness 58, 196
portfolios 131; challenges 131; scope
119, 130–1; tailoring 131
positioning theory 51, 52; episodic
feedback 52
praise 114; constraint 107–8; disparities
60–1; limitations 13, 114
privacy 106, **215**
private industry 160
professional skills and workplaces 3, 72,
174; assessment 119–21; challenges
73, 74–5, 78–9; complexity 78;
constraint 51, 120–1; deference 63;
disparities 166; frameworks 75–87,
79; goals 166; informality 190;
limitations 120; linguistic factors
72, 74; managing conversations 80;
metadiscourse 76; MSF 158, 159–61;
private industry 160; safety and 53–4;
scope 42, 79, 80, 88, 120, 165–6,
190, 200; self-regulation 3; written
feedback 119–20; *see also individual
professions and subjects*
psychology 31–2; complexity 12;
constructivism 126

questionnaires 37, **170**, 192, 193; oral
feedback and 197; pilot tests 163;
scales 163; scope 160, 162–3, 193–4
Quinn, R. et al. 183

Raemer, D. et al. 142
Rafferty, S. E. C. 190
Ramsey, P. G. et al. 161
reflection *see* self-evaluation
reflective knowledge building 35, 42,
43–4, 94–5; complexity 36; evaluative
judgement 38; nesting tasks 37;
patchwork text 37–8; rewriting and
38; scope 36, 45, 46, 47; self-review
39–41; sequences and 37–8; written
feedback 36–7, 39, 45; *see also*
self-evaluation; self-review
Regehr, G. 22, 55, 199
Reina, D. S. 92
Reina, M. L. 92

Reinders, M. E. et al. 191, 192
relationships: constraint 82, 83–4, 176;
    contextual factors 80; continuity
    13, **65**; cooperative learning groups
    178–80, 182–3; dependency 39;
    dialogic feedback 90, 92–3, 97,
    100, **101**; disparities 86; informality
    85, 86; listening and 86–7; novice-
    authority 52, 62–3, 72, 180–1, 183;
    peer coaching 177–8, 181–2, 183,
    184; peer tutoring 177, 178; primacy
    169; prior experience 85; respect and
    86; scope 77, 86, 176; trust 91
rephrasing feedback 37
respect 86
rewriting: limitations 38; primacy 38;
    scope 38, 133
Richardson, W. 127
Ridder, J. M. van de et al. 191, 198
Riggio, R. et al. 175
risk-taking 86, 92, 97
Rock, D. 182
Rorty, R. 63, 115
Roscoe, R. 35, 43–4
Rowntree, D. 13
Rust, C. et al. 43

Sadler, D. R. 15, 34, 40, 56, 61, 109
Saedon, H. et al. 75
safety 53–4, 108, 176, **214**; hazards
    85–6, 87; scope 87, 109, 141, 154
Sandmire, D. 177
Sargeant, J. 158–73
Sargeant, J., Armson, H. et al. 55
Sargeant, J., Mann, K. and Ferrier, S.
    162, 166
Sargeant, J., Mann, K., Sinclair, D. et al.
    166, 191, 192
scaffolding **26**; scope 135
scales 163
SCFF (Socio-Cultural Feedback
    Framework) 75, **76**, 76–8, 81–7
Schmidt, H. 180
Schon, D. 144, 175, 176
Schunn, C. D. 42
Schwartz, J. 182
Seabrook, M. A. 115
Seale, C. 115
self-evaluation 15, 24, **26**, 27, 28,
    34–5, 43, 69, 100, 176, 186;
    debriefing 142–3; disparities
    22–3, 93; frameworks 64, **64–7**,

67; honesty 63; initiation in 23;
    limitations 22, 27–8, 55, **215**; prior
    tasks 23; scope 23, **23**, 24, 47, 50,
    95–6, 112, 118, 119, 154, 182, 204,
    218; short-termism 15; time factors
    14; trust and 15; *see also* reflective
    knowledge building; self-review
self-explaining 39
self-review 14–15, 38; cross-curricular
    40–1; goals 41; limitations 40;
    objectivity and 41; requested
    feedback 46; scope 38–40, 41, 45–6;
    self-explaining 39; *see also* reflective
    knowledge building; self-evaluation;
    written feedback
Seligman, A. B. 92
Shady, S. L. H. 92
Sharifian, F. 77
Sharp, P. 106
Sheull, T. J. 15
Showers, B. 181
Shute, V. J. 61, 109, 110
Siegel, M. A. 125
Siemens, G. 126
SIK (stocks of interactional knowledge)
    74
simulations in interview skills 185
simulations in medicine and healthcare
    140; bench top models 141, **141**,
    146, **147**; briefing 145; challenges
    141; debriefing 142–3; hospital
    placements 197–8; limitations 146;
    manikin based 142, **143**; patient-
    centred feedback 146–50, **151**,
    152–5; safety 141; scope 143–4,
    145–6, 155
Skiffington, S. 182
Slavin, R. 178
Smartphones 131
Smither, J. W. et al. 164, 165–6
Smits, M. et al. 129
social constructivism 126, 176; dialogic
    feedback 176
social interaction 58
social networking 132–3
social sciences 28; group work 27;
    nesting tasks 28; self-evaluation 27–8
social work 28–9
socio-cultural factors: challenges 74,
    87; contextual factors 80; digital
    environments 132, 133; intellectual
    styles 80; non-verbal cues 79; primacy

72; scope 72, 80, 81, 87; workplaces and *see* professional skills and workplaces
Socio-Cultural Feedback Framework (SCFF) 75, **76**, 76–8, 81–7
standards-work variation 6, 7, 21, 55, 56, 67, 77–8, 110, 205–6, 208–9, 216, 218; *see also individual terms*
Stav, J. et al. 134
Stefani, L. A. J. 39
stocks of interactional knowledge (SIK) 74
Strauss, W. 127
stress **53**; scope 53, **54**, 60, 98
Su, F. 133
Sweller, J. 13–14, 108

Tan, M. 186
Tang, C. 131
Tang, C. et al. 131
Taras, M. 40
Taylor, S. 159, 160
teamwork *see* group work
tests and exams *see* assessment
Thomas, J. 78
Timperley, H. 4, 12, 41, 51, 52, 54, 67, 107–8, 109, 110–14, 118, 120, 144
Titchen, A. 180
Topping, K. 175, 177, 178
Towle, A. 192
traceability 106–7
track changes 117
Trompenaars, A. 79
trust 59, 68; constraint 91, **184**; dependency and 97; disparities 93, 96; empathy 97; frameworks 91–4; honesty and 93; limitations 15; listening 92; meaning 91; risk-taking 92; scope 90–1, 92–3, 94, 97, 100, **101**, 101–2; undervalued 91
Tschannen-Moran, M. 91
Tuckman, B. 178–9
Turan, S. et al. 192
Twitter 134
typed feedback 117

Van Dijk, D. 12
vanishing feedback 61, 113, 195–6
Varey, W. 181, **184**
Vehviläinen, S. 74

Vickery, A. 129
video recordings 146, 152–3, 185; disparities 99; oral and written feedback 107; primacy 150; scope 99, 143
videoconferencing 132
Violato, C. et al. 162, 164
voice 79
Vygotsky, L. 126, 176

Waddell, D. 178, 181
Waddell, D. et al. 132
Wager, S. 18
Wager, W. 18
Walker, D. 51
Walsh, C. et al. 183
Wang, Q. et al. 132
web-based environments *see* digital environments
Webb, G. et al. 74, 75, 78
webcams 148, 149
Wenger, E. 74, 118, 144, 146
Wenger, E. et al. 126
Wertsch, J. 52, 176
West, A. 118
White, C. 143, 144
Wiener, N. 17, 18
wikis 133
Wilkinson, J. R. et al. 119
Williams, B. et al. 125–39
Wilson, T. D. 56, 59, 68
Winne, P. H. 14, 22, 34, 55–6, 57
Winter, R. 37
workplaces *see* professional skills and workplaces
Wright, N. 134
written feedback 36, 206, 208, **212**; action plans 37; challenges 118; comments boxes 117; constraint 115; countering 36; cover sheets 118–19; disparities 111, 115, 116, 118; drafts 116–17; handwritten 117; limitations 36–7, 105, 108, 109, 116, 120, 185; oral feedback and 107; personal disparagement 109; portfolios 119; privacy 106; rephrasing feedback 37; safety 108, 109; scope 39, 45, 104, 105, 106, 107, 108, 109, 114, 115–16, 117, 118, 119–20, 121, **213**, **214–15**; tailoring 104; time factors 107, 108; traceability 106–7; uncertainty 104–5; undervalued

104–5, 109; *see also* marking; self-review
Wykurz, G. 191
Wysocki, A. 175

Xiao, Y. 133

Yonge, O. et al. 132
Yorke, M. 16, 19

Zemke, R. et al. 127
Zeus, P. 182
Zimmerman, B. 144, 154